DO-IT-YOURSELF
CAR CARE

LARRY W. CARLEY

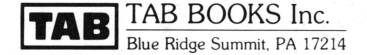

TAB BOOKS Inc.
Blue Ridge Summit, PA 17214

I'd like to thank the vehicle manufacturers,
tool and equipment suppliers, aftermarket trade publishers,
and working mechanics everywhere for the information and
insight that made this book possible. To these people I give my thanks.

FIRST EDITION
FIRST PRINTING

Copyright © 1987 by TAB BOOKS Inc.
Printed in the United States of America

Library of Congress Cataloging in Publication Data

Carley, Larry W.
Do-it-yourself car care.

Includes index.
1. Automobiles—Maintenance and repair—Amateurs'
manuals. I. Title.
TL152.C367   1987   629.28'722   87-1917
ISBN 0-8306-0843-5
ISBN 0-8306-2143-1 (pbk.)

Questions regarding the content of this book
should be addressed to:

Reader Inquiry Branch
Editorial Department
TAB BOOKS Inc.
P.O. Box 40
Blue Ridge Summit, PA 17214

Cover photograph courtesy of Subaru.

Contents

Introduction

Thank you for buying my book. Do-it-yourself car care isn't dead yet, nor is there any less of a demand for basic car-care knowledge. If anything, the demand has grown because of the changes that have taken place in automotive technology and design in recent years. Your decision to buy this book shows that you still believe in and appreciate the importance of taking care of your vehicle.

This book is written for the average person who wants to perform his or her own basic car maintenance and possibly do some light repair work. I'm not going to tell you how to overhaul an engine or how to replace a transmission; those jobs are far beyond the abilities of the average weekend mechanic and are better left to the professional. This book is also written for the person who wants to learn more about car care and repair—even if the work is done by a professional mechanic.

The information you'll find in this book is quite different from that found in ordinary repair manuals. A typical repair manual will give you the step-by-step procedures for taking something apart and, hopefully, for putting it back together again.

It might even give you a few hints on troubleshooting by listing several dozen "possible causes" of a particular problem; beyond that, you're on your own.

The typical repair manual offers nothing in the way of explanation as to how often filters or fluids should be changed, let alone *why* they should be changed. The ordinary maintenance manual usually instructs you to see your owner's manual. If you haven't lost it, your owner's manual does list recommended service intervals. Often the intervals given are intended more for "minimal" maintenance than "real-world" maintenance, however. The factory-recommended service intervals might not be adequate for your kind of driving. But unless somebody tells you otherwise, how are you to know what's best?

Every repair manual has tables of tune-up specifications, but they don't tell you which parts should be replaced or why. The subject of winterizing is totally neglected as is any advice on how to save money on do-it-yourself auto repairs or how to find a competent mechanic when you do need one. Unfortunately, if you depend solely on your owner's manual or an ordinary shop manual for guidance, you won't be getting all the information you need to care for your car properly. Most of your questions will probably go unanswered or be answered incorrectly by well-intentioned but misguided friends who don't know any more about the subject than you do. That's where this book can help.

Think of this book as an encyclopedia of car-care. This book can't answer every question, but it can fill the information void as far as most questions on basic maintenance are concerned.

The opinions expressed herein are primarily my own, but they are based on years of experience of working with and writing for professional mechanics. For more than five years, I served as editor of *Motor Service* magazine, a leading trade magazine for the automotive service aftermarket. (This term refers to independent repair garages, fleet service centers, and the service departments of new car dealerships.) I've written about every conceivable technical subject and have listened to the opinions of industry experts, engineers, training managers, and working mechanics nationwide. I've listened to complaints and I have supervised a number of nationwide surveys as to the kinds of repairs mechanics are performing, the kinds of problems they're experiencing, and the service intervals they are recommending. I'm a certified automobile mechanic by the National Institute for Automotive Service Excellence. I've also worked in various types of service facilities as a mechanic, so I know from firsthand experience what inadequate care can do to an automobile.

I'm trying to stress that the information and suggestions contained in this book are based on experience and are intended for the average person who is interested in saving money and extending the useful life of his or her car.

Chapter 1

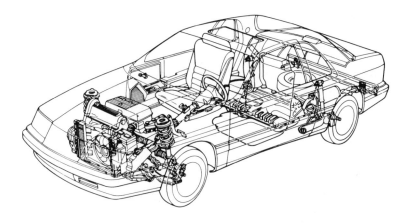

The Best Person
to Care for Your Car

Why pay someone else to do simple jobs you can do yourself? That's a question you've probably asked yourself when you've been handed a huge repair bill for your car. There are lots of reasons why most of us pay someone else to fix our cars. The leading excuse is "I don't know how to do it myself." That's a valid reason, but you pay a hefty price for your lack of knowledge. The typical garage charges an average of $30 to $40 per hour for labor; for every hour you pay a mechanic, how many hours will *you* have to work to pay his wages and his employer's overhead?

Obviously, it's cheaper to do your own repairs because you save the cost of the mechanic's labor plus the overhead of his employer, plus the 30 to 50 percent markup that is usually applied to the parts the mechanic installs in your car. Add it all up and you can see why doing your own maintenance and light repair work can save you a bundle. In addition, you'll gain the satisfaction of knowing you did the work yourself (Fig. 1-1).

Doing your own maintenance and light repair work has other advantages, too. You can forget

about the hassles of making an appointment to have your car serviced and dealing with service people. You also eliminate the inconvenience of having your car tied up for several days because the shop is too busy to immediately work on it.

The latest industry statistics show that there is approximately one mechanic for every 300 cars. The shortage is continuing to grow, because young people today don't want to be automobile mechanics. The profession lacks any social status, starting pay is less than other skilled blue-collar jobs, and fringe benefits are minimal or nonexistent. Computers and electronics are where the action is, so these fields are the ones attracting the technicians of tomorrow. Unfortunately, many people don't realize professional mechanics make almost as much money as plumbers. Average salaries are around $20,000 per year, but nearly one out of ten mechanics earns over $30,000 per year—more if he owns his own shop.

Many would-be mechanics think they lack the necessary mechanical skills when really what they lack is faith in their own abilities. They'd like to

1

Fig. 1-1. All it takes to do your own maintenance work is a willingness to do it yourself—and a willingness to occasionally get your hands dirty.

do their own service work, but they have trouble just opening the hood on their car. If you fall into this category, you're likely intimidated by anything mechanical. You're probably afraid that if you did touch anything under the hood, you'd ruin it, and it would cost you a fortune to get the damage repaired.

There is some truth to this kind of thinking. If you don't know what you're doing, it is possible to cause a lot of expensive damage, especially on late-model cars that are loaded with electronics. On the other hand, with a little guidance (which this book will provide) even a novice can perform most basic maintenance jobs on any car as well as many kinds of simple repairs. You don't need the hands of Mr. Goodwrench to do this kind of work, so why pay Mr. Goodwrench or his associates when you can do it yourself? Unless you're physically incapacitated, there's no reason why any person of average intelligence can't do basic car care. Some people don't even consider blindness to be a handicap when it comes to working on automobiles, and there are quite a few blind service technicians who do everything from tune-ups to transmission overhauls. If they can do it so can you. The only requirements are a desire to do it yourself and a willingness to get your hands dirty.

THE JOY OF DOING IT YOURSELF

Greasy hands might not sound like something to be joyful about, but besides the convenience factor and satisfaction that comes with doing your own work there also comes a peace of mind you rarely get at even the best service facilities.

In spite of the industry's efforts to upgrade their image and to eliminate out the rotten apples, the repair industry still suffers from a bad reputation. Most people are still afraid that they are going to be taken advantage of when they take their car in for repairs. The public generally mistrusts mechanics and there is always that nagging suspicion that the mechanic didn't really do what he said he did.

In defense of the industry, most instances of "repair rip-offs" are greatly exaggerated. Most mechanics are honest, hard-working individuals who are trying to do their best. Mechanics do make mistakes, but many times incorrect repairs are usually the result of misdiagnosis or poor communication between the customer and mechanic. For example, the customer requested the wrong repair or didn't describe the symptoms accurately. The only real "repair rip-off" that's worth writing about is the need for updating and advancing the professional skills of working mechanics. Most mechanics are busy earning a living and their employers can't find time to send them to clinics or schools to learn about the new systems that are being introduced. Or, if they can get the time off to attend a clinic or school, it's often at their own expense. Of course, there are always a few unscrupulous individuals to be found in any trade or profession.

Doing your own work eliminates any worries you might have about being cheated or getting the quality of service you expect. You'll know what items have been replaced, the brand of parts replaced, the condition of the old parts that have been removed, and whether all the work you wanted done has been done.

There's no better way to get to know your car than to get under its hood. Just as you learn where every nick and scratch is when you wash and wax your own car, so too, you'll learn where the various components are located when you do your own maintenance work. You can see for yourself the parts that need to be replaced as well as other things that might need attention.

Learning your way around the engine compartment can also do much to alleviate the fear and intimidation that accompanies unexpected breakdowns. Instead of standing along the road and staring with a dumbfounded look into a mysterious engine compartment, you'll at least have an idea of what's wrong and possibly why it happened and how to fix it.

Because one of the reasons for doing your own maintenance work is to prevent unexpected breakdowns, your car should run better and cause you fewer headaches than one that belongs to the typical gas-and-go driver (Fig. 1-2). By being aware of what's under the hood, you'll be more aware of the overall condition of your car. This will enable you to prevent major problems from developing by keeping your car in good shape and fixing minor problems as they occur.

No car is ever going to be 100 percent trouble free regardless of the brand, the price, or the maintenance. But a well-maintained car is far less likely to cause problems—especially major problems— simply because the owner is concerned enough to take good care of it.

GETTING STARTED

If you've had little or no experience under the hood of an automobile, you would be well advised to attend an adult education class at a local high school or community college. Such courses will give you a hands-on opportunity to get acquainted with the basics before you work on your own car. The fee

Fig. 1-2. Taking good care of your car can prevent scenes like this.

to attend such a course is usually minimal and pays for itself the first time you change your own oil.

In Chapter 2, the kinds of hand tools you'll need for do-it-yourself maintenance and light repairs are discussed along with some recommendations on how and where to buy them. Chapter 3 tells you how to save money on the parts you buy. The remainder of the book covers the basics of maintenance along with some common repairs that are frequently done by do-it-yourselfers. All you need to get started is a little know-how, which this book provides, a few tools, and a desire to do it yourself!

IT'S EASIER THAN YOU THINK

Table 1-1 lists a number of typical automobile repair jobs along with their relative degree of difficulty. As you can see, most don't require a great degree of skill. Even some of those listed in the "for experienced or professional mechanics only" column are often successfully tackled by persons of lesser ability.

The worst problems you're going to encounter are limited access to components and corrosion. Because many of today's cars have been drastically downsized to reduce weight (and thus improve fuel economy), there isn't a lot of elbow room under the hood. Compromises are often made to accommodate easier assembly at the factory or to shave a few pennies off the cost of tooling, so some components aren't located as conveniently as they could or should be. Some, in fact, are downright exasperating to replace. Changing spark plugs on the rear bank of a *transverse-mounted* (sideways) V6 engine might require the dexterity of an octopus. Likewise, it might be necessary to remove half of the components in the engine compartment to get at a starter or to change a belt.

Fortunately, automobile manufacturers have started to pay more attention to serviceability. Perhaps the engineers who design cars have actually tried to work on them. In any event, there does seem to be an organized effort to try to improve

Table 1-1. Maintenance and Repair Difficulty Ratings.

	Anyone can do using simple hand tools	Within the ability of most weekend mechanics	For experienced or professional mechanics only
Check vital fluid levels	●		
Change engine oil & filter	●		
Change air filter	●		
Change fuel filter	●		
Change transaxle fluid & filter	●		
Change coolant	●		
Replace radiator hose	●		
Replace V-belt	●		
Replace spark plugs	●		
Perform a tune-up		●	
Replace thermostat	●		
Replace water pump	●		
Replace alternator	●		
Replace battery	●		
Replace starter	●		
Adjust rear brakes	●		
Reline brakes		●	
Overhaul entire brake system			●
Lubricate chassis	●		
Rotate tires	●		
Replace rear shock absorbers	●		
Replace front MacPherson struts			●
Replace steering gear			●
Replace muffler & tail pipe	●		
Replace headlight or taillight	●		
Adjust engine valves		●	
Perform a valve job			●
Overhaul engine			●
Adjust idle speed	●		
Overhaul carburetor			●
Replace carburetor		●	
Align front end			●
Adjust clutch	●		
Replace clutch			●
Overhaul transaxle			●

serviceability and to locate frequently changed parts where they can be easily reached. They don't always succeed, but on the whole, today's cars are somewhat easier to work on than the V8s of a decade ago. The spark plugs on a typical front-wheel drive car with a transverse-mounted four-cylinder engine, for example, are right up front. Anybody with a plug socket and wrench can reach them (Fig. 1-3).

One area that still needs improvement is the location of tubes and hoses under the hood. Open the hood on some cars and you'll have trouble finding the engine because there is such a spaghetti-like maze of tubes obscuring it. It's tempting to start removing hoses, but many are connected to various emission control components. The tubes and hoses are often located where they are because there's no place else to put them, but often it looks as if the hoses were added as an afterthought. The heater hoses on some transverse-mounted four-cylinder engines are a prime example. The engineers who design some of these systems must have trouble connecting two points with a straight line, because you will usually find half a dozen hoses and crossover pipes running over, under, and around the engine.

One difficulty you will probably encounter is rusty bolts. A new car is a pleasure to work on be-cause the bolts actually come loose when you put a wrench on them. As a car ages, the nuts and bolts that hold it together become less and less willing to release their grip. This is especially true of any fastener exposed to high temperatures (the exhaust manifold and entire exhaust system) or subjected to road splash (the exhaust system, suspension, shock absorbers, bumpers, and trailer hitches).

Professional mechanics have the advantage of using a power impact wrench to break loose stubborn bolts. Muffler shops rarely waste their time trying to fight corroded fasteners, and simply cut them off with an acetylene (gas) torch. The same technique is often used on shock absorber bolts. Few do-it-yourselfers, however, have such tools at their disposal. Instead, most rely on penetrating oil, heat from a propane torch, a hammer and chisel, and muscle to overcome immobile bolts. Only after considerable blood, sweat, and tears does one master the art of freeing rusted fasteners; even then, bolts still break and threads strip. This is unquestionably the worst part of working on cars and

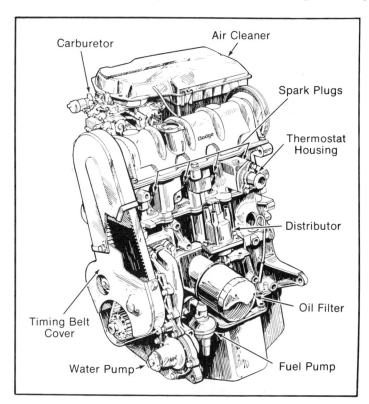

Fig. 1-3. Car manufacturers are placing more emphasis on serviceability these days. By making essential maintenance items and frequently replaced parts more accessible, it's easier for you to care for your own car. (Courtesy of Chrysler Corporation.)

a part that can make even a devout do-it-yourselfer turn the job over to a professional.

By the time you compare the relative advantages and disadvantages, the scale usually tips in favor of doing it yourself—unless, it's a particularly difficult job you'd rather pay someone else to do. It's your option, but being able to perform such work yourself allows you the flexibility to choose.

Chapter 2

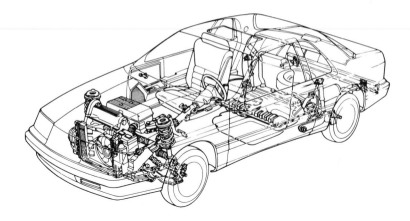

Tooling Up

Before you can start saving money on car care, you first have to obtain tools. You can't play mechanic unless you have proper tools. Don't try to get by with the old pliers, screwdriver, and Crescent wrench that's been in the junk drawer for the past 10 years.

YOUR TOOL BOX IS YOUR BEST FRIEND

Ask a professional mechanic who his best friend is and he'll probably tell you it's his tool box. It's not unusual to find professional mechanics who own thousands of dollars worth of hand tools. They've invested a considerable sum of money in their tools because their livelihood depends on it. They know the value of having the right tool for the right job. In many instances, they'll spend $50 or more for a tool that's specially designed for one particular application. The price is justified by the time the tool can save; it might be the only way to assemble or disassemble a certain component.

A professional mechanic buys the best quality

tools he can find, because he can't afford to have a tool break in the middle of a job. His tools must be durable to withstand the everyday abuse.

BUYING THE BASICS

Like the professional mechanic, you should try to buy top-quality tools backed by a lifetime free-replacement guarantee. There's no need to sink a small fortune into your tool collection. All you need are a few simple hand tools, a couple of specialty tools, and a tool box. Your total investment should be under $50, less if you already own some of the below-mentioned items.

All you need in your basic tool box is a set of combination wrenches, an adjustable wrench, a few regular and Phillips-tip screwdrivers, a pair of pliers, and a few assorted special-purpose tools such as an oil filter wrench, an oil spout, a feeler gauge, and a tire pressure gauge (Fig. 2-1). You may certainly add more (Table 2-1), but these are the minimum requirements.

Table 2-1. Guide to Determining Tool and Equipment Needs.

	Necessary for basic maintenance	Necessary for tune-up & troubleshooting	Nice to have but necessary only for some jobs
Hand wrenches	●	●	
Screwdrivers (straight & Phillips)	●	●	
Pliers (regular & needle nose)	●	●	
Sockets & ratchet	●	●	
Adjustable wrench	●		
Torque wrench			●
Oil filter wrench	●		
Oil spout	●		
Funnel	●		
Tire pressure gauge	●		
Grease gun	●		
Antifreeze tester	●		
Jack stands or ramps			●
Spark plug gap gauge	●		
Spark plug cleaner			●
Feeler gauge set	●		
Timing light		●	
Tachometer/dwellmeter		●	
Volt meter		●	
Compression gauge		●	
Vacuum gauge		●	
Battery charger			●
Jumper cables			●
Battery terminal cleaner			●
Trouble light			●

Wrenches

For simple maintenance jobs, you'll need a set of open-end/box-end wrenches (also called combination wrenches). If your car is an import it uses metric fasteners. A set of wrenches ranging in size from 10-mm through 19-mm should handle all of the nuts and bolts you're likely to encounter. For older domestic vehicles, you'll need a wrench set ranging in size from 3/8 of an inch to 3/4 of an inch. If it's a newer model car, you'll also need to buy a set of metric wrenches, because many of these cars use a mixture of metric and inch-size fasteners. The engine might have metric fasteners while the suspension might use standard sizes.

A 3/8-inch or 1/2-inch drive socket set and ratchet is a good addition to any tool box because it's much faster at removing most fasteners. A few extensions and a swivel can increase the tool set's versatility tremendously. But, socket and ratchet sets are expensive, so if you're buying on a budget, put off the socket and ratchet set. Besides, sometimes a socket on a nut isn't practical because an

Fig. 2-1. A basic beginner's tool set. With these few hand tools you can perform a wide variety of repairs.

open-end wrench is all that will fit. That's why a simple combination wrench set is the most used tool set you can buy. Wrenches should be of drop-forged tempered alloy steel, plated for corrosion resistance, and backed by a lifetime written guarantee.

To loosen large flare nuts or to hold one end of a bolt while you tighten a nut, an adjustable or Crescent wrench is hard to beat. Get one with a wide jaw opening that can handle nuts up to 1 inch in diameter.

Allen wrenches (small six-sided L-shaped wrenches) are rarely needed today. Pre-1975 cars required an Allen wrench to adjust the ignition points. Because all newer-model vehicles have an electronic ignition (which doesn't require a dwell adjustment), Allen wrenches are seldom needed. The only place you'll find Allen-head screws any more is on the dash trim of some performance

cars—and they're usually fake screws molded in plastic!

Box-end ratcheting wrenches can be very useful for tasks, such as removing shock absorber nuts or muffler clamps. If you own a ratchet and socket set, however, you probably won't use box end ratcheting wrenches very often. File these under "nice but rarely necessary" (Fig. 2-2).

If you like gimmick tools, you might consider a set of combination open end/socket wrenches. These have an open jaw on one end and a socket that can bend 180 degrees on the other end. The concept behind these wrenches is that they combine the versatility of open-end wrenches with sockets. In reality, they're not as convenient to use as a socket and ratchet set and they cost more than ordinary combination wrenches. They're certainly not necessary for the basic tool collection and unless somebody gives you a set as a gift, your money is better spent on ordinary combination wrenches and a socket set.

Screwdrivers

For a variety of jobs you'll need at least two different sizes of regular (flat-tip) and Phillips (cross-tip) screwdrivers. The least expensive way to buy screwdrivers is usually in a set. A set will often include an assortment of long and short handles, which gives you more versatility. Plastic or wooden handles are fine, but make sure each handle offers a good grip. Plastic handles with rubber liners might look like they'd give a good grip, but once they become greasy the rubber sleeves slip. The blade tips should be of hardened steel and the screwdriver should be plated for corrosion resistance.

Depending upon the kind of vehicles you own, you might also have to buy a couple of "torx"-head screwdrivers. Torx-head screws have a six-point star-shaped recess in the head (torx-head bolts have a gear-like head and require special torx drive sockets). You'll find them on many headlight and taillight covers. Torx fasteners are also used on seat belt anchor bolts and some carburetor and fuel injection assemblies to discourage tampering. Torx-head screws are used because they're more resistant to stripping than slot, Phillips- or Allen-head fasteners. A six-point Allen wrench can be used to remove a torx-head screw, but doing so can sometimes ruin the screw. Figure 2-3 illustrates the four basic types of screwdrivers.

Pliers

A pair of regular pliers and a pair of long-nose

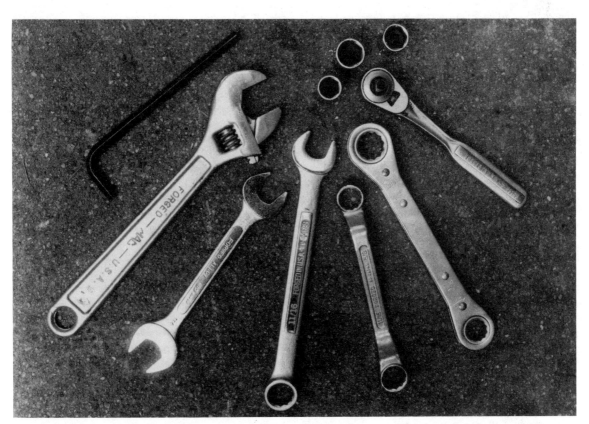

Fig. 2-2. Basic wrench types include (left to right): Allen, adjustable, open end, combination, box end, ratcheting box end, and ratchet and socket.

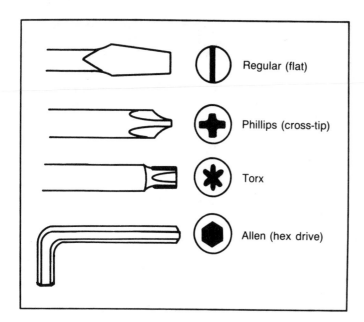

Fig. 2-3. Basic screwdriver types.

Regular (flat)

Phillips (cross-tip)

Torx

Allen (hex drive)

pliers are a must for any tool box. A pair of locking pliers (such as Vise-Grips) can be extremely handy for holding and gripping various fasteners. Likewise, a pair of interlocking pliers (often called waterpump pliers) are very useful to own.

Pliers should be of tempered steel and plated for corrosion resistance. Grip is also extremely important. Some pliers come with plastic covers on the handles. The covers look nice and they help protect both the pliers and hands. If the covers don't fit tightly, however, they'll slip off when the pliers become greasy.

If you think you'll be going beyond basic maintenance and light repair, a pair of snap ring pliers will be necessary. The needlelike tips on these pliers are needed to remove snap rings from parts such as master brake cylinders, U-joints and starter drives.

Oil Filter Wrench

For changing oil, one item you can't do without is an oil filter wrench. Buy the best one you can find, because the inexpensive ones don't grip very well and they usually bend or break after being used a few times. There are a variety of oil filter wrenches from which to choose, but those that work best have a metal band that wraps all the way around the fil-

ter. The kind that resemble a large socket and are designed to grip the filter can on its fluted end won't remove a stubborn filter.

Before you buy an oil filter wrench, be warned that they come in different diameters to handle different sized filters. Make sure you get the right size wrench for your car (Fig. 2-4). If you don't know what size it takes, look up your car's oil filter on an application chart, then use the filter to select the correct wrench.

Oil Spout

This is a tool for which the need is rapidly disappearing. One of the nicest favors the oil companies ever did for the consumer was to start putting oil in plastic containers with a funnel-type spout. The new packaging eliminates spills and allows you to reseal the container if you don't need the entire quart. You can still buy oil in the traditional cardboard or metal cans, and some oil companies insist that they'll never change their packaging. So if you buy your oil "the old-fashioned way" in a can you'll also need an oil spout.

A lot of people use a can opener and a funnel. Some even jab a hole in the top of the can with a screwdriver and splatter oil all over everything. And when they try to pour it in, half of the oil drib-

Fig. 2-4. You can't change your own oil unless you have a good filter wrench. Filter wrenches come in different sizes, so make sure you get the one that is right for your filter.

bles all over the engine. A spout is definitely better than the latter technique and is usually faster and less messy than using a funnel.

Feeler Gauge

For checking and gapping spark plugs, adjusting valve lash on many import engines, and adjusting contact points on older ignition systems, a set of feeler gauges is necessary. If you're going to stick with basic maintenance only, the least expensive type of feeler gauge you can buy is a simple wire gauge for gapping spark plugs. For a few dollars you can set plugs like a professional.

Many spark plugs supposedly come "pre-gapped" from the factory so some people might question the need for this particular tool. Spark plug gaps should always be checked before installation because the gap might not be correct for your car.

Recent improvements in spark plug construction (copper cores for example) have allowed spark plug manufacturers to drastically reduce the number of different types of plugs needed to cover all the various engine applications. One spark plug part number today might replace a dozen or more older spark plug numbers. Even though the heat range of the plug will work in a wider variety of engines, the gap requirements might vary.

Tire Pressure Gauge

Here's a tool that many people own but seldom use. Once bought, it is often tossed in the glove box and quickly forgotten. It makes a great toy for the kids because they love to pull the little plastic indicator stick in and out of the housing.

Believe it or not, this tool is very useful and necessary to own. Every time one of the tire companies does a survey on consumer maintenance habits they find most tires are either under- or over-inflated. Underinflation is bad because it causes the tires to heat up from excessive flexing. Not only does this wear out the tread faster, but it's also very damaging to the tire casing. Overinflation is just as bad because it makes a tire too hard. This makes the tire more vulnerable to road damage, not to mention that it causes a rough ride. Overinflation can also accelerate tire wear (in the middle area of the tread), and it can often cause a blowout because the tire heats up and builds up excessive pressure.

You can't accurately judge tire inflation by simply looking at or kicking a tire. Because the sidewalls on radial tires tend to bulge out, many people think they look underinflated. They pull into a service station and add air until the tire looks nice and round, which probably overinflates the tire by 10 to 20 pounds per square inch.

The only way to keep the tires on your car properly inflated is to check them with a gauge. The best time to do it is in the morning while the tires are still cold. Driving even a short distance heats the air inside the tires causing a higher than normal reading.

Other Handy Tools

A grease gun is one item you might consider adding to your tool inventory, but only if your vehicle has greaseable suspension components such as ball joints, tie rod ends, idler arm, pitman arm, and U-joints. Although most car manufacturers now use "greaseless" or "lubed-for-life" suspension components to eliminate the need for periodic greasing, most older cars, many pickup trucks, and some imports still have need for a grease gun. If you don't know whether your vehicle falls into this category, check in your owner's manual to see if periodic chassis lubrication is required. If it is you need a grease gun. Another way to tell is to look at the tie rod ends and ball joints to see if they have a grease fitting. If they do you need a grease gun. The best kind to buy is one that uses slip-in mini-cartridges and is equipped with a flexible rubber snout. The flexible snout is much easier to connect to fittings than those with a rigid pipe or short coupling (Fig. 2-5).

A spark plug socket is a necessary item for changing spark plugs. A spark plug socket is available in one of two sizes: 5/8 inch or 13/16 inch. The only thing that makes it different from an ordinary deep-well socket is a rubber sleeve or cushion inside the top to protect the spark plug insulator against breakage. Of course, if you have a spark plug socket you'll need a ratchet wrench or extension handle with which to turn it. A 1/2-inch drive gives more leverage than a 3/8-inch drive, so you'll probably find the job much easier with the larger drive size.

A pair of jack stands should be standard equipment in every do-it-yourselfer's garage (Fig. 2-6). Even the smallest cars weigh close to a ton. The bumper or post jack that comes with your car is barely adequate for changing a tire and should never be used to support the vehicle while you're under it. Bumper jacks have a rather nasty reputation for slipping when you least expect it. Because of this, the weight of the vehicle should always be supported on jack stands after raising it. Always use them in pairs and always position them under the frame, subframe, crossmember, or other substantial part of the chassis or suspension. The jack stands should carry a minimum rating of 1 1/2 tons or half the vehicle's weight—whichever is greater.

In addition to jack stands, you'd also be wise to invest in a small hydraulic floor jack. A good floor jack is both faster and easier to use than a bumper, scissors, or frame-post jack, and it's safer. (Under no circumstances should you ever rely on the jack alone to hold the car up while you're under it; always use jack stands.) Such a jack needn't be expensive. You can find 1 1/2 ton rated jacks for under $30. Of course, the more you spend, the better the quality and reliability of the jack. The average home mechanic will likely find one of the small portable units to be much more versatile and easier to use than one of the larger (and considerably heavier) long-handle floor jacks.

Some people prefer to buy a pair of steel ramps (Fig. 2-7) instead of a floor jack and jack stands for

Fig. 2-5. Here are some of the "specialty tools" you might need for basic maintenance and repair work: timing light, tach/dwell meter, compression gauge, vacuum gauge, tire pressure gauge, feeler gauge, spark plug gap gauge, battery post puller, battery post cleaner, trouble light, and grease gun.

undercar work. Steel ramps are less expensive, but they can slide when you try to drive your car onto them, there is always the danger of driving off of them, they can get in the way, and they aren't as versatile. However, if that's what you want, go ahead and buy a pair. Just make sure they're rated to handle at least half the weight of your vehicle.

For changing tires you should consider buying a four-way lug wrench. It's obvious that whoever designed the L-shaped lug wrench that comes with most cars never changed a tire. It works fine as a jack handle, but it's virtually useless for removing lug nuts. It's awkward and the leverage is all wrong. The harder you pull on it, the more it slips off the lug nut—often rounding off or damaging the nut in the process. A good four-way lug wrench will

give you excellent leverage and won't damage the lug nuts (Fig 2-8).

A trouble light comes in handy when working under the hood or under the car. Flashlights are okay for emergency use, but chances are your need for light will outlast the batteries. Both 110-volt and 12-volt trouble lights are available. The 110-volt variety plug into an ordinary electrical outlet, which might require an extension cord when working outside. On the positive side, a 110-volt light can give more light when fitted with a 100-watt bulb. On the negative side, there is always a shock hazard when working outdoors or on wet ground. Ordinary light bulbs are also easily broken if the trouble light is dropped. As for the 12-volt lights, they offer the greatest utility. They can be plugged into the ciga-

Fig. 2-6. Safety stands and a floor jack are a must for undercar work (oil changes, chassis lubrication, transmission fluid and filter changes, etc.).

Fig. 2-7. Ramps can also be used to raise a car. Just make sure they are strong enough to support the weight of the vehicle.

Fig. 2-8. A four-way lug wrench is essential for changing tires. The lug wrench that comes with the jack in most vehicles is virtually useless because it doesn't give enough leverage.

rette lighter or clamped onto the battery. This makes them highly portable which also makes them ideal for emergency roadside repairs. The 12-volt bulbs don't give quite as much light and replacement bulbs are not as easy to find. But all things considered, the 12-volt version is probably the best.

A pair of jumper cables (Fig. 2-9) is another item you'll eventually acquire if you live in the Northern states, or if you've found yourself stranded because of a rundown battery. You don't need jumper cables for routine maintenance or repair work, but there's nothing you can use in their place if you're stuck with a dead battery. When it comes to buying jumper cables, you definitely get what you pay for. The sets that sell for $3.98 are virtually worthless. The gauge of wire is too small to carry an adequate current between batteries. The

clamps usually break after a few uses. A good pair of jumper cables will use heavy gauge (size 4 or 6) copper wire (not aluminum) and have sturdy clamps. The cables should be long enough to reach from one end of your car to the other. Shorter cables are usable if you can get another vehicle nose-to-nose with your own, but you can't always do that. Therefore, it is better to pay more for longer cables.

Besides jumper cables, you might find some other battery tools useful. These include a post puller (for prying battery cables off battery posts without damaging either) and a battery post cleaner (for cleaning battery posts and cable clamps). Most no-starts and many dead batteries are due to corroded battery terminals. A wire brush can be used to clean the posts, but a post cleaner is faster and works better for cleaning out the inside of the clamps.

You might find yourself in need of a battery charger at some point to recharge a low or dead battery. Unless your car has a charging system problem or an old battery, you'll probably have little use for a charger. The money would be better spent fixing the problem instead of treating the symptom. However, a battery charger can be quite useful for recharging a dead battery after someone has left the lights on all day, for recharging the battery in a vehicle that has been sitting for a long period of time, for recharging a boat or lawn tractor battery, or for cold morning starts. If you buy a charger, get one with at least a 10-amp capacity. The little 2- and 4-amp trickle chargers are too slow. It's also nice if the charger has a "boost" feature for winter jump starting.

More Advanced Tools

As your skill level increases, it is a good idea to buy yourself an inexpensive torque wrench. The beam indicator type is the least expensive (usually under $20) and is accurate enough for most home repairs. The scale should show both standard (pounds-foot) and metric (Newton-meters) torque values. Treat a torque wrench with care; its accuracy will vary depending on how much abuse it receives (Fig. 2-10).

For checking ignition timing, you might con-

Fig. 2-9. Jumper cables are a handy item for cold morning starts or for starting rundown batteries.

sider buying an inexpensive timing light (Fig. 2-11). A timing light is basically a strobe that shows you the timing marks on the crankshaft pulley or flywheel while the engine is running. The light is triggered by connecting it to the number one spark plug wire. The light itself can be powered by ignition voltage or by battery voltage. The xenon battery-powered lights give the most light while the low-cost neon ignition-powered lights are barely visible. There's no need to spend a lot of money on a professional-grade adjustable timing light, because the added feature confuses more people than it helps. The only reason for using an adjustable timing light is to check total timing advance, and that's something best left to someone who is skilled in ignition service.

As far as test equipment is concerned, the sky's the limit. An inexpensive vacuum gauge can help you diagnose a variety of ills ranging from vacuum leaks to bad engine valves. A compression gauge

is useful for keeping an eye on the condition of your engine's rings, valves, and head gasket. Either of these might be useful additions to your tool collection if you plan to do your own tune-ups or try your hand at diagnosis (Figs. 2-12 and 2-13).

On older vehicles with point ignition systems, a hand-held dwell meter/tachometer provides a more accurate means of adjusting the points and making carburetor adjustments, but a feeler gauge works just as well. A dwell meter can also be used on late-model General Motors vehicles (1981-86) with feedback carburetors to monitor the relative richness or leanness of the air/fuel mixture. There are even plug-in testers for displaying trouble codes stored in the vehicle's on-board engine control computer. This is advanced stuff for a home mechanic. Therefore, unless you plan on becoming a semi-professional, there's no need to spend your money on these tools.

One tester that you will find to be very useful,

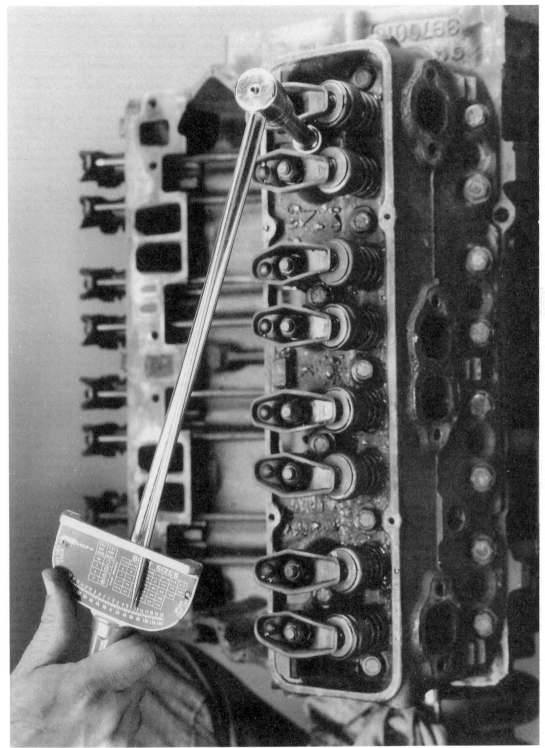

Fig. 2-10. A torque wrench shows how much force is being applied to a fastener. Shown is a beam type wrench, the most common wrench used by do-it-yourselfers.

Fig. 2-11. You will need a timing light to check the ignition timing marks on the crankshaft pulley or flywheel. Xenon bulbs provide the brightest light.

doesn't require much skill to operate, and is inexpensive is an antifreeze tester (Fig. 2-14). Some use floating balls, a needle indicator, or a calibrated hydrometer to measure the strength of the antifreeze in your radiator. For all practical purposes, the least expensive floating-ball type tester gives just as meaningful (though not as precise) readings as the more sophisticated testers. In fact, the floating-ball testers are about as goof-proof as you can get.

You can buy all kinds of special testers and gadgets for checking this and adjusting that on your car, but before you spend any money for such "toys," ask yourself if you'll ever get your money's worth out of them.

A portable mini-air compressor might be one item that falls into the "don't need" category. At first glance, it looks like a great product. It plugs into the cigarette lighter and can be used to inflate everything from beach balls to flat tires. In real-

ity, it is better suited for beach balls than tires because it's extremely slow. Although a typical mini-compressor might be able to pump up to 100 *psi* (pounds per square inch), it takes a very long time—perhaps half an hour—to inflate a flat tire to just 30 psi. The time factor might not be important in a roadside emergency situation, but chances are, if the tire is flat, the air will leak out of it faster than the little pump can put it in.

ALL TOOLS ARE NOT ALIKE

When it comes to buying hand tools, you'll soon discover that there is a world of difference in quality—often depending on what part of the world a tool comes from. India, Korea, Taiwan, and Japan have earned a reputation for being exporters of inferior-quality tools. This doesn't mean that every tool that comes from overseas is of inferior quality. We have some cheap tool manufacturers in the United States, too. In fact, many quality brand-name tools are now manufactured overseas because of lower labor costs.

What you do want to watch out for, however, are junk tools that reflect a lack in both workmanship and quality. The most important difference, yet the difference that's most difficult to see, is in the quality of the steel used to make the tools. A set of sockets that retails for $14.95 might look as good to the uneducated eye as a quality name-brand set that sells for several times as much. They both look the same, yet the quality tools might be anywhere from two to ten times stronger, and thus better able to withstand repeated use without breaking.

The reason for the difference in price is that the inexpensive sockets are probably made of cast steel rather than forged alloy steel. Casting produces a finished-looking socket in one easy step while forging requires several steps. The best quality sockets are often machined out of solid bar stock and go through multiple machining operations.

Each step adds to the cost, but it also adds to the strength and quality of the finished tool. That's what you pay for when you buy a quality tool.

You can usually identify a quality tool by its guarantee. Most of the junk tool manufacturers don't offer guarantees, because they know their tools won't hold up. Some are being more clever and have started to put guarantees on their packaging to mislead consumers into believing their tools are of a higher quality than they really are. Sometimes you'll find the "catch" in the fine print; instead of exchanging the tool where you bought it, you have to send it back to Taiwan or wherever.

Better quality tools are always backed by a written guarantee that allows an over-the-counter exchange of a defective tool at the place of purchase. Most quality tool manufacturers offer a free lifetime replacement guarantee if the tool fails for any reason other than obvious misuse or abuse. Even then, they'll often exchange it anyway as long as you don't reveal what you really did to break it.

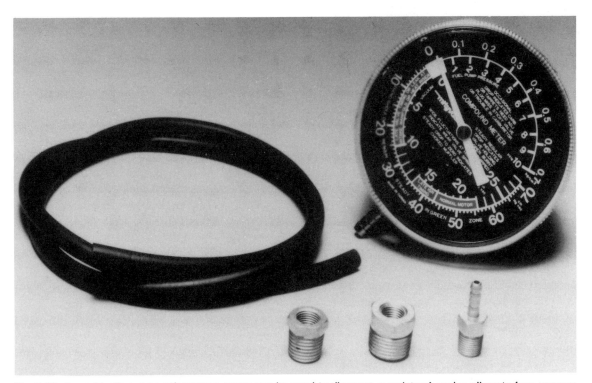

Fig. 2-12. A combination vacuum/pressure gauge can be used to diagnose a variety of engine ailments from vacuum leaks to valve problems to fuel pumps. (Courtesy of Neward Enterprises, Incorporated.)

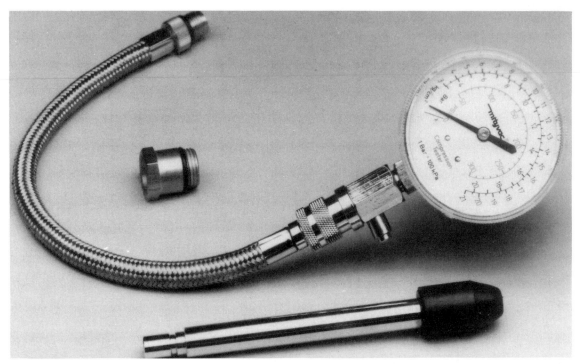

Fig. 2-13. A compression gauge checks engine compression to determine the condition of the rings, valves, and head gasket. (Courtesy of Neward Enterprises, Incorporated.)

One of the most misleading phrases you'll find on tool packaging is "professional quality." The implication is that this tool is of the same quality that is used by a professional mechanic. In reality it is meaningless, because a so-called "professional-quality" tool can be absolute junk next to a true professional-grade tool. Name brands such as Sears Craftsman, Stanley, S-K, Master Mechanic, and their counterparts are all quality brands you can trust.

HOW TO FIND THE BEST DEALS ON TOOLS

The least expensive way to buy tools is to buy a complete set. The greater the number of tools in the set, the greater the savings. Buying tools in a prepackaged set can save anywhere from 30 to 50 percent over what it would cost to buy each tool individually.

Most retailers offer basic beginner sets for around $50 that include the wrenches, screwdrivers, and pliers needed for basic maintenance

and simple repair work. There's no need to buy a 200-piece tool set if a 40-piece set will satisfy your needs (Fig. 2-15).

Timing can also save you quite a bit of money on tool purchases. Most retailers offer basic sets as well as individual tools at significant savings during special sales throughout the year. Retailers promote every holiday imaginable as well as the coming of a new season for tool sales.

As far as finding the best place to buy tools is concerned, the bargains are where you find them. A supermarket or a drug store is probably the worst place to buy tools because the quality of tools they carry is usually junk. Such tools are for light housework, like hanging curtain rods, not automotive service work.

Another place to avoid is flea markets. Normally a flea market is a place to go to find a good bargain. Sometimes you can find an individual selling good used tools for a fraction of the original cost. The real problem with flea markets, however, is that they've become saturated with en-

Fig. 2-14. To check the strength of the antifreeze you need an inexpensive antifreeze tester like this.

trepreneurs hawking cheap tools from Taiwan. These tools are mostly junk, so save your money for good-quality tools.

Automotive parts stores, hardware stores, and the automotive departments of large retailers are where you'll find the better-quality tools. You still have to be careful, however, because retailers will often have a mixture of better and lesser quality tools to appeal to every budget.

There's no need to buy true professional-quality tools, but if you want them, you'll often have to go to an automotive parts store. But all automotive parts stores are not the same. Is the store retail (do-it-yourself) oriented or does it cater primarily to the professional trade? It's not easy to tell because virtually every automotive parts store does some retailing. Even so, you can usually tell which is which by where the parts counter is located. If it's way in the back with a lot of display shelving up front, it's oriented more toward the do-it-yourself clientele rather than the professional customer. Such a store probably won't have the top-quality tools as does one that sells to the professional trade.

Another place to buy professional tools is from the "wagon vendors" who sell tools direct to mechanics (Snap-On, Mac, Matco, etc.). Their trucks have regular routes that include dealerships, service stations, and independent repair garages. The tools they sell are unquestionably the highest quality (and highest priced) tools you can buy, if you can buy them. It isn't easy because you first have to find one of their tool trucks. Look up the local distributor in the telephone directory and give him a call.

GENERAL SAFETY PRECAUTIONS

A tool is only as safe as the person who uses it. The following list of tool precautions is included along with some general suggestions on repair safety. Please take a few minutes to read through them carefully—especially if you're a novice to automotive repair. Working on your car need not be any more dangerous than changing a light bulb providing you use good common sense and observe these rules. When accidents do happen, they're often the result of carelessness or ignorance. Don't let that happen to you.

Before starting any kind of repair work dress for the part. Remove jewelry such as rings, watches, and bracelets, and don't wear loose-fitting clothing such as ties, scarves, or jackets that might become tangled or caught.

Some means of eye protection such as safety glasses, goggles, or a face shield is highly recommended whenever you're using a hammer and chisel, when drilling or grinding, when working under the car, when working on the car's battery (when jump starting or charging the battery for example), or when servicing the air conditioning system (Freon can cause frostbite if it comes into direct contact with your skin, so always protect your eyes when recharging the system or disconnecting hoses).

Use tools for their intended purpose. Screwdrivers make lousy chisels and pry bars, just as pliers make poor hammers. Socket extensions are not designed to double as punches, nor are ordinary hand sockets designed to withstand the abuse of an impact wrench. Vise-grips are great for holding,

23

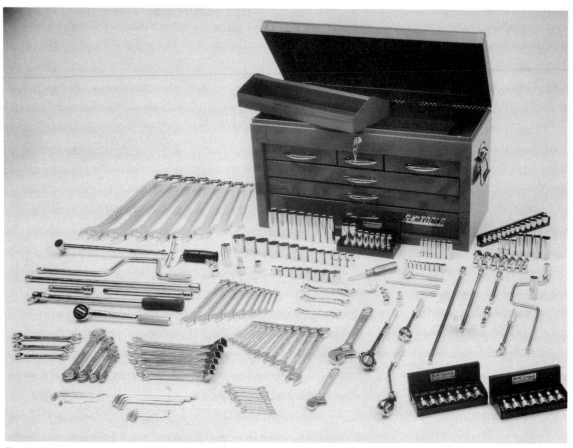

Fig. 2-15. The most economical way to buy tools is in a set. A set like this is more than most do-it-yourselfers need, but for more advanced repair work it provides all the essentials (Courtesy S-K Tools).

but they can also damage nuts and bolts. Use your tools the right way and they'll serve you well.

Avoid breathing dust from brake linings or clutches. Many vehicles use friction linings that contain asbestos fibers. The dust from these linings accumulates inside brake drums and bell housings. Asbestos dust should be avoided because it is suspected of causing cancer. Scientists don't know for certain how much of it you have to inhale before it causes a problem, so the best advice is to avoid it altogether. To remove dust from brake or clutch parts, use liquid brake cleaner and a rag. Don't blow off dusty parts with an air hose or try to clean them with an ordinary vacuum cleaner, because doing so can blow thousands of asbestos fibers into the air. If you have an attached garage, airborne asbestos

fibers can find their way into the rest of the house where they can endanger you and your family.

The Environmental Protection Agency (EPA) states that contact with oil and grease can be hazardous. The warning is now printed on some oil containers. After soaking some laboratory rats for months in dirty crankcase oil, the rats eventually developed skin cancer. It is doubtful that oil and grease pose any real health threat; if they did, professional automotive mechanics, who are up to their elbows in grease everyday, would have a higher-than-usual incidence of skin cancer. They don't, so there's no need to consider yourself doomed if your hands get dirty. Just wash them thoroughly when you're through with a good hand cleaner (Goop or Go-Jo are two excellent products).

Hair shampoo is also good, but ordinary soap is not very effective at removing grease.

Never crawl under a car that isn't adequately supported, and never rely on a jack alone to hold up the vehicle. The car should be parked on level ground with the emergency brake set and the transmission in park (automatic) or in gear (manual). Wheels should be chocked with a block of wood to prevent the car from rolling. Once the vehicle has been raised, place a pair of jack stands underneath to carry the weight. Position the stands under something solid such as the frame, frame rails, control arms, axles, or bumper supports. Don't put them under the rocker panels, floor pan, or oil pan. If you don't have jack stands, use something that can support several thousand pounds such as wooden 4- × -4 blocks or concrete blocks. Don't use milk crates, foot stools, garbage cans, or your kid's toy wagon.

Treat a running engine with respect. Keep tools, fingers, hands, hair, and clothing away from all moving parts. It's also a good idea not to stand in direct line with the fan blades on a rear-wheel-drive vehicle with an engine-driven fan. Should an item fall into the blades, it becomes a projectile.

You can get a real charge out of do-it-yourself auto repair, especially if you touch a high-voltage source such as the spark plug wires, distributor cap, or ignition coil while the engine is running. Today's ignition systems put out more than 40,000 volts, and should you become part of the circuit between the secondary ignition system and ground, you'll get a nasty shock. The 12-volt part of the electrical system (battery & wiring), isn't dangerous because it doesn't carry enough voltage to cause a shock.

Leave your cigarettes in the pack when working on any part of the fuel system (especially the carburetor and fuel tank) or the battery. Most people are smart enough to treat gasoline with respect, but not everyone is aware of the danger associated with batteries. Hydrogen gas is produced inside the battery during recharging; all it takes is a tiny spark in the immediate vicinity of the battery to touch it off. Remember the Hindenberg? It was filled with hydrogen. Treat the stuff with the same respect you would a bomb. Batteries have been known to ex-

plode because someone tried to use a match or cigarette lighter to see how much "water" was inside.

There's also a danger of blowing up the battery by using jumper cables incorrectly. The final jumper connection should never be made to the negative post on the battery itself but to a good ground such as the engine block or frame. The final jumper connection usually sparks as the voltage starts to flow. Making this connection away from the battery reduces the chance of igniting any hydrogen that might be present.

Batteries also contain sulfuric acid. Use care when removing, installing, or carrying a battery so that you don't spill the acid. Hands can be protected by wearing rubber gloves and eyes should be protected with goggles or safety glasses. If you do get acid on your skin, wash it immediately with plenty of water. Acid can also be neutralized with baking soda. Corrosive residue on the outside of the battery can get on clothing where it will leave holes the next time the clothing is washed. When carrying a battery, therefore, use a battery strap or hold it away from you. Don't cradle it like a baby or you'll ruin your clothes.

Never use gasoline to clean greasy parts; it's much too dangerous. The slightest spark can cause it to ignite. Even the pilot light on a nearby water heater or furnace can be enough to cause an explosion. Always use a degreasing solvent, detergent, or kerosene to clean parts.

Never run an engine inside a closed garage. Carbon monoxide fumes can build up to lethal levels in minutes. You can't see it and you can't smell it. In fact, you won't even be aware of it until it's too late. Don't take foolish chances. If you must run the engine in a garage, open the garage door or use flex tubing to vent the exhaust outdoors.

Never open the radiator cap on a hot engine. The cooling system builds up considerable pressure, and if the engine is hot, you run the risk of being scalded by hot steam and/or hot water. Let the car sit for several hours before you open the cap. If you can't wait that long, shut the engine off and pour cold water over the radiator (not the engine) to help cool it off. Then place a rag over the cap and slowly turn it to the first safety catch. Wait until the pressure has vented itself before completely removing the cap.

Use care when working on a hot engine or around a hot exhaust system. It's always best to let a car set and cool off before you start to work on it. If you can't wait, you can protect yourself against burns by wearing a long-sleeved shirt and gloves.

ENVIRONMENTAL CONCERNS

One of the drawbacks of doing your own maintenance is the problem of what to do with the old fluids you've drained from your car. This includes such things as dirty crankcase oil, used antifreeze, transmission fluid, power steering fluid, brake fluid, gear oil, and gasoline.

The worst thing you can do is dump any one of these fluids down the drain or into a storm sewer. You should never dispose of it by pouring it in your back yard, either. The reason you shouldn't dump it is because it gets into the ground water where it can pollute local water supplies. This is especially a concern in areas that rely on ground water wells for drinking water. Petroleum distillates and antifreeze are also toxic to both plant and animal life. Old antifreeze makes great weed killer, but it also kills the grass, trees, and other vegetation.

The best way to dispose of used crankcase oil, transmission fluid, and gear oil is to pour it into a sealed container and take it to a local recycling center. Most service stations and quick-lube oil change facilities will also accept it provided it doesn't contain gasoline or anything hazardous. This might be changing, however, because of the EPA's crackdown on hazardous wastes. Some businesses might be reluctant to accept oil for recycling because they don't know what it contains. This can create disposal problems for them if the oil turns out to be contaminated with toxic substances.

The other alternative is to put the old oil or antifreeze in a sealed container and throw it in the trash. Most municipalities will still accept such wastes for landfills, but this too might change in the near future. Unfortunately, we live in a throwaway world and, as yet, nobody has come up with a good solution for disposing of or recycling hazardous wastes.

Chapter 3

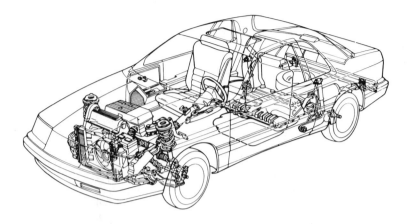

Replacement Parts

One of the most important aspects of do-it-yourself car care is buying filters, fluids, and replacement parts. The savings can really add up if you shop wisely. Easy as it might sound, shopping for the best bargains on automotive parts takes a certain amount of skill and luck, because the retail jungle is full of snares waiting to trap the unwary.

THE GREAT "LIST PRICE" RIP-OFF

To help you better understand the pricing of automotive parts in the marketplace, I will explain some facts about how automotive parts are distributed and sold in the *aftermarket* (this means the auto parts stores and garages that cater to cars after they're new; it does not include the new car dealers).

The story of how an automobile part gets from the factory to you is long and often complicated, but one that has a tremendous influence on the price you ultimately pay for a product. The essence of it all is the longer the path from factory to consumer, the higher the end price (Fig. 3-1).

When an automobile part is manufactured at the factory, the manufacturer establishes a basic selling price for each step in the chain of distribution. The "suggested" selling prices guarantee each player a certain amount of profit. Whether the amount of profit each step in the chain grabs is justified is another question, but at each stage there is a certain amount of "traditional" markup. The selling price at each stage and the amount of markup is then printed on price sheets and distributed to the various players.

The first player in the game of distribution is usually a *warehouse distributor*. His job is to be a middleman for the manufacturer. He stores the parts in a huge central warehouse for delivery to various auto parts stores that make up his clientele. The markup at this stage of distribution ranges from 15 to 30 percent.

The next player is the *jobber*. This is the name the industry gives the person who runs an auto parts store. If the jobber caters primarily to the do-it-yourself trade, he is called a *retail jobber*. If he

Fig. 3-1. Bargains are where you find them. Everyone claims to sell "discount" auto parts, but prices can vary widely depending on where you shop. Stick with recognized brand name products; the quality is usually superior. (Courtesy of Ford Motor Company.)

caters more to the professional trade, he is said to be a *traditional jobber.*

The jobber maintains only a small inventory of parts in his store, partly because of limited shelf space but primarily to minimize his inventory stocking costs. The parts he does carry tend to be only the most popular parts that he's most likely to sell. The less popular parts, such as parts for older model vehicles, would just sit on his shelf and gather dust. He usually relies on his warehouse distributor when he needs such parts. He also relies on his warehouse distributor to keep him stocked. In fact, he might deal with several different warehouse distributors; if one doesn't have the part he needs, he can get it from another. If the jobber doesn't have a part on hand when a customer asks for it, he'll call up his warehouse distributor and order it. The warehouse distributor can usually have it delivered the same day. The jobber's markup depends on what the item is, but it ranges from 30 percent to 100 percent.

Next comes the great "list price" rip-off. Depending on who walks into the jobber's store to buy a part, one of several different price sheets might be used. If the customer is a professional mechanic, he becomes the next player in the distribution scheme. The jobber will give him at an *installer's price*—which is usually 30 percent to 40 percent less than the final or *list price* that you pay if you walk through the door. The mechanic gets a bigger discount so that he can charge you the full list price and make a profit on the installation of the part.

How does it all add up? Let's say a manufacturer makes a muffler and it costs him $3 to build it at the factory. The manufacturer needs a profit so he'll sell it to the warehouse distributor for $8. The warehouse distributor tacks on his markup and sells the muffler to a jobber for $14. The jobber needs his profit to stay in business so he sells it to the local garage for $22. You walk in the door and the service manager quotes you a price of $34—plus installation, pipes, and clamps.

These facts make a lot of consumers angry. After all, you're already paying the garage $30 per hour for labor to install the muffler, so why should they make a profit by marking up the parts as well? That's a good question for which there is no good answer. It doesn't seem fair that the consumer pays the full freight for every markup in the entire chain of distribution, but that's the way automobile parts (and virtually every other kind of product) are sold in this country. If you think the markup on automobile parts is bad, the markups on clothing and furniture are outrageous by comparison.

With automobile parts, however, you at least have a way to fight back. By eliminating the professional installer from the last step, you can knock as much as 30 percent to 40 percent off the final price of the part. Let us go back to our friendly jobber store for a minute. The jobber, remember, has several price sheets from which he can sell parts. Obviously, he wants to make as much profit as he

can. He is therefore going to try to sell each customer off the highest price sheet. His professional customers get the best deal because they buy the most parts. You, on the other hand, are usually charged the full list price because that is the way the system works—or at least that is the way it used to work.

The system is changing for the better as far as consumers are concerned, because the traditional price structure is breaking down. Competition has put more pressure on every stage in the distribution system to cut prices. As a result, some jobbers now buy direct from factories. Others have become part of huge program groups who can buy at better discounts. Distributors have set up their own auto parts stores to be more price competitive. One of the most important changes in recent years has been the rise of the so-called *discount jobber* who sells parts direct to do-it-yourselfers at a price somewhat higher than the professional trade but at significant savings compared to full list price.

Nowadays when you walk into a retail-oriented auto parts store, the counterman will first quote you the list price, then the discount price. You are still paying for the jobber's and distributor's markups, but at least you save a few dollars off the list price. How much do you actually save? Maybe 20 to 30 percent depending on the item and the jobber's discount policy.

Unfortunately, the discount structure has held its ground as far as the new car dealer is concerned. In fact, even professional installers can have a tough time getting a discount on new parts, particularly from import car dealers who are reluctant to give anybody a discount.

New car dealers historically charge the highest prices for the parts they sell. Why? Because they have a captive audience. Many parts are simply not available outside the dealer network. This applies to virtually all body parts, many chassis parts, and major components such as the engine and drive train. If the car is not a new model, you can buy spark plugs, filters, shock absorbers, starters, and alternators almost anywhere, and you can scour the local salvage yards for other parts. But if the car is a new one, chances are, the dealer will be your only source of supply. Dealers use this to the maximum advantage by pricing hard-to-get parts as high as possible. Because the dealer enjoys a virtual monopoly on most of the parts he sells, supply and demand dictates a sky-high price.

This arrangement creates other headaches for consumers as well as professional mechanics. Parts availability is often limited, because most of the parts are being used for new car production rather than repair. Consequently, you can find yourself waiting weeks on end while a part is backordered from the manufacturer. Import car dealers seem to be somewhat worse than domestic car dealers, although both can experience agonizing delays in parts delivery.

The new car dealer gets most of his parts from the car manufacturer's warehouse, who in turn gets its parts from either the factory or the original equipment supplier. Believe it or not, car manufacturers do not make most of their own parts. They buy them from outside supplier companies—often the same companies who make replacement parts for the aftermarket.

A Ford Motorcraft oil filter, for example, might be made by an independent manufacturer who also makes the same filters for dozens of other companies. The same Motorcraft filter that would cost you $6 at a Ford dealership might sell for $5 at a traditional auto parts store, for $4 at a discount auto parts store, or for as little as $2 on sale at K-Mart.

DOES EVERYBODY REALLY SELL "DISCOUNT" AUTO PARTS?

It would seem that the least expensive place to buy parts is at a "discount" auto parts store or large retailer. Yet, one store's so-called "discounts" might not be nearly as good as another's.

"Discount" pricing has become a catch phrase for merchandising virtually everything today. The actual selling price might be discounted below the manufacturer's suggested list price, but in many instances the list price is a phony. It is artificially inflated to make it look as if the retailer is giving the consumer a big discount when, in fact, he is paying the same price, or sometimes more, than the item sells for elsewhere. Just because a store has "DISCOUNT" banners plastered all over the walls and windows does not mean you are truly getting a discount. You still have to shop and compare to know whether you are getting a bargain.

One thing is for certain, if you are paying full list price for your parts, you are paying too much. Sometimes you do not have a choice, especially when it comes to dealer only parts that simply are not available elsewhere. But when the parts you need are readily available at a variety of outlets, you can save a bundle by shopping around.

You know you are getting a bargain when you find a brand name item that already sells for a discount on sale at an even lower price. That is a deal that is hard to beat. Let us take oil as an example. Let us say you prefer Superduperlube brand oil. If you buy a quart of Superduperlube at the local service station, you will pay $2.25 a quart. The same oil sells for $1.30 a quart in the supermarket. The best price you have ever found is 99 cents at the Big Discount Auto Parts store. Then the Big Discount Auto Parts store decides to have a special sale on Superduperlube for $9.60 a half case (12 quarts); that is only 80 cents a quart. Now there is a bargain. Compared to the per can price you would pay at the service station, you are saving $1.45 a can or $5.80 on every oil change, if you do it yourself.

Seasonal sales can provide good savings. Batteries are a prime example of seasonal pricing. The dead of winter is obviously the peak season for battery sales; not lower price type sales but sales of thousands of batteries to people who desperately need them. During this time, you will usually pay top dollar for a new battery. What is more, the lower-priced batteries are the first to sell out, forcing you to spend more than you really intended for a new battery. Yet, in the middle of July when nobody buys batteries, retailers typically advertise specials offering as much as $20 or $30 off their best batteries. If your battery is more than four years old, chances are, it will not make it through another winter. If that is the case and your budget can handle it, buy one in July and save yourself some money—and aggravation.

SHOPPING FOR THE BEST
DEAL: USED VS. REBUILT VS. NEW

As mentioned earlier in this chapter, one of the alternatives to buying new parts is to shop for used parts. Your local salvage yard (they prefer not to be called junkyards or boneyards anymore) can be an alternative source for such things as body parts, radios, glass, trim moldings, taillight lens, engines, transmissions, starters, carburetors, alternators, radiators, even tires. The savings can be considerable, but you have to know how to "source" your parts.

You will find that prices for used parts vary considerably from one salvage yard to another depending on their relative level of sophistication. If it is one of those places where you take your life in your hands trying to get past the guard dogs, then wade through knee deep mud to scrounge the wrecks for the parts you need; chances are you will get the lowest price. You find the parts, you take them off the wrecked car, and you take the risks (no guarantees), so you save yourself money. And, depending on how skilled you are at dickering, you might even get the "junkie" to knock a few dollars off his price.

Of course, this kind of bargain hunting is not for everyone. If you do not feel comfortable searching through piles of wrecked automobiles or dealing with tattooed people who look as if they steal motorcycles to support a drug habit, you can opt for a more "upscale" junkyard.

Many salvage yards today are run in a more business-like manner. Instead of piling the wrecks out back where nature and vandals can take their toll, each car is totally disassembled as it arrives. The salvageable parts are removed, cleaned, tested, numbered, and inventoried. The parts are stored indoors in a warehouse and are categorized by year, make, and model. When you walk into one of these places, you will be greeted by a salesperson, not a snarling dog. The guy might still have tattoos on his arms and rings in his ears, but at least he will help you find the part you need. He will check to see if they have the part on the computer, then he will get it and bring it to you. He might also give you a 10-day exchange guarantee. Naturally you pay for the added service, but still the savings can be considerable compared to buying new parts at a dealer or auto parts store.

The salvage dealer is in business to make money too, and many times he will charge almost as much for certain hard-to-find parts as they cost new. This is particularly true on most late-model cars as well as newer luxury models and high-priced or exotic imports.

Your only other alternative to buying new parts for your car is to buy rebuilt parts. The traditional savings of rebuilt versus new is usually 30 to 50 percent. What is a rebuilt part? It includes such things as starters, alternators, carburetors, water pumps, clutches, fuel pumps, distributors, rack and pinion steering assemblies, brake calipers, master brake cylinders, brake shoes, air conditioning compressors, transmissions, and even complete or partial engines. There is no exact definition as to what *rebuilt* actually means, but, generally speaking, it is a part that has been tested and reconditioned so it works like new. A popular phrase is "equals or exceeds original equipment specifications." In plain English, this means the part is supposed to be as good as a new one; sometimes it is true and sometimes it is not (Fig. 3-2).

One of the risks of buying rebuilt parts is the wide variety in rebuilding procedures employed by parts rebuilders. Some are backyard businesses that buy scrap parts from a junkyard, clean them up, patch whatever is wrong with the part, and then sell it to a jobber as being rebuilt; others virtually remanufacture the part. They will disassemble hundreds of similar parts, clean and test individual components, and routinely replace all wear-prone items to bring the part back into original equipment specifications. Such parts are typically backed by a written guarantee (some even offer lifetime guarantees) and are generally the best value for the money. The problem is in distinguishing quality rebuilt parts from the others.

YOU GET WHAT YOU PAY FOR

The highest-quality rebuilt components are obviously those that have been totally reconditioned to like-new or better-than-new condition. In many in-

Fig. 3-2. Remanufactured parts are a less-expensive alternative to buying new parts.

stances, a rebuilder will make small improvements on the original design to improve durability or performance. This might include increasing the size of the bolts or the wiring, using a stronger casting, installing a better grade of bearing, using a higher-quality seal or gasket, etc. Such improvements cost money, so the higher quality parts command a higher price.

Unfortunately, many people demand the absolute lowest price regardless of quality. Consequently, a lot of poor-quality rebuilt parts have appeared on the market. These bargains are no bargain at all. What good does it do you if you initially save $10 on a rebuilt starter but the starter fails in another 6 months? Some parts do not even work right out of the box!

Given a choice between a quality remanufactured component and a bargain-priced rebuilt, you are always better off spending a few dollars more for the better part. Most of the better-quality

remanufactured parts are sold under national or regional brand names. Beware of the plain white box or generic packaging. It could be an indication of cost cutting that stretches beyond the packaging itself.

Another way to tell good quality from not-so-good quality is to look for a guarantee—the longer the better. Many rebuilders now offer lifetime guarantees (to the original purchaser only) on many components. Even if you plan to sell or trade your car in the near future, a lifetime guarantee is your assurance that the part will not fail and leave you faced with another repair bill. Even if the guarantee cannot be transferred to the new owner, it can be a positive selling point because it indicates you cared enough to install only the best.

One item to watch out for with respect to brand name automobile parts is "look-alike" or counterfeit packaging. When a manufacturer has established a good reputation for building quality parts, there are always unscrupulous suppliers who try to capitalize on someone else's good name. In some cases they resort to product names that sound similar to recognized brand names (Motorcare, which sounds like Ford Motorcraft, for example) or look-alike packaging (using a red, white, and blue box that resembles a Chrysler Mopar box, or a streaking race car that looks like the one used by Ford).

The best way to protect yourself against this kind of deception is to read the packaging carefully. If it says "replaces" Chrysler, Ford, GM, or whatever on the box, it is not a genuine original equipment part. That does not necessarily mean the part is of lesser quality, but it does imply the supplier lacks enough faith in its own reputation to sell products under its own brand name.

Then there are the rip-off artists who use outright fraud to deceive the public. There have been numerous instances of inferior quality products (mostly from Taiwan and other overseas sources) being sold in brand name boxes or with bogus brand name trademarks printed on them. In some instances, the auto parts store is the guilty party out to pad their profits by selling cheap merchandise at brand name prices. Oftentimes they, too, are the victims.

The only form of protection against outright fraud is to buy parts that come in sealed boxes or boxes that have obviously not been opened. It is easy for a dishonest retailer to slip a cheaper part into a brand name box, especially if he keeps the box after he sells you the part. Be suspicious, therefore, of any retailer who either brings you the part out of the box or who wants to keep the box. Some rebuilders might ask auto parts stores to return exchange parts in the original packaging because it offers better protection than a steel drum (which is the way most parts are returned for rebuilding), but this usually only applies to such things as carburetors, distributors, or other components with breakable parts. If you suspect fraud— especially if you have trouble with the part—do not hesitate to write directly to the manufacturer.

Another aspect of buying rebuilt parts that should be mentioned is that of a *core exchange*. When you buy a rebuilt part, an alternator for example, you usually have to surrender your old alternator. If you do not happen to have your old alternator with you when you buy the rebuilt alternator, the store will charge you a core deposit (usually around $10 to $20 for an alternator) that is refundable when you bring in your old alternator.

This might seem like an unnecessary hassle, but the rebuilding business depends on a steady supply of exchange parts. Ideally, a rebuilder would like to receive one rebuildable core for every rebuilt product sold. It rarely turns out this way because many parts are so badly damaged that they cannot be salvaged. This means the rebuilder has to pay a premium price for the cores he needs by buying them from salvage yards or other suppliers. Thus, the core deposit on hard-to-get parts runs higher than those on more common parts. If your part is not salvageable, you forfeit the core deposit.

In conclusion, the best deals are where you find them. You can always save money when buying automobile parts by calling around and checking various sources. Do not be afraid to compare prices and do not be afraid to buy used or rebuilt parts rather than new. Stay with brand names whenever possible and try to buy parts backed by a written guarantee.

Chapter 4

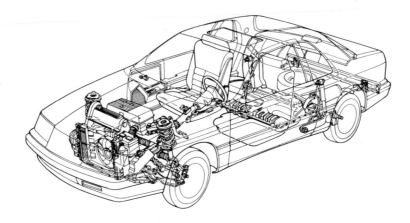

Preventive Maintenance

The basic theory behind preventive maintenance is if you maintain your vehicle in good condition, it will give you fewer problems and last longer than one that has not been maintained. The theory is not flawless, but generally speaking, it holds true most of the time.

We have all heard stories from people who claim they have never changed a filter or spent a nickel on preventive maintenance. "Do not fix it unless it breaks" is their philosophy. Others will say preventive maintenance is nothing but a scam to sell a lot of unnecessary parts and service. Fortunately, such narrow-minded views are limited to a minority of motorists. Most people are smart enough to recognize the merits of preventive maintenance whether they actually practice what they preach.

In the following sections of this and subsequent chapters, you will learn why certain fluids and filters require periodic replacement. You will also learn why certain parts wear out and why others need to be readjusted from time to time. In short,

you will discover that there are many sound reasons for preventive maintenance, not the least of which is to protect your investment.

The average new car today sells for approximately $12,000, with some luxury models costing twice that figure. Even a good used car will cost $3000 or more. Are you willing to risk your investment to save a few dollars on parts and service? Obviously not, or you would not be reading this book.

One recent consumer survey found that 70 percent of motorists claim they now maintain their vehicles better than they did 10 years ago to keep their vehicles running smoothly. Fifty-two percent said they perform routine maintenance to prevent costly repairs. Yet the same survey found that 56 percent of professional mechanics think motorists do not maintain their cars as well as they did 10 years ago. The mechanics believe motorists are not taking care of their cars the way they should, because of the high cost of professional services and the longer service intervals recommended by the car companies.

THE EVILS OF GAS-AND-GO DRIVING

You will not find a definition for gas-and-go driving in *Webster's Dictionary* (maybe because Webster did not drive a car), but it is an appropriate description for the most common kind of driving today. Gas-and-go driving means exactly what it says; the only thing the driver does in terms of maintenance is put gas in the tank.

Gas-and-go drivers do not check their oil when they fill up or check their tires or check anything else. Unless the car acts up, makes weird noises, or leaves a puddle in the driveway, they do not even open the hood. They just keep on gassing up and going—until something goes wrong! In time, neglect will manifest itself. The result is often an unexpected breakdown and a tow to the local garage.

In the good old days when gas was inexpensive and service stations performed routine services, the attendant usually opened your hood and checked your oil. Belts, hoses, the battery, and sometimes even the air filter would receive a quick inspection while your tank was being filled. Most attendants would even check the air in your tires and add air if necessary for no extra charge. Today the pump island attendants are gone. A lone attendant sits behind bulletproof glass, and reads comic books while you pump your own gas. What about the free air? It is rapidly becoming a thing of the past; the oil companies have discovered yet another "convenience" for which the consumer is now expected to pay.

Maintenance neglect was not such a serious problem in the days of full-service filling stations because the hood was routinely opened nearly every time you bought gas. Consequently, low fluid levels were more likely to be caught and corrected before they could cause any serious damage. Likewise, a frayed fan belt, a bulging radiator hose, a clogged air filter, or even a leaky water pump stood a better chance of being noticed because someone was always looking under the hood. Of course, some motorists resented the idea of a stranger poking around under the hood of their car—especially if they did not ask first—and they were always suspicious whenever the attendant told them their engine needed a quart of oil. Someone at least was making the necessary checks and trying to bring obvious problems to your attention. You could also always ask the attendant for free diagnostic advice; he might not have always known the correct answer, but he was there and willing to serve. Not so anymore; ask for help today at a self-service pumper station and all you will get is a blank stare.

Thousands of dealer-operated, full-service filling stations have been revamped or bulldozed and replaced by company-operated "pumper" stations. By eliminating service from the service station, so the argument goes, more gasoline can be sold at a lower price. The convenience store concept has taken over and today you can buy everything from soda to pantyhose at the filling station—but not service.

The direct consequence of this change is an alarming rise in maintenance neglect. Motorists do not open their hoods anymore because there is no one at the pump island to do it for them. The attendant's job has been sacrificed to satisfy the public's demand for lower prices and the oil company's desire for greater profits. A recent survey showed that out of every 100 customers who fill up at a self-service filling station, fewer than 5 will take the time to open their hoods and check the oil level. Rarely is anything else ever checked. The rest are apparently gas-and-go drivers.

To determine the impact such driving habits are having on vehicle maintenance, Shell Oil Company, which still believes service stations should provide service, inspected 100 cars that pulled up to a self-service pump. Shell found that 56 of the vehicles were down one quart or more of oil, 33 had at least one underinflated tire, 34 needed coolant added to their radiators, 29 were low on power steering fluid, 28 had low brake fluid, and 27 needed water added to the battery.

The Car Care Council conducted a similar survey on randomly sampled cars in service stations and parking lots and found a similar lack of care. Half of all the vehicles the Council checked had air filters that needed replaced, a third of the cars had improperly inflated tires, a third were down one quart or more of oil, and another third had low coolant levels in their radiators.

The perils of gas-and-go maintenance habits are summarized in Table 4-1. Maintenance neglect can cost you money. How much money? Worn-out transmission fluid that would have cost approximately $30 to change at a quick-lube place could cost you $500 to $900 for a new transmission. A dirty oil filter and four quarts of oil that would have cost you less than $10 to change yourself could mean a $1500 repair bill for a new engine! A $2 fuel filter that takes about 10 minutes to change could cost you hours of inconvenience and $50 for a tow truck. A few more pounds of air in your car's tires, which would cost you less than $1, could cost $60 to $200 for a new tire. Even something as simple as a worn spark plug could cut your fuel efficiency by as much as 25 percent, cause your car to fail a vehicle emissions inspection, or possibly even ruin your car's $300 catalytic converter. Yes, maintenance neglect can cost you money and cost you dearly (Fig. 4-1).

HOW TO ENJOY TROUBLE-FREE DRIVING

The obvious answer for preventing unnecessary repairs and expenses is to take good care of your car. You do not have to devote your life to the care and feeding of your car or give up much of your precious free time. A few weekly and monthly service checks and an hour or two for some simple maintenance jobs two to four times a year are all that is required.

The following list of preventive maintenance recommendations is intended for the typical passenger car or light truck that is driven 12,000 miles per year, and used mostly for short trips (less than 4 miles). The suggested service intervals are a compilation of various recommendations from vehicle manufacturers, fleet practices, and surveys of professional mechanics' opinions by *MOTOR SERVICE* magazine, Champion Spark Plug Company, Goodyear Tire & Rubber Company, and Fram Filters.

Preventive Maintenance Recommendations:

Weekly
☐ Check engine oil level (before starting engine in morning).
☐ Check coolant level (when cold).
☐ Check tire pressure (when cold).

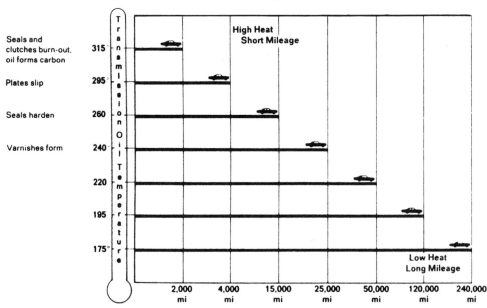

Table 4-1. Transmission Fluid Life. (Courtesy of Hayden Incorporated.)

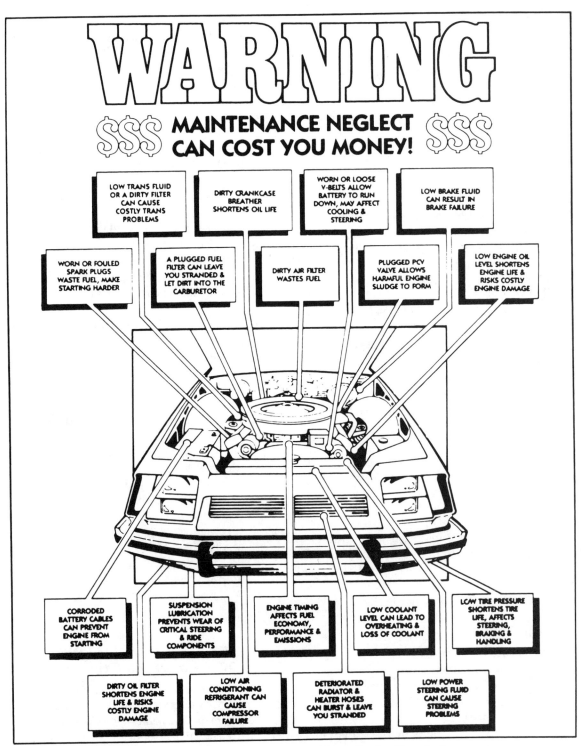

Fig. 4-1. Maintenance neglect can cost you money. (Courtesy of *Motor Service Magazine.*)

☐ Check washer fluid level.

Monthly

☐ Check automatic transmission fluid level (hot, idling in park).

☐ Check brake fluid level.

☐ Check power steering fluid level (hot or cold).

☐ Inspect drive belts (must be tight and free from cracks).

☐ Inspect radiator and heater hoses (replace if cracked or mushy).

☐ Check all lights (headlights, taillights, turn signals, etc.).

☐ Check battery (water level or charge indicator) and terminals.

Twice Per Year

☐ Change engine oil *and* filter (every 6 months or 3,000 miles).

☐ Lubricate chassis, door hinges, locks, and latches.

☐ Inspect suspension for loose parts or leaky shock absorbers.

☐ Check differential and/or manual transmission fluid level.

☐ Inspect driveshaft U-joints (RWD) or CV-joint boots (FWD).

☐ Inspect condition of exhaust system and muffler.

☐ Check condition and strength of antifreeze in radiator.

☐ Check air pressure in the spare tire.

☐ Check operation of the emergency brake.

☐ Wax body and touch up paint nicks and rust spots.

☐ Check windshield wiper blades.

Yearly

☐ Replace air filter.

☐ Replace fuel filter.

☐ Replace PCV filter and check PCV valve.

☐ Check the operation of the air conditioner (recharge if needed).

☐ Inspect vacuum hoses (must be tight and free from cracks).

☐ Replace windshield wiper blades.

☐ Flush and refill radiator with a 50/50 mixture of fresh antifreeze and water (cars with aluminum engine parts or radiators only).

☐ Rotate tires.

Every 2 Years.

☐ Flush and refill radiator with 50/50 mixture of fresh antifreeze and water; check radiator cap seal and radiator for leaks.

☐ Replace fluid and filter in automatic transmission.

☐ Replace spark plugs (30,000 miles average change interval for vehicles that use unleaded gas, 12,000 miles for regular gas).

☐ Check ignition timing (reset if needed).

☐ Check ignition components (distributor cap, rotor, and wires).

☐ Repack wheel bearings (unless bearings are sealed variety).

☐ Inspect brake linings.

Every 3-4 Years   Note: By this time the following items have usually deteriorated to a point where replacement will soon be necessary.

☐ Replace V-belts.

☐ Replace radiator and heater hoses.

☐ Replace PCV valve.

☐ Replace spark plug wires (carbon core type only).

☐ Replace distributor cap.

☐ Replace battery.

☐ Replace shock absorbers.

☐ Replace exhaust system (muffler and tail pipe).

SERVICE INTERVALS: HOW OFTEN IS OFTEN ENOUGH?

One of the difficulties in trying to make a list of specific service interval recommendations is that differences in driving habits and vehicle design affect the frequency that service is required. In most new car owners' manuals, for example, a distinction is made between "normal" driving and "severe" driving. The so-called "normal" driver can supposedly get by with 5,000 to as many as 7,500 mile oil change intervals because his kind of driving is not as hard on his engine's oil as the severe driver. Most motorists think of themselves as normal drivers, when in fact, research has shown that 80 percent of all drivers fall into the severe service classification (Fig. 4-2).

According to a maintenance handbook published by General Motors, "severe" driving is:

☐ When most trips are less than 4 miles.

☐ When most trips are less than 10 miles and outside temperatures remain below freezing.

☐ Prolonged high speed driving during hot weather.

☐ Idling for extended periods and continued low speed operation such as that encountered in heavy stop-and-go traffic.

☐ Towing a trailer.

☐ Operating in dusty areas.

If these things define severe, what is normal?

Normal use, according to vehicle manufacturers, is driving mostly on open roads, taking mostly long trips, avoiding dusty areas not, driving short distances during freezing weather, and not towing a trailer. That leaves very few people who qualify as normal drivers. In other words, when you examine the facts, most of us are actually severe drivers. Consequently, most vehicles require more frequent maintenance than suggested by the owners' manual. Severe service is actually the norm for most drivers, and normal is the exception.

Confusing? You bet it is. Unless you are absolutely certain that you do not do any of the things that would qualify you as a severe driver, the best advice is to follow the maintenance recommendations given in this book or those listed in the severe service maintenance schedule in your owners' manual.

DETERMINING THE SERVICE SCHEDULE THAT IS RIGHT FOR YOU

Some types of vehicles, no matter how they are driven, require more frequent service intervals than others. Diesel engines, for example, have much

Fig. 4-2. Determining who is a "severe" driver and who is a "normal" driver can be confusing. Most normal drivers are in fact severe drivers, which means their vehicles require more frequent fluid and filter changes. (Courtesy of Ford Motor Company.)

higher compression ratios than gasoline engines. This results in increased crankcase blowby, which causes the oil to become contaminated much more quickly. Most vehicle manufacturers, therefore, suggest 3,000 mile oil change intervals for diesel engines, regardless of the type of driving to which the engine is subjected.

Air-cooled engines (such as old Volkswagen Beetles, motorcycles, and lawn mowers) run considerably hotter than water-cooled engines. The higher temperatures shorten the useful life of the oil and therefore require shorter change intervals. Changing the oil every 1500 miles or every 40 to 50 hours of engine operation is highly recommended for air-cooled engines.

Turbocharged engines require more frequent oil change intervals. Most manufacturers recommend 3,000 mile intervals for turbocharged engines because most are in high-performance automobiles. Such engines are more likely to be driven at high speeds and pushed to the limit; therefore, they require better lubrication. Equally important is the fact that turbocharger bearings can be easily damaged by dirty or oxidized oil. The high temperatures inside the turbo housing can literally cook the oil, turning it into a thick, black goo that sticks to the bearing shaft and can plug up the oil lines. Unless the oil is renewed periodically, it can lose its ability to lubricate and protect the engine and turbocharger (Fig. 4-3).

High-mileage engines (those with over 60,000 miles on the odometer) also need shorter oil change intervals regardless of how they are driven. As the cylinders and piston rings in an engine wear, the amount of blowby into the crankcase goes up. The combustion gases and unburned fuel dilute the oil and reduce its ability to lubricate. Replacing the oil and filter every 3,000 miles can compensate for the accumulated wear and significantly extend the life of the engine.

Trailer towing can be especially hard on both engine oil and transmission fluid. Because the engine and transmission have to work harder when pulling a load, operating temperatures go up. The higher the temperature, the faster the oil oxidizes. Automatic transmission fluid, for example, can last up to 100,000 miles if operating temperatures remain below 175 degrees Fahrenheit. But a rise of only 20 degrees in temperature cuts the life of the fluid in half. At highway speeds, most passenger car automatic transmissions run around 190 to 195 degrees. Add a trailer behind the car and the operating temperature skyrockets. At 235 degrees, the useful life of the transmission fluid is reduced to 12,000 miles; at 255 degrees, it is down to 6,000 miles. If the temperature goes over 300 degrees, you will burn up the transmission within a few hundred miles. The fluid, therefore, should be changed in direct proportion to the amount of towing miles driven, the size of the load, and the amount of fluid cooling provided. A vehicle equipped with an auxiliary transmission oil cooler can get more life out of the transmission fluid than one without a cooler.

Some engines can have their oil change intervals safely extended. Alternative fuels such as propane are exceptionally clean burning. There is little dilution of the crankcase oil so the oil does not have to be changed as often. Engines with larger capacity crankcases hold more oil. This spreads the dilution factor over more quarts so each quart can go somewhat further. Thus, an engine with a 5- or 6-quart oil capacity can probably run more miles between changes than one with the standard 4-quart capacity. The problem, of course, is determining the best service intervals for your vehicle. Wait too long and you might regret it. Service it too often and you are only wasting money.

Truck fleets have solved this problem by relying on oil analysis to tell them when a truck's oil needs changing. A small sample of oil is sent in to a lab that analyzes it and records the presence of trace elements and other contaminants. Based on this information, the truck mechanic can determine the condition of the oil as well as the engine. An oil analysis usually costs $10 to $20, which is worth the money for a large truck engine that holds several gallons of oil and runs tens of thousands of miles between changes. But for an ordinary passenger car, the cost of oil analysis is more than the cost to change the oil. Even if such a service were readily available to the motoring public, which it is not, few people would use it because of the cost.

Fig. 4-3. Turbocharging has grown enormously in recent years as a means of boosting power. It also means more frequent service intervals. (Courtesy of Chrysler Corporation.)

Truck fleets have also established maintenance schedules based on experience. They have learned that after a certain number of miles, the failure rate of certain components such as belts, hoses, ignition parts, filters, etc., goes up drastically. By replacing these parts before they reach the age where failure becomes a problem, they are able to avoid a lot of unnecessary downtime. Because the average motorist does not keep detailed records on his own car,

he has to rely on somebody else for such experience. That is where the vehicle manufacturers', parts manufacturers', and professional mechanics' recommendations come into play.

How a Vehicle Manufacturer Develops Service Schedules

Vehicle manufacturers are required by law to put their cars and light trucks through a vigorous test-

Table 4-2. Engine Oil Life. (Courtesy of Hayden Incorporated.)

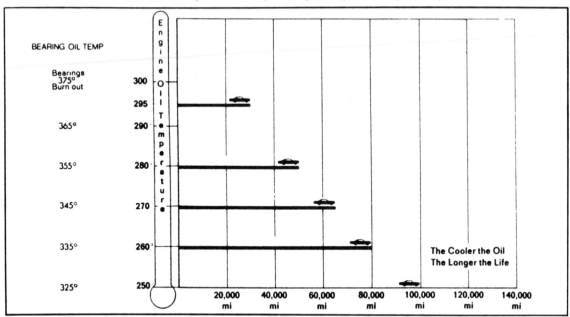

ing program to certify the vehicles as complying with the Environmental Protection Agency clean air standards. Each car make, model, and engine combination is tested, then run 50,000 miles, and retested to make certain it does not exceed the exhaust emission standards. The service recommendations in your owners' manual are based in part on the service the vehicle required to pass its 50,000 mile certification. That is why some manufacturers say a once a year or 7,500 mile oil change interval is satisfactory.

There are three objections to recommendations based on such tests. One is that a 50,000 mile certification program is run over a period of several months, not years, unlike vehicles driven in the real world. The engine does not experience as many starts and stops as it would in real life. Second, a significant portion of the miles are simulated miles, not real road miles. The wheels of the car are placed on rollers and the engine is operated automatically to run the odometer up to the required mileage. A third factor is a lack of extreme temperature changes, dust, or other environmental factors that can shorten the life of various fluids and components. The cars are driven on a test track by profes-

sional drivers under controlled conditions. They are not driven for hours on end in stop-and-go traffic, run in sub-zero weather, or subjected to dusty roads or industrial pollution. Thus, any service information that comes from manufacturers' certification tests can be inconclusive and unreliable. Of course, vehicle manufacturers also do a tremendous amount of durability testing and the results of these tests are usually used to temper the final recommendations.

Who Do You Believe?

The companies that make the various components and fluids that are used in your car are probably in the best position to make service recommendations. They do their own testing or hire independent test labs to do it for them. These test results are then used to market their products to the vehicle manufacturers who in turn subject the parts or fluids to tests of their own. Thus, if a rubber company that manufacturers fan belts states a belt normally lasts about four years or 50,000 miles, you would better believe them. There is always the suspicion that some manufacturers recommend replacing parts or fluids more often than is really necessary to sell more products, and some no doubt do. But most are being truthful when they make specific recommendations. With today's product liability laws, you can feel confident that any claims of a product's longevity are backed by solid research.

That leaves the professional mechanic as a third source of service interval recommendations. Mechanics are not engineers, nor are they researchers. They do not conduct durability tests on various products, nor can they always give you a correct explanation for why certain parts fail or wear out. A mechanic's job is to service his customers' vehicles, and based on his day-to-day experiences, he quickly develops a sense for what sort of parts fail and when.

A professional mechanic spends all of his working day in a service bay. He sees the cars that have not had their oil changed regularly and what is happened to the engine as a result. He sees the transmissions that were ruined because of overheated, worn-out fluid. He sees the broken fan belts, the corroded radiators, the dead batteries, the brake problems, the ignition problems, and the driveability problems that result from maintenance neglect. Based on such real-world experiences, the mechanic forms definite opinions about how often

certain things should be changed or adjusted in spite of what the owners' manual or service guide recommends. That is why the service recommendations in this book rely more on the professional mechanic's experience than what the car companies or others have to say.

New Car Warranties

One final thought to keep in mind about service schedules is that all new car warranties require a certain amount of minimal maintenance to be performed at specific mileage intervals. There is nothing that says you cannot service your car more often than the required intervals, but if you don't perform the essentials, it can void your warranty.

Sometimes a dealer will tell a customer the warranty is void unless the dealer does all the maintenance work. This is nonsense! Even if put in writing such threats are illegal. The only item the dealer has a monopoly on is warranty repair work. As far as general maintenance is concerned, you can have your vehicle serviced anywhere or you can do it yourself. To prove the work has been performed, however, you should keep all receipts and a detailed log describing the type of service performed and the date and mileage when it was performed.

Chapter 5

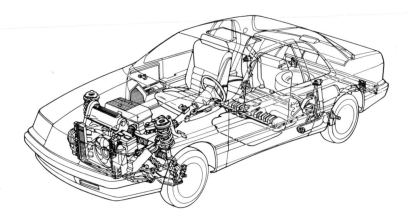

Vital Fluids and Filters

Your vehicle has seven vital fluids that are essential for safe and trouble-free operation. They are engine oil, automatic transmission fluid, gear oil, coolant, brake fluid, power steering fluid, and battery water. Also included is chassis and wheel bearing grease. Checking these fluids regularly and adding or replenishing as needed is the single most important thing you can do to maintain your vehicle, prolong its useful life, and prevent costly breakdowns.

CHECKING ENGINE OIL LEVEL

Oil is the lifeblood of your engine. It not only lubricates the moving parts inside your engine, it also helps to cool many components such as bearings and pistons. The average engine holds 4 quarts of oil. If the oil level is low, the remaining oil in the crankcase must do the work of a full 4 quarts. This can cause the oil to run hot, or worse yet, to starve vital components of much needed lubrication. That is why the oil level should be maintained as close to the full mark as possible. Do not wait until it is

down to the "add" line before adding a quart. Running 1 quart low might not provide adequate lubrication, especially when high-speed driving during hot weather or when towing a trailer.

Tools Needed. Clean rag.

How Often. Check the dipstick level once a week or every time you fill the vehicle with gas.

Location. The dipstick is located at the front or side of your engine (check your owner's manual for the exact location if you can not find it). The dipstick has a long handle with a finger loop at the end. Be careful; the dipstick might be hot if the engine has been running.

What To Do. First turn the engine off. Checking the oil level with the engine running will result in a low oil level reading because some of the oil will be circulating inside the engine. Wait about 30 seconds after turning the engine off before checking the level. This will give the oil time to drain back down into the crankcase.

1. Pull the dipstick out and wipe the oil off the end with your clean rag (Fig. 5-1).

Fig. 5-1. Checking the engine oil dipstick.

2. Insert the dipstick back into its hole and push it all the way down.

3. Pull the dipstick back out and read the oil level. However far up the dipstick you can see wet oil indicates the oil level inside the engine.

If the crankcase is full, the oil level will be up to the full mark on the dipstick. If the oil level is low, add only enough to bring the level back up to the full mark (the add line is one quart below the full mark). Do not overfill the crankcase because this can cause the oil to foam or to leak past various engine seals (Fig. 5-2).

If there is no oil on the dipstick when you check it, add enough oil to bring the level back up to the full mark—and cross your fingers that the engine has not been ruined. Then look for an oil leak by looking for puddles or greasy deposits on the engine itself. Return the dipstick to its hole when you are finished checking the oil level.

Oil Appearance. New oil is clear to yellow in color (except for certain types of Kendall brand oil that appear green). The oil turns medium to dark brown in a short time, so you cant judge the oil's age or condition by color alone. If the oil has a tar-

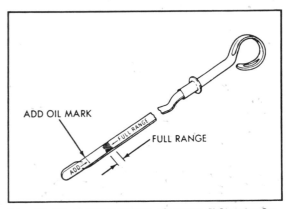

Fig. 5-2. Oil dipstick markings. (Courtesy of Chrysler Corporation.)

like consistency, however, the engine is long over-due for an oil change.

A brownish to yellowish foamy appearance indicates moisture contamination. Moisture accumulates inside your engine's crankcase during normal driving. Using your vehicle for short trips only or driving during cold weather accelerates this accumulation because the oil never gets hot enough to evaporate the moisture. A vehicle that is only used for short-trip, stop-and-go driving will likely show a lot of moisture contamination in the oil.

In time, the water will combine with other contaminants to form acids and sludge inside the engine. Your oil filter can trap dirt and sludge but not moisture or acids. That is why the oil *and* filter must be changed periodically.

A possible source of severe moisture contamination is a plugged *Positive Crankcase Ventilation* (PCV) valve or hose. The PCV system draws fresh air through the crankcase to remove fumes and moisture. If the system plugs or fails to work, the moisture will remain in the crankcase and rapid oil contamination results. A large accumulation of brownish-yellow foam or gunk on the underside of the oil filler cap might indicate such a problem.

Coolant is another contaminant that can enter the crankcase through a leaky head gasket or cracks in the engine block or cylinder head. Coolant is usually half antifreeze and half water, neither of which can lubricate an engine. You will get the same accumulation of brownish-yellow crud and, most likely, serious engine damage in the form of scored cylinder walls and bearings. The presence of tiny metal flakes or particles in the oil is definitely bad news because it means the engine has suffered some sort of major damage.

Adding Oil. Unscrew or pull out the round filler cap on the top of the valve cover and pour in as much oil as needed to bring the level back up to the full mark on the dipstick. Use only SF-rated oil (or CC-CD-rated oil if you have a diesel) of the same viscosity as the oil already in the engine. If the oil container doesn't have its own pour spout, use an oil spout or funnel to keep oil from spilling on the engine. Wipe any excess oil that spills because it will attract dirt and create a greasy mess.

Oil also attacks rubber, so be careful not to spill any on hoses or belts (Fig. 5-3).

Viscosity Recommendations. Refer to your owner's manual for specific oil viscosity recommendations. For most applications, multiweight 5W-30, 10W-30, or 10W-40 oils are satisfactory. For easier cold weather starting, 5W-20 or straight 10W oil may be used, but such oils should not be used for sustained high-speed driving or during warm weather, they are too thin to provide adequate high temperature lubrication (Fig. 5-4).

Straight weight oils such as 10W, 20W, and 30W are rarely used any more, because multiweight oils combine the cold starting and low friction characteristics of a lightweight oil with the high

Fig. 5-3. Oil filler cap.

Fig. 5-4. Oil viscosity and grade markings are printed on the oil container. Follow the recommendations specified in your owner's manual.

temperature protection of a heavier oil. Nondetergent oils should not be used in modern engines.

The most popular oil weight is 10W-40, although General Motors has issued bulletins warning that it might be too heavy for some applications and gum up the piston rings. GM recommends 10W-30 or 5W-30 for most applications. Many new cars are factory filled with 5W-30 because the lighter oil reduces friction, which helps improve fuel economy. Trucks subjected to hard use or high-performance engines often use 20W-50 oil. The oil viscosity you select, therefore, should be based on

the type of driving you do and the anticipated climactic conditions in your area (Table 5-1.)

CHANGING ENGINE OIL AND FILTER

Tools Needed. Oil filter wrench; wrench for oil pan drain plug; pan of at least 1-gallon capacity to catch the oil as it drains from the engine; oil spout or funnel (unless oil can is self-pouring); clean rag; ramps or a jack and jack stands to raise and support the car if extra working clearance is needed.

Parts Needed. Oil filter; 4 quarts of oil.

How Often. Oil and filter should be changed every six months or 3000 miles, whichever comes first, or according to the recommended service schedule in your owner's manual.

Location. The oil drain plug is located at the lowest point on the bottom of your engine's oil pan. The oil filter will be located somewhere on the engine block. Some can be easily reached from above while others can only be reached from under the car (Figs. 5-5 and 5-6).

What To Do. It really does not make any difference if you change the oil while the engine is hot or cold. Some people say it is better to drain the oil while it is hot (such as right after driving), because hot oil drains more quickly and is more likely to flush all the contaminants out of the crankcase. Others say it is better to change it while it's cold (such as first thing in the morning after the car has been sitting all night), because all the oil is in

Table 5-1. Oil Viscosity Recommendations.

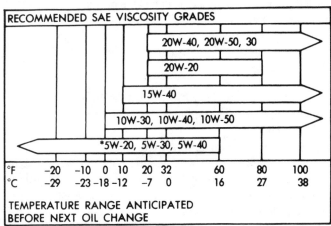

RECOMMENDED SAE VISCOSITY GRADES

20W-40, 20W-50, 30
20W-20
15W-40
10W-30, 10W-40, 10W-50
*5W-20, 5W-30, 5W-40

| °F | -20 | -10 | 0 | 10 | 20 | 32 | | 60 | 80 | 100 |
| °C | -29 | -23 | -18 | -12 | | -7 | 0 | 16 | 27 | 38 |

TEMPERATURE RANGE ANTICIPATED
BEFORE NEXT OIL CHANGE
*SAE 5W-20 NOT RECOMMENDED FOR
SUSTAINED HIGH SPEED VEHICLE OPERATION

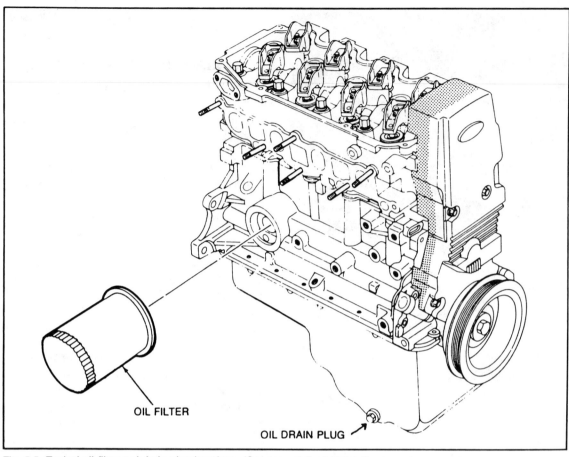

OIL FILTER

OIL DRAIN PLUG

Fig. 5-5. Typical oil filter and drain plug locations. (Courtesy of Ford Motor Company.)

the crankcase, and the gunk in the engine will have settled to the bottom of the oil pan. This means you don't have to wait while oil dribbles down from the upper parts of the engine. You're also less likely to burn your fingers if you change it while it's still cold.

1. Turn the engine off. Never, ever drain oil from an engine that's running if you want it to continue running.

2. Set the parking brake, put the transmission in park (automatic) or in gear (manual), then raise the car if you need more room to work underneath. If you raise the car, make certain the vehicle is parked on level ground before lifting. Then support the vehicle with a pair of jackstands. Never rely on the jack alone to hold it up.

3. Position your catch pan under the engine so it will catch the oil as it drains out. Oil will usually squirt out several inches if the drain plug is located on the side rather than the bottom of the oil pan, so be sure to position your catch pan accordingly.

4. Loosen the drain plug with your wrench by turning it counterclockwise, then back it out until it's almost free. Protect your fingers with a rag if the oil is hot, then quickly twist the plug the rest of the way out.

5. While the oil is draining out of the engine, locate the oil filter and loosen it by turning it counterclockwise with your filter wrench. Don't take it all the way off yet because it's full of oil. Wait until the engine has finished draining, then reposition your catch pan under the filter and spin the filter the rest of the way off.

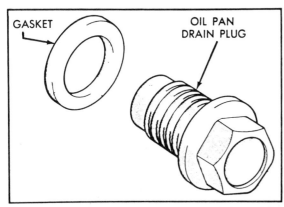

Fig. 5-6. Most drain plugs have a gasket to help seal the plug. Don't lose the gasket or the plug will leak. (Courtesy of Chrysler Corporation.)

Most spin-on filters say "hand tighten only" on the side. Overtightening makes the filter nearly impossible to remove, and it can sometimes squeeze the seal on top of the filter out of position, resulting in a very messy (and possibly costly) oil leak.

If the filter won't budge, there are three ways to get it off. The first is to spear the filter with a screwdriver. It's messy, but using the screwdriver as a handle gives you more leverage and will usually loosen even the most stubborn filter. If there isn't enough room to use a screwdriver, a second technique is to use a hammer and chisel to knock it loose. The chisel should be carefully positioned against the lip of the filter so the hammer blows will twist the filter counterclockwise. Care must be used not to nick or gouge the filter mating surface. If both of these methods seem too difficult, a third option is to refill the engine with oil and take the vehicle to a professional mechanic. He might have a better filter wrench or he might have better luck using either of the two techniques just described. You should never skip the filter because it's too hard to change. If the filter plugs up, oil will bypass it and circulate unfiltered through the engine. This accelerates engine wear tremendously and can, if the bypass valve fails to open, completely ruin the engine.

6. Once all the oil has drained from the engine, replace and tighten the drain plug. Be careful not to overtighten or crossthread the plug. If the drain plug leaks and appears to be damaged, self-tapping repair plugs are available in most auto parts stores.

7. Place a few drops of fresh oil on your finger and wipe it around the rubber seal on the new oil filter. This will help the seal seat properly when the filter is installed. Then hand tighten the new filter until snug. The filter should be turned about three-quarters of a turn with your filter wrench after the rubber seal makes contact with the engine, but do not overtighten it (Fig. 5-7).

8. Add the required amount of oil to the engine to refill the crankcase (check your owner's manual if you don't know how many quarts it takes). Most engines hold four quarts, although some V8s hold five.

9. Check the dipstick after adding oil. It should read above the full mark because some of the oil will be pumped into the filter once the engine starts.

10. Start the engine and let it idle. Don't race it, because it takes a few seconds for the oil to pump through the new filter and come up to pressure. The oil pressure warning light will probably remain on for a few seconds until the oil pressure reaches normal. Look under the car and around the oil filter to make sure the drain plug and filter are not leaking. If the filter isn't tight or if its seal slipped out of place, oil will be leaking around the filter.

11. Dispose of the used oil by pouring it into a sealed container and taking it to a service station for recycling. Don't pour it down the drain, a storm sewer, or on the ground; used oil can seep into ground water supplies.

12. Wash your hands, then make a note of the date and mileage at which you changed the oil and filter. You should also write down the brand and viscosity of oil used. This will help you remember when to change your oil next and what kind to use should your engine need oil. Maintenance forms are included at the back of this book for your convenience.

CHECKING AUTOMATIC TRANSMISSION FLUID LEVEL

Automatic transmissions use a special kind of lubricating oil called automatic transmission fluid

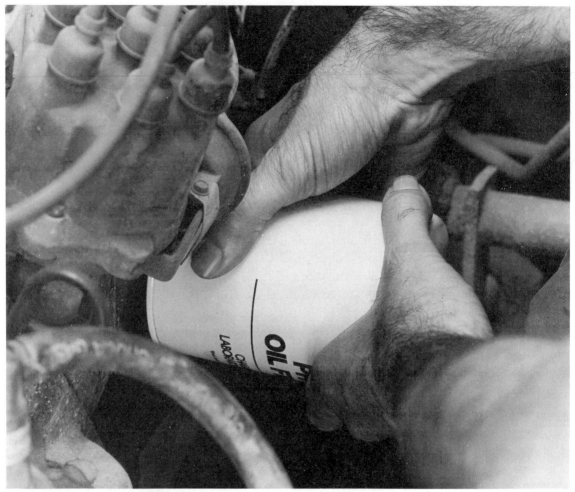

Fig. 5-7. Hand tighten the oil filter. (Courtesy of Champion Laboratories.)

(ATF). There are two main types: Dexron II and Type F. Most Ford transmissions use the Type F while most others use Dexron II. There are exceptions so check your owner's manual to be sure. Sometimes the type of fluid required is printed right on the dipstick.

A few late-model Ford transmissions use a third kind of fluid called Type H. It's important to always use the correct type of fluid in a given application because Dexron II, Type F, and Type H all have different friction characteristics. Using the wrong fluid can cause performance problems and possible damage.

ATF fulfills several roles inside an automatic transmission. It acts as a lubricant for the gears, bearings, and shafts within the transmission, it carries hydraulic pressure through various control circuits to actuate transmission engagement and gear shifts, and it serves as the working fluid inside the torque converter to transmit engine power through the transmission.

ATF has a much easier life than engine oil because it isn't subjected to combustion blowby gases and moisture contamination. Its one weak point, however, is its vulnerability to overheating. As long as operating temperatures remain below 175 degrees, the fluid lasts indefinitely. But the average operating temperature in most automatic transmissions ranges from 190 to 195 degrees—or higher. The higher the temperature, the shorter the life of the fluid (see Table 4-1 in Chapter 4).

Few vehicle manufacturers recommend changing the fluid periodically unless the vehicle is used for towing or is operated in an extremely dusty environment. Most professional mechanics, however, advise that changing the fluid and filter every 25,000 miles can help the transmission last the life of the car.

Tools Needed. Clean rag.

How Often. Check the transmission fluid level at least once a month and always before taking a long trip or towing a trailer.

Location. The transmission dipstick is usually located on the passenger's side of the engine compartment near the firewall. It has a long handle with a finger loop at the end (Fig. 5-8). On some front-wheel-drive vehicles, you'll find it on the transaxle. Check your owner's manual for the exact location.

What To Do. The vehicle must be parked on a level surface for an accurate reading. The transmission fluid must also be hot, which means driving at least 10 miles if the fluid is cold.

1. Set the parking brake firmly. With the engine idling, momentarily place the gear selector in each gear range ending with the lever back in PARK.

2. With the engine idling and the transmission in PARK, get out of the car and open the hood. Pull out the dipstick, wipe it clean, and push it all the way back down into its tube. Feel the fluid with your fingers to make sure it's hot.

3. Now pull the dipstick back out and note the fluid level. If the fluid is hot, the level should be to the ''full'' mark or up to the top of the cross-hatched area marked ''okay.'' If the fluid level is low, additional fluid should be added to bring it up to the full mark.

Note: The ''add'' mark on most transmission dipsticks is 1 pint below the full mark. Do not over-fill the transmission; doing so can cause the fluid

Fig. 5-8. Automatic transaxle dipstick.

to foam (foaming interferes with lubrication and pressure control inside the transmission) (Fig. 5-9).

Fluid Appearance. ATF normally has a pink to red color. If the fluid has overheated or is old, it will be a brownish color. A strong, burnt odor means the fluid has oxidized and must be changed. Continuing to drive with burned fluid can ruin the

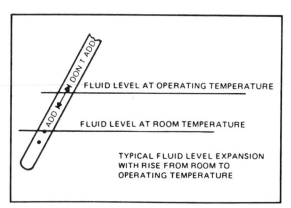

FLUID LEVEL AT OPERATING TEMPERATURE

FLUID LEVEL AT ROOM TEMPERATURE

TYPICAL FLUID LEVEL EXPANSION
WITH RISE FROM ROOM TO
OPERATING TEMPERATURE

Fig. 5-9. Automatic transmission dipstick markings. Check the fluid level when hot and don't overfill. (Courtesy of Chrysler Corporation.)

transmission. Metal flakes or particles indicate internal transmission damage. Changing the fluid at this point won't do any good; better find a good transmission mechanic.

Adding Fluid. If the transmission is low and needs fluid, the ATF is poured directly down the dipstick tube. You will probably need a clean funnel or oil spout to keep from spilling the ATF as you pour it down the tube. Do not allow any dirt or foreign material to fall down the dipstick hole.

Add fluid a little at a time. Remember, the add line is only a pint below the full mark on most transmission dipsticks. Give the fluid time to drain down the tube, then recheck the fluid level and continue adding as necessary.

CHANGING AUTOMATIC TRANSMISSION FLUID AND FILTER

This task is not terribly difficult, but it does require working under the car. It can also be messy. You might prefer to take your vehicle to a garage or quick-lube facility to have the transmission fluid and filter changed. A professional mechanic should be able to complete the job in 30 minutes or less.

Tools Needed. Wrench for transmission pan bolts; oil spout or funnel; wide catch pan; rubber mallet; putty knife or gasket scraper; wire brush; ramps or a jack and jack stands.

Parts Needed. Transmission pan gasket (or a tube of RTV silicone sealer); transmission filter;

several quarts of automatic transmission fluid (check your owner's manual to determine the type and quantity required).

How Often. Every 25,000 miles, or every 15,000 miles if the vehicle is used for off-road excursions, trailer pulling, or operated in an extremely dusty environment.

Location. No drain plug is provided on most transmission pans. This means the pan must be removed to drain the fluid and change the filter (which is located on the bottom of the transmission inside the pan). On front-wheel-drive vehicles, the transmission is part of the transaxle. The pan on the bottom of the transaxle must be removed to change the fluid and filter (Fig. 5-10 and 5-11).

What To Do. Transmission fluid can be changed hot or cold.

1. The car should be parked on level ground. Set the parking brake and put the transmission in PARK. Then raise the vehicle and support it with a pair of jackstands. Never rely on the jack alone to hold it up.

2. Place your catch pan under the transmission. It should be positioned so fluid can drain into it when one side of the transmission pan is lowered.

3. Loosen and remove all but two opposing transmission pan bolts. *Caution:* The transmission pan is full of fluid; as soon as either of these two remaining bolts is removed, one side of the pan might drop and spill its contents.

4. Tap the pan sideways with a rubber mallet to help loosen it from the transmission. A screwdriver might be needed to pry it free, but be careful not to dent the pan or gouge the transmission mating surface. Loosening the two remaining bolts a couple of turns will hold the pan while you loosen it.

5. Now comes the messy part. Support the transmission pan with one hand while removing one of the two remaining pan bolts with your other hand. Remove the bolt on the side furthest from you so that when the pan swings down it will spill the fluid away from you. As soon as the bolt is free, slowly let the pan swing down so the fluid dumps into your catch pan.

6. Remove the remaining pan bolt and lower

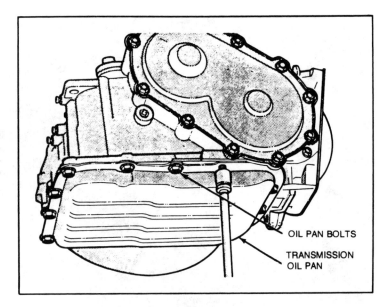

Fig. 5-10. To change the transmission fluid and filter, the oil pan on the bottom of the transmission or transaxle must be removed. (Courtesy of Chrysler Corporation.)

OIL PAN BOLTS

TRANSMISSION OIL PAN

the pan from the transmission. You can now scrape all the old gasket material from both pan and transmission. Use care when scraping the transmission because the case is aluminum and nicks easily. Wipe out the pan to remove any sediment. If you clean it with solvent or wash it out, make certain it's absolutely dry and perfectly clean before it's reinstalled.

7. Replace the filter on the bottom of the transmission. The filter is a flat pad-like component bolted to the underside of the control housing with two or three bolts holding it in place. Use care when tightening the bolts because the threaded holes in the aluminum housing can be easily stripped. Make sure the new filter is installed in exactly the same position as the old. Pay attention to any markings that indicate "This side up" (Fig. 5-12).

8. Coat both sides of the new transmission pan gasket with gasket sealer and position the gasket on the pan. Raise the pan, insert, and finger tighten all the bolts to make sure the gasket is correctly positioned. Then tighten the pan bolts in a side-to-side alternating sequence so the pan is clamped down evenly against the transmission. Don't overtighten the bolts; doing so can crush the gasket (and possibly break it) as well as deform the pan flange (Fig. 5-13).

If you're using RTV silicone sealer instead of

a pan gasket, make sure both pan and transmission mating surfaces are clean and dry; any oil or grease will interfere with a good seal. Then apply a 1/8-inch bead of sealer all the way around the pan flange (the bead should go along the inside edge of

Fig. 5-11. After all the bolts except one have been removed, the fluid can be dumped into a catch pan.

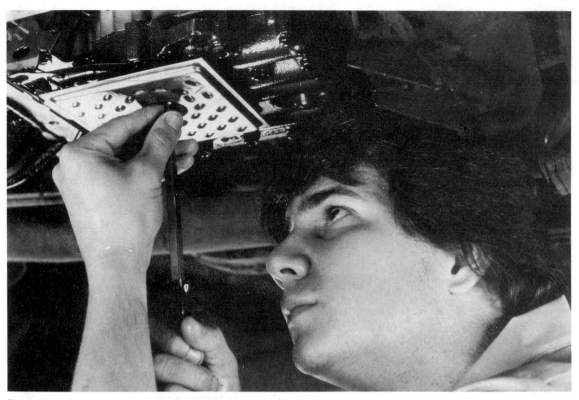

Fig. 5-12. The automatic transmission filter is located inside the transmission pan.

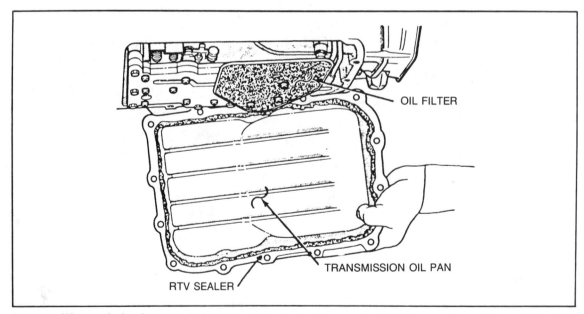

OIL FILTER

TRANSMISSION OIL PAN

RTV SEALER

Fig. 5-13. When replacing the transmission pan, use a new gasket or apply RTV silicone sealer as shown. Be sure the bead of sealer runs along the inside (not outside) of the bolt holes. (Courtesy of Chrysler Corporation.)

the bolt holes). Put the pan in position, tighten the bolts, and wait an hour before refilling the transmission with fluid.

9. Refill the transmission with the required type and amount of ATF.

10. Start the engine and check for leaks. Drive the car for 15 minutes, then check the transmission fluid level once the fluid is hot. Add fluid if needed.

11. Dispose of the old transmission fluid by pouring it into a sealed container and taking it to a service station for recycling.

12. Wash your hands, then make a note of the date and mileage at which you changed the fluid and filter. This will help you remember when to change the fluid next. Maintenance forms are included at the back of this book for your convenience.

CHECKING MANUAL TRANSMISSION GEAR OIL LEVEL

On rear-wheel-drive vehicles, checking the manual transmission gear oil level involves raising the entire car. Adding fluid is also tricky, so you might want to have this job performed by a professional mechanic. On front-wheel-drive applications you can do it yourself.

Most manual transmissions in rear-wheel-drive vehicles use 80- or 90-weight gear oil for lubrication. The same type of lubricant is also used in some front-wheel-drive vehicles, but many manual transaxles require Dexron II automatic transmission fluid instead of gear oil. Check your owner's manual for the type of transmission fluid recommended.

The oil level can be checked hot or cold.

Tools Needed. Clean rag; 1/2-inch wrench or hex drive wrench, or adjustable wrench (to remove the transmission inspection plug where required); ramps or jack and jack stands (RWD only).

How Often. Unless the transmission is leaking fluid and leaving puddles in the driveway, checking the fluid level once or twice per year should be sufficient. Rear-wheel-drive transmissions typically leak around the driveshaft seal. Front-wheel-drive transaxles typically leak around the halfshaft (right and left driveshafts) seals.

Location. An inspection plug is provided on the side of the transmission case (rear-wheel-drive). On front-wheel-drive transaxles, an inspection plug might be located on the end of the transaxle or a dipstick might be used (Figs. 5-14 and 5-15).

What To Do. The vehicle must be parked on level ground for an accurate indication of the oil level. If you have to raise the car, you must raise the ENTIRE car evenly. Tilting the car will affect the level of the fluid inside the transmission. For this reason, it might be better to have the oil level checked by a mechanic while the car is up on a hoist.

For rear-wheel-drive transmissions:

1. Raise the car on a hoist or raise it evenly and support it with four jack stands. Make certain the stands are properly placed and the vehicle is stable before going under it.

2. Locate the inspection plug on one side of the transmission. It will either be an inverted square or hex drive plug, or a squarehead protruding plug.

3. Remove the plug and insert your finger through the hole. The oil level inside should be within half an inch of the bottom of the inspection hole. If low, add oil until it starts to dribble back out of the hole. Then replace the plug.

Adding gear oil to a manual transmission isn't as easy as it sounds. There's usually little elbow room between the transmission and floor pan. Professional mechanics use a drum and pump setup with a long hose and filler neck to add oil. Because you don't have such equipment, you'll have to improvise.

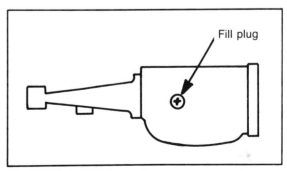

Fill plug

Fig. 5-14. Typical fill plug location on a rear-wheel-drive manual transmission.

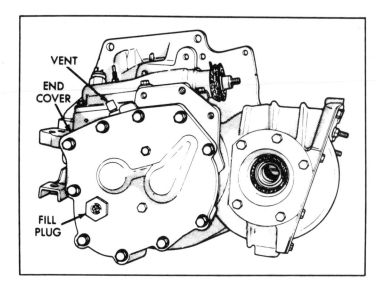

Fig. 5-15. Typical fill plug location on a front-wheel-drive transaxle. (Courtesy of Chrysler Corporation.)

One method that works well is to fill an empty plastic mustard container with oil, then use it to squirt oil through the inspection hole. You might also use a very long length of lightweight plastic tubing and a funnel. Insert one end of the tubing into the inspection hole, then snake it up through the engine compartment and add oil from above.

For front-wheel-drive transaxles:

1. Locate the inspection plug. You'll find it on the end of the transaxle (which is usually located on the driver's side of the engine compartment just behind the left front wheel) or on top of the transaxle if a short dipstick is used.

2. If the transaxle has a dipstick, pull it out, wipe it off, push it all the way back in, then pull it out again and read the level. If low, add lubricant as required to bring it up to the full mark.

If an inspection plug is used, remove the plug and insert your finger into the inspection hole. The oil should be within half an inch of the bottom of the hole. If low, add the required lubricant until it starts to dribble back out of the hole. Then replace the plug.

CHECKING DIFFERENTIAL GEAR OIL LEVEL

The differential in rear-wheel-drive vehicles requires 80- or 90-weight gear oil, the same as a manual transmission. In front-wheel-drive vehicles, the differential oil level does not require checking because it's part of the transaxle, and both share a common supply of lubricant. The only exceptions are 1981 and 1982 Chrysler front-wheel-drive transaxles that have a separate oil compartment for the differential gears. The oil level in these cars is checked via a filler plug on the end of the transaxle.

The oil level can be checked hot or cold.

Tools Needed. Half-inch wrench or hex drive wrench, or adjustable wrench; jack and jack stands (RWD only).

How Often. Unless the differential is leaving puddles in the driveway, checking the oil level once or twice per year should be sufficient. The differential in a rear-wheel-drive vehicle might be losing oil if grease or oil is observed on the underside of the chassis just above the point where the driveshaft couples with the rear axle. Oil can also be lost through leaky rear axle seals or through leaks in the differential cover gasket.

Location. For rear-wheel-drive differentials, an inspection plug is located on one side or the back of the differential housing (Fig. 5-16).

What To Do.

1. Make sure the vehicle is parked on level ground. Block the front wheels to keep the vehicle from rolling, then raise the back end slightly and

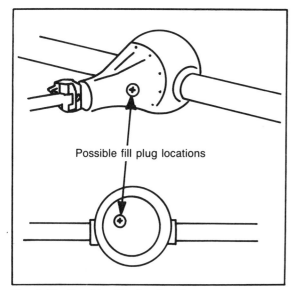

Fig. 5-16. Possible fill plug locations on a rear axle differential.

support it with jack stands. You don't want to raise it too high; doing so will affect the oil level inside the differential.

2. Locate the inspection plug and remove it, then insert your finger through the hole and feel the oil level inside. It should be within half an inch of the bottom of the hole. If low, add 80- or 90-weight gear oil until oil starts to dribble back out of the hole, then replace the plug.

CHECKING COOLANT LEVEL

The coolant level inside your vehicle's radiator should be checked periodically to make certain the cooling system has enough coolant. If the coolant runs low, either as a result of leakage or overflow, it can cause the engine to overheat.

Tools Needed. A rag.

How Often. Monthly.

Location. On most vehicles, the coolant level can be checked by simply looking at the plastic reserve tank on or near the radiator. The reserve tank is connected to the radiator cap with a rubber hose (Figs. 5-17 and 5-18).

What To Do. On the side of the reserve tank are usually markings that indicate the correct coolant level. The upper mark usually says "hot full"

or "maximum" and the lower mark "cold full" or "minimum." As long as the coolant is visible in the reservoir and is between these two lines, there should be adequate coolant in the radiator. The different levels are indicated because coolant expands as it gets hot. Thus, a hot engine will show a higher level than a cold one.

Opening the radiator cap to check the coolant level inside shouldn't be necessary as long as the coolant level in the reserve tank can be seen. *Caution:* The coolant inside the radiator is near 200 degrees when the engine is running at normal operating temperature. It is also under considerable pressure, so *never* open the radiator cap on a hot engine. If you want to check the coolant level inside the radiator, shut the engine off and wait until it has cooled enough to do so at least 15 to 30 minutes. The best time to check the level is first thing in the morning before the vehicle has been driven (Fig. 5-19).

To Check the Coolant Level Inside the Radiator:

1. Place a rag over the radiator cap and turn the radiator cap counterclockwise until it comes to the first safety catch. If there is any pressure in the

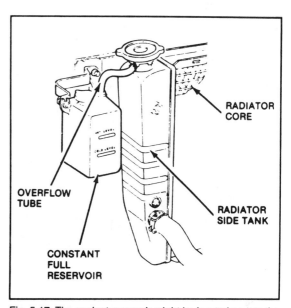

Fig. 5-17. The coolant reservoir might be located next to the radiator as shown elsewhere in the engine compartment. (Courtesy of *Ford Motorcraft Shop Tips,* Vol. 19, No. 2.)

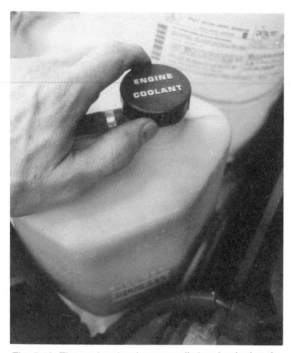

Fig. 5-18. The coolant level can usually be checked at the coolant reservoir or overflow tank.

system, it will vent at this point (you'll hear a slight hissing sound).

2. Wait until any pressure has vented itself through the overflow tube, then press down on the cap and continue turning it off.

3. On some vehicles, the coolant level will be right up to the top of the opening; on others, the correct level is several inches below the cap opening. Look on the side of the radiator to see if there are any marks that indicate "hot" or "cold" full levels. If the radiator is low, add a 50/50 mixture of water and antifreeze.

Adding Coolant: If the fluid level in the coolant reservoir is low, you don't have to add coolant directly to the radiator. You can add it to the fluid reservoir instead by simply opening the lid and pouring in a 50/50 mixture of antifreeze and water.

Never use straight water; it offers no corrosion, freezing, or boil-over protection. Straight water should only be used in an emergency to temporarily refill the cooling system. It should be drained out of the cooling system as soon as repairs have

Fig. 5-19. Never open a radiator cap when the engine is hot. Always wait until the engine has cooled off before opening.

been made and replaced with a 50/50 mixture of antifreeze and water. Straight antifreeze should not be used either because it doesn't offer as much freezing or boil-over protection as it does when it is mixed with water.

If the coolant reservoir is empty and/or the engine has overheated, it will be necessary to add coolant directly to the radiator. Remove the radiator cap using the procedure just described and add a 50/50 mixture of antifreeze and water until the radiator is full. Replace the cap, then add coolant to the reservoir to bring it up to the appropriate full mark. Be careful not to splash antifreeze on the exterior of your vehicle because it can damage paint.

Overheated Engine: If the engine has overheated and lost coolant, or if coolant has been lost due to a leak which in turn caused the engine to overheat, shut the engine off and wait until it has cooled before adding coolant. Pouring coolant into a hot engine can crack or warp hot metal parts. Steam trapped inside the engine can also cause the coolant to boil back out of the radiator with extreme force. So always wait until the engine has cooled before removing the radiator cap and attempting to add coolant.

After the engine has cooled for 30 minutes or more, carefully remove the radiator cap, start the engine, and add coolant while the engine is idling. As the coolant begins to circulate inside the engine, the level inside the radiator might drop, requiring more coolant to be added.

CHANGING THE COOLANT

Tool Needed. Catch pan or bucket; pliers; funnel; rag.

Parts Needed. Antifreeze and water (distilled water recommended for optimum corrosion protection).

How Often. Once every two years or 24,000 miles minimum; yearly or every 12,000 miles for maximum protection against internal corrosion in vehicles with aluminum radiators, engine blocks, cylinder heads, or water pumps.

Location. A drain plug or T-valve is usually located at one corner of the radiator along the bottom side (Fig. 5-20).

What To Do. It makes no difference whether the cooling system is drained hot or cold, although it's safer for you to drain it when it's cold.

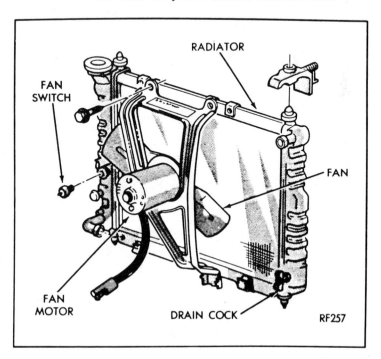

Fig. 5-20. The drain plug can usually be found toward the bottom of the radiator. (Courtesy of Chrysler Corporation.)

1. The engine must be off. Never drain coolant out of a radiator while the engine is running.

2. Position your catch pan or bucket under the radiator drain plug or T-valve to catch the coolant as it drains. The coolant can squirt several inches so take that into account in positioning your pan.

3. Remove the radiator cap.

4. If your radiator has a drain plug, simply remove the drain plug and allow the coolant to dribble out. If your radiator has a T-valve, you'll need pliers to loosen it. Carefully turn the T-valve in to open the drain. The threads on the T-valve are often reverse (left hand) threaded so make sure to turn it in the right direction. If it doesn't want to turn, try turning it the opposite way. Applying moderate heat with a propane torch can sometimes loosen up a frozen T-valve (don't apply heat if it's a plastic radiator!).

5. Let the radiator drain until the coolant stops dripping out the drain opening or T-valve. This doesn't mean your cooling system is completely drained, however. Coolant will still remain inside the engine block and the only way to get it out is to flush the cooling system with fresh water. Flushing or back flushing (see below) isn't absolutely essential, but it is highly recommended if the old coolant is rust-colored or contains a lot of residue.

Flushing: Close the drain plug or T-valve and refill the cooling system with water. Then start the engine, let it run for a few minutes or until hot water can be felt circulating through the upper radiator hose. Then shut the engine off and redrain the radiator. It might be necessary to repeat this step several times to remove all of the old coolant from the engine. Nevertheless, it should be done if the coolant is especially dirty or if the engine has an aluminum cylinder head or radiator.

Back-Flushing: A better method for removing the old coolant and residue from both radiator and engine, and one that is used by most professional mechanics, is to back-flush the cooling system. Special equipment is often used for back-flushing, but a do-it-yourselfer can get by with a garden hose T-adapter fitting that is installed in the heater return hose. The fitting allows you to circulate water backward through the cooling system to flush out old coolant and corrosion. Once the fitting is installed, just open the radiator drain plug (the radiator cap must be in place) and turn on the hose. Continue to flush water through the system until only clean water comes out the drain. Then turn off the hose, drain the radiator, and refill the system with a mixture of antifreeze and water.

Refilling The Cooling System: Always use a 50/50 mixture of antifreeze and water.

1. Close the radiator drain plug or T-valve.

2. Pour coolant into the radiator until full. To get the right 50/50 mixture, pour in a quart of antifreeze, then a quart of water, then a quart of antifreeze, and so on. You should probably add an extra quart of antifreeze to make up for the water that remains in the engine block if you flushed or back-flushed the cooling system.

3. Start the engine and let it idle for 15 to 20 minutes until coolant starts to circulate through the radiator. Carefully feel the upper radiator hose. When it starts to feel hot, the thermostat has opened and coolant is flowing into the radiator.

4. Turn the heater on maximum and continue to add coolant to the radiator until the system will take no more. Then replace the radiator cap and add coolant to the reservoir to bring it up to the appropriate full mark.

On some vehicles, notably front-wheel-drive cars with transverse (sideways) mounted engines, air pockets can form in the heater core and prevent the system from being completely refilled. If the heater fails to blow hot air after you've refilled the system and the engine is hot, it might be necessary to "burp" the heater core by loosening the heater hose clamp on the return hose so air can bleed out of the system.

CHECKING POWER STEERING FLUID LEVEL

Tools Needed. A clean rag.

How Often. Monthly

Location. The fluid level is checked at the power steering pump, which is mounted on a bracket attached to the front of the engine. The pump is driven with a V-belt attached to the crankshaft pulley. On most rear-wheel-drive cars, you'll find the pump mounted on the driver's side of the engine compartment. On front-wheel-drive cars with transverse mounted engines, the pump is usually positioned behind the motor on the passenger's side of the engine compartment (Fig. 5-21).

What To Do. Make sure the vehicle is parked on a level surface and the engine is off.

1. Wipe the top of the pump off to remove any grease or dirt that might be around the filler cap.

2. Unscrew the filler cap and note the fluid level inside or on the cap's dipstick. Some have "cold full," "hot full," and "add" marks on the dipstick or inside the filler neck. If the fluid is hot, it should be up to the hot full mark. If the vehicle hasn't been driven, it should be at the cold full mark. Add just enough power steering fluid to bring it up to the appropriate level. Don't overfill the reservoir because the fluid needs room to expand as it heats up.

When adding fluid, make certain that no dirt or grease falls into the pump. Even a small bit of dirt can play havoc with the system. Check in your owner's manual to see if your pump requires regular power steering fluid or automatic transmission fluid.

A low fluid level means there is a leak somewhere in your power steering system. You should check the pump, hoses, hose connections, and power cylinder or rack to determine from where the fluid is leaking. On power rack and pinion steering, an internal leak will allow fluid to accumulate in the rubber bellows on either end of the rack. If you squeeze the bellows and feel fluid inside, the seals are shot and the rack must be rebuilt or replaced. Rebuilding a power rack is a job few professional mechanics can do competently. Most replace the rack with a new or remanufactured assembly because the internal seals are so difficult to replace. This is an expensive job, so you might find it less expensive to add fluid as long as the steering itself isn't acting up.

Fig. 5-21. Checking the power steering fluid reservoir.

CHECKING BRAKE FLUID LEVEL

Tools Needed. None.

How Often. Monthly.

Parts Needed. Brake fluid (from a sealed container).

Location. The master cylinder fluid reservoir is located on the driver's side of the engine compartment. The master cylinder is mounted on the firewall (Fig. 5-22).

What To Do. Make sure the vehicle is parked on a level surface. Wipe away any grease or dirt from around the fluid reservoir caps or lid. Remove the caps or lid and note the fluid level inside. On some vehicles, you don't even have to remove the caps because you can see the level through the transparent sides of the reservoir.

Fig. 5-22. A low brake fluid level might mean there's a leak somewhere in the brake system.

If the fluid level is low, add clean, fresh brake fluid from a sealed container. Never use fluid from a container that has been left open because brake fluid absorbs moisture from the air. Moisture in the fluid lowers the fluid's boiling point, which can cause the brakes to fail under hard use. Moisture-contaminated fluid will also accelerate rusting inside the brake lines, calipers, and wheel cylinders. Also, never dump oil or any other fluid into the fluid reservoir. Petroleum-based liquids can ruin the seals in the master cylinder, caliper, and wheel cylinders.

The fluid level will gradually drop over time as the brake linings wear. This is because the disc brake pads and drum shoes move further out allowing more fluid to enter the calipers and wheel cylinders. A low fluid level can also mean there is a fluid leak somewhere in the brake system (leaky hose, caliper, wheel cylinder, or master cylinder), so check the system for wet spots.

After adding brake fluid, make sure the caps or lid are put back on and are tight. Be careful not to allow dirt, grease, or any other foreign matter fall into the fluid reservoir where it could plug up the metering ports inside the master cylinder. Also avoid splashing brake fluid on the fender because it can damage paint.

Brake fluid should be replaced periodically (every 2 to 3 years) or when relining the brakes to remove moisture contamination from the system. This is covered in Chapter 11 under Bleeding Brakes.

CHECKING BATTERY WATER LEVEL

Maintenance-free batteries do not require periodic additions of water but regular batteries do. The water level inside the battery is critical because it affects the life of the plates. A low water level will expose the tops of the cell plates, which changes their chemistry and reduces their ability to store electricity. This reduces battery output and eventually ruins the battery.

The water level in all types of batteries (including maintenance-free) should be checked because it can help you detect a variety of problems. A low water level in a maintenance-free battery or a sudden increase in water usage in a conventional battery means one of two things: a leaky battery case or a defective charging system that is putting out too much voltage.

Tools Needed. A clean rag; funnel.

How Often. Monthly.

Parts Needed. Distilled water.

Location. The battery is usually located in the front of the engine compartment. On some vehicles, such as vans, pickups, or certain imports, you might have to hunt for it; try looking under the passenger side floor, in the trunk, or under the back seat.

What To Do. Make sure the vehicle is parked on a level surface and the engine is off. *Caution:* Do not smoke when checking the level of the water inside the battery or use a match or cigarette lighter to see inside the battery. Batteries give off explosive hydrogen gas that can be ignited by a spark or flame.

On conventional batteries, use a rag to remove the caps on the top of the battery and check the water level inside. The rag is important because it will protect your fingers from any battery acid residue. The water level should be up to the top of the split ring or ledge in the cap opening.

On maintenance-free batteries the water level inside can be determined one of three ways. Usually you can see the water level through the sides of the semitransparent case. On some, the caps can be pried off with a screwdriver to check the water level inside. Others include a small charge indicator eye on top of the battery. A green dot means the water level is satisfactory and the battery is at least 75 percent charged. A dark indicator eye means the water level is satisfactory but the battery needs recharging. A clear or yellowish eye means the water level is low and unless you can pry open the caps and add water the battery will have to be replaced (Fig. 5-23).

Adding Water: Use only distilled water. Ordi-

Fig. 5-23. Maintenance-free batteries might never need water, but they can sometimes get low on water. If low, the hydrometer window will appear light or yellowish in color.

nary tap water contains dissolved minerals that will react with the acid inside the battery, weakening the solution and shortening the life of the battery. Add water slowly to bring the level up to the full mark. The cells fill rapidly and are easy to overfill. Overfilling isn't good because it can flush acid out of the cell.

REPLACING THE AIR FILTER

The air filter keeps dirt out of your engine and fuel system. The pleated paper filter element has a large surface area relative to the amount of air that passes through it. In time, however, the gradual accumulation of dirt and debris begins to restrict air flow through the filter. When the filter reaches this point, it's time to replace it. In most areas of the country that means once a year. But for vehicles that are driven on gravel roads or off-road, the filter should be checked several times a year and replaced as needed.

Tools Needed. Screwdriver and/or pliers.

Parts Needed. New air filter.

How Often. Yearly or as needed.

Location. The air filter is located inside the air cleaner housing. The housing will be a large metal or plastic canister or box over or near the carburetor. On fuel injected engines, the air cleaner housing is usually located in the intake ducting ahead of the engine (Fig. 5-24).

What To Do. Make sure the engine is off and the vehicle is parked on a level surface.

1. Remove the wing nut or pry loose the snap tabs that hold the top of the air cleaner housing in place. On some applications you might have to loosen the duct work from the housing to open the top.

2. Remove the top and lift out the filter element. On vehicles that use a flat rectangular filter, note which side of the filter goes up (Fig. 5-25).

3. Hold the filter up to a bright light to determine how dirty it is. If the paper is heavily clogged with dirt, replace it. Paper elements are not washable.

4. Compare the new filter element to the old to make certain both are the same size. Then drop the new filter in place and replace the top of the air cleaner housing. Finger tighten center wingnuts or plastic wingnuts only. Overtightening can break plastic components.

5. Note the date and mileage you replaced the filter in your maintenance record.

REPLACING THE FUEL FILTER

The fuel filter keeps your fuel system clean by trapping dirt and rust particles before then can cause trouble. Unfortunately, in so doing, the filter itself can sometimes cause problems if it plugs up. The best way to prevent such woes is to change the filter periodically whether it needs it or not.

Tools Needed. Pliers and/or a wrench; and a clean rag.

Parts Needed. New fuel filter.

How Often. Once a year.

Location. Different vehicles use different types of fuel filters. Some are *in-line* filters that can be found in the fuel line between the fuel pump and carburetor. On some carburetors, a tiny sintered brass or paper filter element is located inside the inlet fitting on the carburetor. On fuel-injected applications, a large canister in-line filter is usually mounted near the fuel tank just after the electric fuel pump (Figs. 5-26 and 5-27).

What To Do. *Warning:* do not smoke while changing the fuel filter. The best time to change the fuel filter is when the engine is cold. This reduces the fire hazard that might be created by splashing gasoline on a hot engine. If the engine has not been driven, there will be little or no pressure inside the fuel lines, allowing you to open the line without too much fuel squirting out.

1. With the engine off, locate the fuel filter (refer to your owners manual or a shop guide). It might be necessary to remove the air cleaner and some of the ducting. If you disconnect vacuum hoses, note where they go so you can reconnect them correctly.

2. Loosen the filter connection by removing the hose clamps and/or unscrewing the filter from the carburetor. If the engine is equipped with fuel injection, the fuel system might still be under pressure. Wrap a rag around the filter to catch any fuel that spills.

3. As you loosen the filter, gas will begin to seep out. Wait until the seepage has stopped before completely removing the filter.

4. Compare the new filter to the old to make certain you have the right replacement, and note any markings on the new filter that indicate which way to install it. If some filters are installed backward fuel will bypass the filter element.

5. Screw the filter into place—be careful not to overtighten it or you might strip the threads in the carburetor—or install it in the fuel line. Most in-line filters come with new clamps and short pieces of hose; use these because rubber hoses deteriorate over time and clamps lose tension.

6. Replace any other hardware you had to remove to gain access to the filter, and make sure the hoses and ducts are tight and routed correctly.

7. Start the engine and check for any fuel leaks.

8. Make a note of the mileage and date you replaced the filter in your maintenance record.

Fig. 5-24. A dirty air filter can hurt fuel mileage and performance. If the filter is clogged with dirt, it's overdue for a replacement.

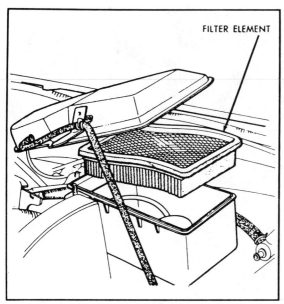

Fig. 5-25. On engines that use flat air filters, pay attention to which side goes up when changing the filter. (Courtesy of Chrysler Corporation.)

CHASSIS LUBRICATION

Tools Needed. Jack; safety stands; grease gun; clean rag.

How Often. The chassis should be greased twice a year or when changing oil. Many suspension components, however, are "lubed-for-life." This means they have grease fittings and do not require periodic lubrication.

Location. The parts that need greasing usually include the ball joints and tie rod ends. On vehicles with parallelogram steering (not rack and

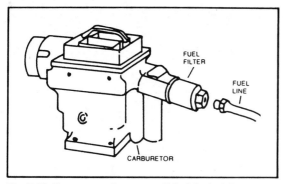

Fig. 5-26. On many engines, you will find the fuel filter where the fuel line connects to the carburetor.

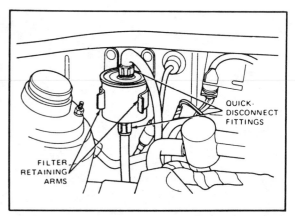

Fig. 5-27. The fuel filter on some engines will be found in the fuel line, usually between the fuel pump and carburetor. On fuel-injected engines, an in-line filter is often positioned under the vehicle near the fuel tank. (Courtesy of Chrysler Corporation.)

pinion steering) the idler arm, steering links, and control arm bushings may require greasing. On some rear-wheel-drive vehicles, the driveshaft U-joints can also be greased.

What To Do. Use a high-quality, multipurpose chassis grease.

1. Set the emergency brake, and put the transmission in Park (automatic) or gear (manual).

2. Raise the vehicle and support it on safety stands.

3. Use your rag to wipe old grease and dirt away from the grease fittings on the suspension components. Inspect the rubber boots for splits or damage that would indicate replacement is necessary.

4. Connect the grease gun to the fitting on each component and pump in grease until the rubber boot is swollen. Don't pump in grease until it squirts out past the boot seal. Some people recommend doing this to flush out water and dirt, but it also loosens the boot seal, which can let more water and dirt into the joint.

5. If the vehicle is a rear-wheel-drive, check the U-joints to see if they can be greased. The fitting will be located in the center cross of the joint.

6. Make a note of the date and mileage at which you lubricated the chassis in your maintenance record for future reference.

LUBRICATING WHEEL BEARINGS

The front wheel bearings on many rear-wheel-drive vehicles and the rear wheel bearings on many front-wheel-drive vehicles require periodic lubrication (often called *repacking*). Not all wheel bearings require lubrication, however, because some are sealed. Check in your owner's manual for lubrication recommendations.

Tooks Needed. Jack; safety stands; lug wrench; adjustable wrench or channel pliers; drift and hammer; screwdriver; block of wood; newspaper.

Parts Needed. New grease seals; wheel bearing grease; cleaning solvent.

When. The wheel bearings should be cleaned, inspected, and repacked with fresh grease every two years or 24,000 miles for maximum longevity. For vehicles that operate off-road or in hub-deep water, more frequent greasing might be needed. Refer to your owner's manual for wheel lubrication recommendations.

Location. The wheel bearings are located inside the front and rear wheel hubs. On rear-wheel-drive vehicles, the rear wheel bearings are located on the axle shafts inside the axle housing. They are lubricated by the differential oil and do not require greasing. On some foreign front-wheel-drive cars (Honda, for example), the front wheel bearings are very difficult to reach. It might be better to have a professional mechanic do the job for you in this case (Fig. 5-28).

What To Do. Use a high-quality wheel bearing grease. Ordinary chassis grease might not provide adequate lubrication.

1. If repacking the front wheel bearings, set the emergency brake. If you're doing the rear wheel bearings, don't set the brake. Block the front wheels to keep the vehicle from rolling.

2. Remove the hubcap and loosen the lug nuts half a turn.

3. Raise the vehicle, support it on safety stands, then remove the wheel.

4. On front disc brakes, remove the brake caliper from the rotor. There's no need to disconnect the hose, but don't let the caliper hang from the hose. Lay it on the suspension control arm or support it with a piece of wire.

5. Remove the grease cup (channel pliers work best), then the cotter pin, locknut, hub nut,

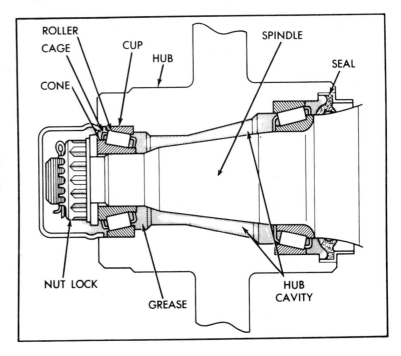

Fig. 5-28. Typical wheel bearing assembly. Always install a new rear grease seal when repacking the bearings with grease. (Courtesy of Chrysler Corporation.)

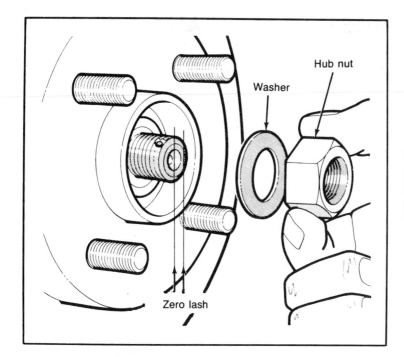

Fig. 5-29. Most vehicles call for "zero preload" on the wheel bearings, meaning finger tighten only (check your owner's manual or a repair manual for specific recommendations). (Courtesy of Chrysler Corporation.)

and washer from the wheel hub.

6. Pull the wheel hub (and drum on drum brakes) off the axle spindle. The hub will contain an inner and outer bearing. The outer one will fall out as soon as the hub is pulled off the spindle, so be ready to catch it.

7. Pry the old grease seal out of the back of the hub or drum, then remove the inner bearing.

8. Throughly clean all the old grease from the hub cavity and bearings. Place the bearings on newspaper and let them air dry.

9. Inspect the bearings and races for pitting, galling, damaged rollers, balls, or tracks. Replace the bearing if damaged or worn. An outer bearing race can be extracted from the hub or drum by using a special puller (which you can rent at an auto parts store), or by pounding from the backside with a hammer and brass drift. To reinstall a race, pound it back in with the hammer and drift (be careful not to cock it) or use a bearing driver.

Fig. 5-30. Always install a new cotter pin after repacking and adjusting the bearings. Bend the pin as shown to hold it securely in position. (Courtesy of Chrysler Corporation.)

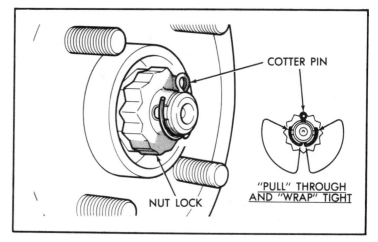

10. Repack the wheel bearings with fresh grease. Hold the bearing in the palm of your hand and work grease into it with your fingers (make sure your hands are clean when you start so no dirt or grit gets into the bearing). Coat the bearing races in the hub or drum with grease and add several tablespoons of grease to the hub cavity (pack it about one-third full). A light coating of grease can also be applied to the hub spindle.

11. Put the inner bearing back in the hub, then install a new grease seal over it. Hold your block of wood over the seal and gently tap it into place. Be careful not to twist or deform the seal or it will leak.

12. Remount the hub back on the spindle, then replace the outer wheel bearing, washer, and hub nut.

13. Tighten the hub nut with moderate pressure while slowly rotating the hub. Most wheel bearings call for zero preloading. When the hub nut is as tight as it will go, back it off and retighten with your fingers only (Figs. 5-29 and 5-30).

14. Install the locknut and a new cotter pin.

Fig. 5-31. Adding washer fluid to the fluid reservoir.

On some vehicles, a staked washer or second hub nut is used to secure the bearings.

15. Replace the grease cap on the hub (gently pound it on with a rubber hammer), then put the wheel back on and tighten the lug nuts. To check wheel bearing freeplay, try rocking the wheel in and out. If the wheel bearings have been adjusted correctly, you should feel no looseness. The wheel should also turn easily when spun by hand.

16. Now lower the vehicle, finish tightening the lug nuts, and replace the hub cap.

17. Make a note of the date and mileage at which you repacked the wheel bearings in your maintenance record for future reference.

CHECKING AND REFILLING WINDSHIELD WASHER FLUID

Although windshield washer fluid isn't really a vital fluid, it's included in this chapter because it can be a safety factor. Washer fluid helps clear road grime, mud, and insects from your windshield for better visibility. Run out of it at the wrong time and your driving visibility can be seriously impaired.

Tools Needed. Funnel.

How Often. Check monthly or more frequently depending on use.

Location. The windshield washer fluid reservoir is usually a white plastic rectangular container. It can be located on either side of the engine compartment, at the base of the windshield, or next to the radiator coolant reservoir.

What To Do. The fluid level inside the reservoir is usually visible through the semitransparent sides of the reservoir. If low, add fluid to bring the level up to the top of the reservoir (Fig. 5-31).

Adding Washer Fluid: Never use cooling system antifreeze (ethylene glycol) or straight alcohol in the washer reservoir (either can damage your vehicle's paint). Use water, water and window cleaner, or premixed washer fluid. During cold weather, always use premixed washer fluid or add washer antifreeze concentrate to protect the system against freezing. Use care to keep dirt out of the reservoir because dirt can plug the spray nozzles (you can usually unclog a nozzle with a straight pin).

Chapter 6

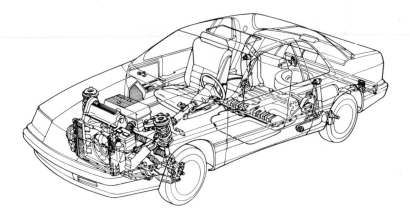

Maintenance and Safety Inspection

An essential aspect of caring for your vehicle is periodically checking the various fluid levels, mechanical components, and safety items. This should always be done as part of a tune-up, but there is no reason why you cannot do it more often. In fact, some of the items included in this section should be checked quite frequently. Giving your vehicle a good once-over both spring and fall is an excellent idea. You should also check it over carefully before going on vacation.

Table 6-1 lists the items that should be included in your maintenance and safety check. You should also use this checklist when inspecting a used car.

INSIDE YOUR VEHICLE

Steering Play. Steering play should be less than half an inch when the steering wheel is rocked back and forth, Looseness means trouble. Looseness indicates that there are worn components in the steering linkage or steering gear. If not repaired the tires will wear quickly. The vehicle might also wander or pull to one side when driven.

Brake Pedal. The brake pedal should feel firm and travel no more than a few inches when pressure is applied. A low pedal can indicate worn brake linings or a low fluid level. A "spongy" pedal can mean air bubbles in the brake lines or a worn master cylinder. If the brakes need repair work, *do not* put it off. Brakes are too important to take needless risks.

Emergency Brake. The emergency brake should lock the rear wheels when applied and hold the vehicle on an incline or when the automatic transmission is placed in drive. If it does not, readjust the linkage. The brake should hold when the pedal or handle is about one-third applied. Also note whether the brake warning light comes on when the emergency brake is applied. No light means the bulb might be out or the switch on the brake handle or pedal might need adjusting or replacement.

Horn. Try the horn to see if it honks easily. If it makes no sound and you are certain you are pressing the right spot, it might indicate a blown fuse or horn relay (check the fuse panel). Corrosion

Table 6-1. Maintenance and Safety Checklist.

INSIDE VEHICLE	OUTSIDE VEHICLE
* Steering play	* Headlights
* Brake pedal	* Taillights
* Emergency brake	* Brake lights
* Horn	* Turn signals
* Windshield wipers	* Backup lights
* Windshield washers	* License plate lights
* Mirrors	* Wiper blades
* Defroster	* Tire inflation
* Spare tire & jack	* Tire condition

UNDER HOOD	UNDERNEATH
* Fluid levels	* Fluid leaks
* Air filter	* Shock absorbers/struts
* V-belts	* Tie rod ends & steering linkage
* Radiator hoses	* Ball joints
* Heater hoses	* Brake hoses
* PCV valve	* Exhaust system & muffler
* Vacuum hoses	* CV joint boots
* Battery terminals	* Differential lube level

on the horn mounting or a loose wire can also silence an otherwise good horn.

Windshield Wipers. The wipers should work at all speeds and should clean the windows without streaking. Dead wipers can be caused by a bad motor, a defective dash switch, or a loose wire. A blown fuse usually indicates overloading due to binding. Check the cowl area for debris or under the dash for interference between the wiper linkage and defroster or air conditioning ducts.

Windshield Washers. Washers should spray on both sides of the windshield when activated. If the stream is weak or the squirters just dribble, try cleaning out the nozzles with a pin. Dirt or kinks in the washer hose or dirt in the bottom of the washer reservoir can restrict fluid flow. If the washers fail to squirt and you hear a buzzing noise, it just needs fluid. Silence means a bad washer pump motor, a defective switch, or loose wire.

Mirrors. Inside and outside mirrors should be free from obstructions, provide clear vision, and be firmly attached. Missing or broken mirrors should be replaced; loose mirrors should be tightened.

Defroster. You can get by without a defroster during warm, dry, weather, but it is absolutely essential on rainy or cold days. Set the heater to de-

frost, turn the blower on high, and feel for warm air blowing up from the top of the dash toward the windshield. No air usually means the ducts under the dash have pulled loose or the air flow control door inside the heater box is not working. Also check the electric rear window defogger. The glass should feel warm three to five minutes after you turn it on. No heat might be due to a loose wire, poor ground, or defective relay or switch.

Spare Tire and Jack. One of the most neglected parts of your vehicle, the spare tire, should be checked for proper inflation pressure—unless it is the deflateable temporary variety, in which case, check to see that the inflation canister contains a full charge. Make certain all the parts for the jack are there and that the jack works.

UNDER THE HOOD

Fluid Levels. Check the engine oil, coolant level, brake fluid, power steering fluid, battery water, and windshield washer fluid levels while the engine is off. Check the automatic transmission fluid level after the car has been driven, the fluid is warm, and the engine is idling (the transmission must be in park). Add whatever fluid is necessary to maintain the fluid levels at the full mark.

Air Filter. Remove the top of the air cleaner and take out the filter. Hold the filter up to a bright light to see the dirt. If you see more dirt than paper, replace it.

V-belts. Check the engine's drive belts for tightness and wear. As a rule of thumb, the longest span between two pulleys should deflect no more than half an inch under moderate pressure (Fig.6-1). If the belt needs tightening, see Chapter 11. On vehicles equipped with *serpentine* belts (one long, flat belt that snakes around all the pulleys), tension is maintained automatically and no adjustment should be required. Any belt that shows fraying, broken strands, or heavy cracking should be replaced (Fig. 6-2).

Radiator Hoses. Check hoses by squeezing them; hoses should feel soft and pliable, not hard, brittle, swollen, or mushy. If the hose is full of tiny cracks, replace it. Also check clamps for tightness and hose connections for leaks. Another problem to watch for is chafing. A hose can wear through if it rubs against a bracket or sharp object. If you see a shiny spot on the side of a hose and it appears to be chafing, reposition the hose away from the object and/or wrap several layers of heavy plastic tape around it for protection (Fig. 6-3).

Heater Hoses. Do the same checks on the heater hoses as you did for the radiator hoses. On front-wheel-drive vehicles with transverse-mounted (sideways) engines, metal pipes are often used to route hoses around the engine. Check the pipes for excessive corrosion or leaky connections.

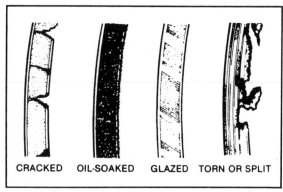

CRACKED   OIL-SOAKED   GLAZED   TORN OR SPLIT

Fig. 6-2. Replace any drive belt that looks like any of these. (Courtesy of *Ford Motorcraft Shop Tips,* Vol. 19, No. 2.)

PCV Valve and Hose. A free-flowing PCV valve is essential to the health of your engine. If the PCV valve or hose clogs, it can lead to rapid sludge buildup inside the engine. Check the PCV valve by removing it from the valve cover and feeling for vacuum while the engine is idling. With the engine off, the valve should rattle when shaken. If the valve or hose is clogged, replace it immediately.

Vacuum Hoses. Plastic and rubber vacuum hoses must be tight and free from cracks, kinks, or burns. Check for possible rubbing against brackets or other sharp objects in the engine compartment. Vacuum is used to control a variety of engine functions; therefore, leaks can result in many different kinds of problems.

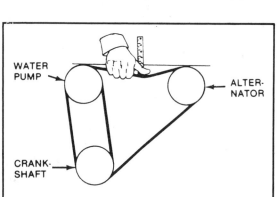

WATER PUMP

ALTER-NATOR

CRANK-SHAFT

Fig. 6-1. A properly adjusted belt should deflect about half an inch under moderate pressure. (Courtesy of *Ford Motorcraft Shop Tips,* Vol. 19, No. 2.)

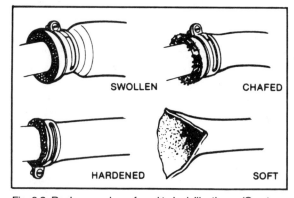

SWOLLEN   CHAFED

HARDENED   SOFT

Fig. 6-3. Replace any hose found to look like these. (Courtesy of *Ford Motorcraft Shop Tips,* Vol. 19, No. 2.)

Distributor Cap. Look at the outside of the cap. It should be free from cracks or signs of electrical arcing (carbon tracks). Use a screwdriver to pop it off. The inside should be clean and dry. Replace the distributor cap if the terminals are worn or corroded (Fig. 6-4).

Spark Plug Wires. The boots should fit tightly around the spark plugs and the ends should attach firmly to the distributor cap. Wires should be free from cracks, burns, or frayed insulation. Check for possible chafing or burning if the wires are routed close to the exhaust manifold.

Battery Terminals. Voltage cannot get through unless the battery terminals are free from corrosion and the cables fit tight (try to wiggle the clamps). Corrosion should be removed by taking off the cables and using a wire brush, sandpaper, or a terminal cleaner to scrape away the crud (Fig. 6-5).

ON THE OUTSIDE

Headlights. Check both high and low beams. The aim can be checked by shining the lights at a garage door or wall. The beam should not be too high or too low or in the left lane. Once adjusted correctly the aim should not change (Fig. 6-6).

Taillights. Check to see that all bulbs are working when the lights are on. If neither the tail-light or brake light on one side works, check for a bad socket or wiring connection.

Brake Lights. The brake lights should illuminate when the brake pedal is depressed. No light on one side usually indicates a burned-out bulb. No lights on either side is usually due to a defective switch on the top of the brake pedal.

Turn signals. Try both left and right turn signals and the four-way emergency flasher. If one side blinks but not the other, the problem is a burned-out bulb. If neither side blinks, the flasher is bad (it is located on the fuse panel and can be replaced by plugging in a new flasher).

Backup Lights. The white backup lights should come on when the ignition is on and the transmission is placed in reverse. No light means either burned-out bulbs, a misadjusted or defective backup light switch on the transmission shift linkage, or a wiring problem.

License Plate Light. The license plate should be illuminated when the headlights are turned on. No light usually means a bad bulb or poor socket connection.

Wiper Blades. Check the rubber blades for cracking and see if they clean without streaking. The average wiper blade usually needs to be replaced once a year.

Tire Inflation. Check tire inflation pressures while the tires are cold. Inflation pressures are

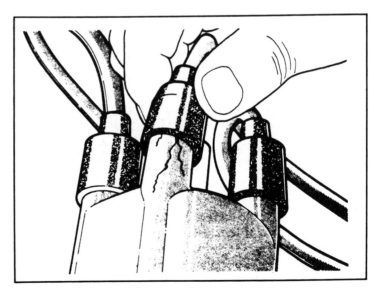

Fig. 6-4. If the distributor cap has cracks, it must be replaced. (Courtesy of Chrysler Corporation.)

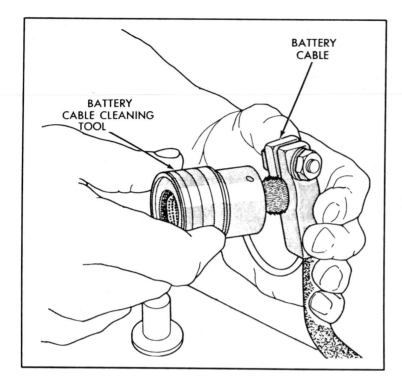

BATTERY
CABLE

BATTERY
CABLE CLEANING
TOOL

Fig. 6-5. Corroded battery terminals and clamps should be cleaned. (Courtesy of Chrysler Corporation.)

usually given in both your owner's manual and on a decal in the glovebox or door sill. A low reading on any tire means it is losing air. It might be leak-

ing around the base of the valve stem, through the valve itself, where the tire seats on the rim, or through a puncture or crack in the tread or side-

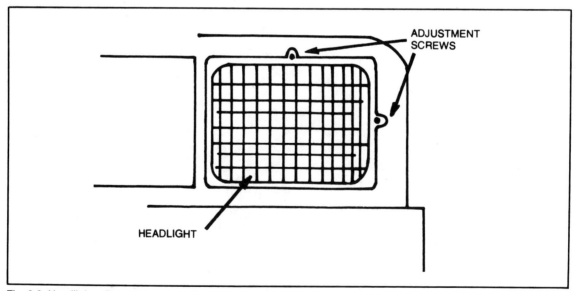

ADJUSTMENT
SCREWS

HEADLIGHT

Fig. 6-6. Headlight adjustment screws. The top screw adjusts the beam up and down. The side screw adjusts the beam left to right. (Courtesy of Chrysler Corporation.)

wall. Applying soapy water to the valve stem and around the rim and tire itself can help pinpoint the problem. If you find a leak, get it fixed so that it does not leave you flat.

Tire Condition. Check the tread for rapid or uneven wear; rapid or uneven tire wear means trouble. If it is a newer vehicle (less than 25,000 miles), chances are it needs to have the wheels realigned. If it is an older or high-mileage vehicle, chances are suspension components are worn and need to be replaced. Tires should also be inspected for splits, cracks, missing hunks of tread, bulges, or sidewall damage (Fig. 6-7).

UNDERNEATH

Fluid Leaks. Check the engine compartment and under both ends of the vehicle for possible fluid leaks. Puddles in the driveway or heavy accumulations of grease or oil on the engine or other components mean trouble. Fuel leaks can be especially dangerous because of the fire hazard they create.

Check the hose connections, the gasket seams and seals on the engine and transaxle, and the transmission and rear end for signs of leakage. A blue or green slimy liquid is antifreeze. Red or pink oily liquid is automatic transmission fluid. Pink or clear strong-smelling liquid is gasoline. Yellow or brown slippery liquid is oil. Clear and oily liquid is brake fluid or power steering fluid. If you find a leak, check the fluid level and add as needed.

Fuel leaks can occur at gas line connections, the fuel pump, the carburetor, or along fuel tank seams. A pump, line, or carburetor leak might not show itself unless the engine is running and the fuel is under pressure.

Engine oil leaks occur most often at the valve cover and oil pan gaskets and at the front and rear crank shaft seals. Valve cover gaskets are usually easy to replace, but pan gaskets and crank shaft seals are much more difficult. Crankcase additives sometimes help by causing leaky seals to swell, but it will not stop a major leak.

Automatic transmissions often leak fluid at the driveshaft seals and around the pan gasket. Either can be replaced by a do-it-yourselfer in a rear-wheel-drive vehicle, but driveshaft seal leaks in a front-wheel-drive transaxle are tough to change because the axles have to be removed.

Coolant leaks most often occur at the water pump (through the shaft seal) and radiator (look around the seams that separate the end tanks from the finned core). Small leaks in the radiator can sometimes be plugged by dumping a can of stop-leak in the radiator, but stop-leak will not help a leaky water pump or hose. Stop-leak can also seal small leaks inside the engine.

Power steering leaks are common at hose connections. Replacing the leaky hose is the only way to stop fluid loss. On rack and pinion steering units, internal leaks in the steering gear can allow fluid

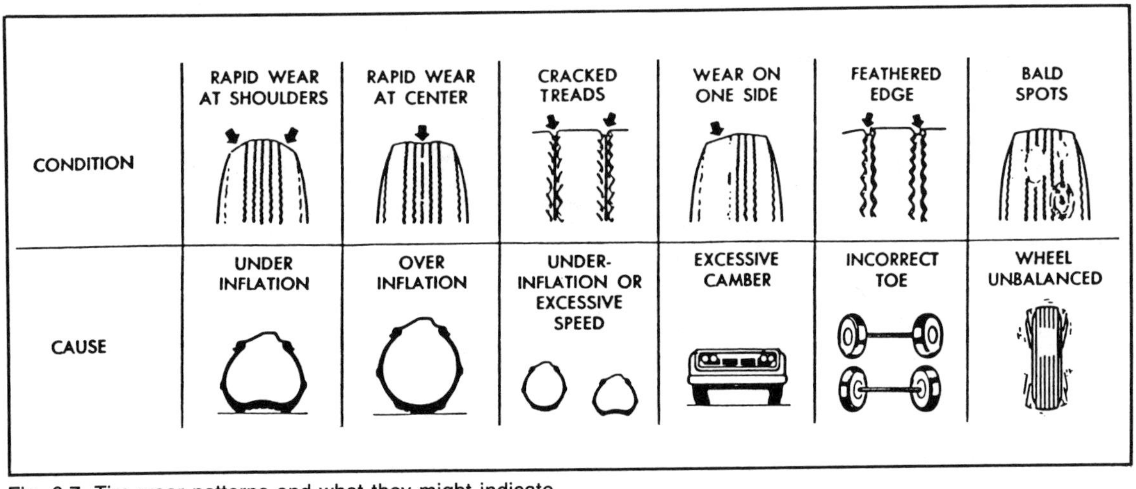

CONDITION	RAPID WEAR AT SHOULDERS	RAPID WEAR AT CENTER	CRACKED TREADS	WEAR ON ONE SIDE	FEATHERED EDGE	BALD SPOTS
CAUSE	UNDER INFLATION	OVER INFLATION	UNDER-INFLATION OR EXCESSIVE SPEED	EXCESSIVE CAMBER	INCORRECT TOE	WHEEL UNBALANCED

Fig. 6-7. Tire wear patterns and what they might indicate.

to seep into the rubber bellows on either end of the unit. If you feel liquid inside the bellows, it means the seals are bad and the unit needs to be replaced by a professional.

Brake fluid leaks can occur in the rubber or metal hoses, hose connections, disc brake calipers, drum brake wheel cylinders, or at the master cylinder. Wetness or fluid on the outside of any of these components means trouble. A leaky drum brake wheel cylinder or disc brake caliper is especially bad because the fluid can get on the linings and make the brakes slip.

Shock Absorbers/Struts. You can get a fairly accurate reading on the condition of the shocks by doing a "bounce" test. Rock one side of the bumper up and down several times, then let go. If the car continues to rock more than once or twice,

the shocks are worn out and need to be replaced. Repeat this test at each corner of the car.

If you find oily streaks on the outside of the shock absorbers, it means the oil seal has failed and the shock is leaking. It will need to be replaced. Also check shock mountings for loose or missing rubber bushings.

If shocks need replacing, they are usually replaced in pairs (both front and/or both rear shocks). A MacPherson strut is simply an overgrown shock absorber; struts, however, can be more difficult to change because many have coil springs around them. This requires the use of a spring-compressor tool (which you can usually rent) to disassemble the strut. Shock and strut replacement are covered in Chapter 11.

Tie Rod Ends and Steering Linkage. The

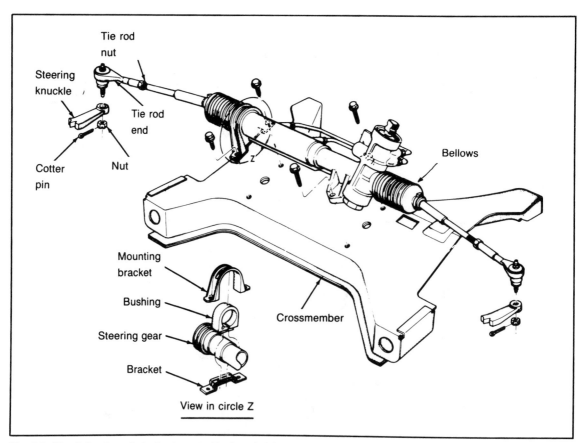

Fig. 6-8. Check the tie rods for looseness. Rack-and-pinion steering units should also be checked for damaged bellows or loose rack mounts. (Courtesy of Chrysler Corporation.)

76

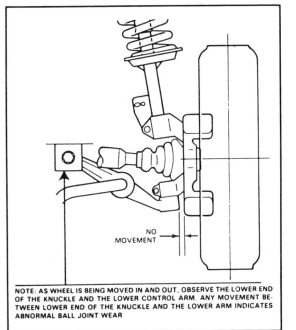

NOTE: AS WHEEL IS BEING MOVED IN AND OUT, OBSERVE THE LOWER END OF THE KNUCKLE AND THE LOWER CONTROL ARM. ANY MOVEMENT BETWEEN LOWER END OF THE KNUCKLE AND THE LOWER ARM INDICATES ABNORMAL BALL JOINT WEAR

Fig. 6-9. Ball joints should show no movement when un-loaded.

tie rod ends connect the steering linkage to the arms on the steering knuckles. They are a high-wear item and should be checked if the tires show uneven or rapid wear or if there is play in the steering wheel. Have a friend rock the steering wheel while the front wheels of the vehicle are on the ground. The wheels should be on the ground to "load" the steering linkage. If you see or feel any looseness in the connection, the tie rod ends need to be replaced (Fig. 6-8).

On vehicles without rack and pinion steering, the idler arm should also be watched for play. The *idler arm* holds the linkage on the side opposite the steering gear; like the tie rod ends, it is a high-wear item. On vehicles with rack and pinion steering, also check the rubber bellows on both ends of the steering gear. These must be tight and free from cracks to protect the steering gear from dirt and moisture. If the bellows are worn, replace immediately to save your steering gear from possible damage.

Also watch for any movement between the rack and pinion gear housing and chassis while the steering is rocked back and forth. The rubber mount-ing bushings or grommets between the housing and chassis can shrink or deteriorate, resulting in steering play, wander, and noise.

Ball Joints. Ball joints connect the front wheels to the suspension control arms. Some vehicles have two on each side, while those vehicles with MacPherson struts have only one on each side. Clunking noises when passing over bumps, or uneven tire wear might indicate worn ball joints.

Ball joints can be checked by raising the front wheels off the ground, grasping the tire at the top and bottom, and rocking the wheel in and out. There should be no looseness or wobble in the wheel. (Note: loose or worn wheel bearings can sometimes make a wheel feel loose Fig. 6-9).

Some ball joints have built-in wear indicators. If the joint has a grease fitting and the fitting feels loose in the housing or has receded into the housing, it indicates excessive wear (Fig. 6-10). On some vehicles, the ball joints remain "loaded" (under spring tension) even though the weight of the vehicle is off the ground. To check the load-carrying ball joints in this type of suspension, the control arm must be supported to relieve spring tension on the ball joint.

Brake Hoses. All rubber brake hoses should be checked to make certain they are not cracked,

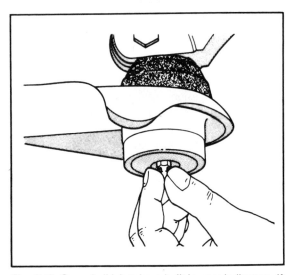

Fig. 6-10. Some ball joints have built-in wear indicators. If the grease fitting has receded into the housing or feels loose, the ball joint is worn and needs to be replaced.

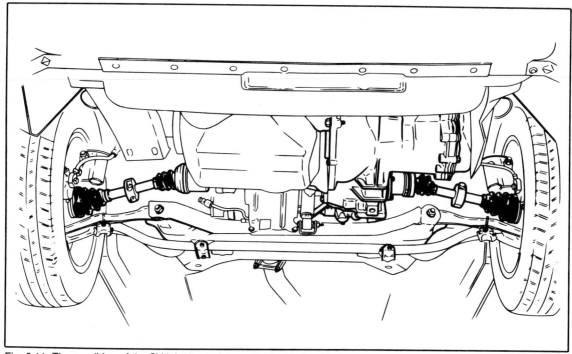

Fig. 6-11. The condition of the CV-joint boots (shown in black) should always be checked on front-wheel-drive vehicles.

bulging, or leaking. Replace any defective hoses.

Exhaust System/Muffler. The exhaust system must be leak-free, and the tailpipe should extend beyond the underside of the car. Check for broken exhaust hangers, holes in the muffler, loose or leaky connections, and crushed or missing pipes. If the vehicle is a 1975 or later model, the exhaust system should have a catalytic converter to be emissions legal. If you live in an area that requires periodic vehicle emissions testing, your vehicle will not pass if the converter has been removed.

CV Joint Boots. This is an extremely important item to check on front-wheel-drive vehicles. The four rubber boots that surround the constant-velocity joints on the driveshafts protect the joints from dirt and moisture. If the boots are loose or damaged, the joints will soon ruin. Replace defective boots immediately.

If you hear a clicking noise while turning, or if there is a "clunk" when you put the transaxle into gear, it is too late. The CV joints are bad and must be replaced (Fig. 6-11).

Differential Lube. On rear-wheel-drive vehicles, do not forget to check the fluid level in the differential. The lube does not usually require changing, but the level is very important. If it becomes low, it can lead to failure of the differential and/or the rear wheel bearings.

Chapter 7

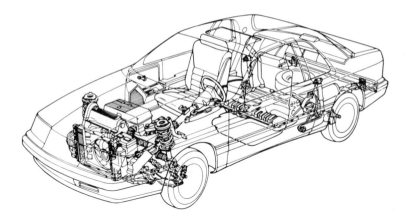

The Essentials Of A Tune-up

A tune-up is one of the basic jobs that must be periodically performed. What is a tune-up? It's not easy to say because the word means different things to different people. A tune-up is basically replacing those parts that have worn out, and readjusting those components that need readjusting to restore peak performance and fuel economy. When it comes to making a list of which parts need to be replaced and which components need adjusting, however, opinions differ.

Ask a dozen professional mechanics to list the parts that should be routinely changed as part of a tune-up and you'll get a dozen different answers. Most mechanics will probably agree that a bare-bones tune-up should include new spark plugs and a new rotor, plus new points and condenser if the vehicle is pre-1975. Some will suggest including a new fuel filter and air filter and there are those mechanics who will insist on replacing the distributor cap and possibly even the spark plug wires.

As for adjustments, the basics include setting point dwell on older point ignition systems, checking the ignition timing and advance, checking and

adjusting idle speed, and on older cars, adjusting the carburetor idle mixture.

IS THE TUNE-UP DEAD?

Some people might try to tell you that because of electronic ignition systems (which all cars have had since 1975), timing adjustments are seldom needed. There are no contact points to wear, so timing doesn't change unless somebody moves the distributor. On many vehicles, timing is totally controlled by the computer and the distributor has even been eliminated on some engines, so there's nothing to adjust.

Idle speed on many 1981 and newer cars is computer controlled. The computer uses a little stepper motor to adjust the idle. Unless the system is not performing properly (stalling or idling too fast) or the stepper motor is defective, there's no need to adjust idle speed.

Idle mixture adjustments on carburetors have been made nearly impossible by factory-sealed adjustment screws. The idle mixture is factory set and sealed to prevent tampering, which could adversely affect engine emissions. On some cars, plastic *idle limiter* caps are placed over the ends of the screws to limit the amount of adjustment within a predetermined range. Even if the caps are pulled off, internal restrictions in the metering orifices prevent much change in the mixture. Forget about trying to change the idle mixture on an engine equipped with electronic fuel injection; it can't be done. The computer controls the task of fuel management as well as idle speed and ignition timing.

In spite of all the parts that don't need to be replaced and can't be adjusted, the tune-up isn't dead yet. Certain items still require periodic attention (Fig. 7-1).

BEWARE OF SNAKE OIL SALESMEN!

There are a lot of tune-up-in-a-can products on the market that claim to "tune your engine while your drive." Some are fuel tank additives while others are dumped into the crankcase. If any of these products do anything at all, the benefits are so marginal that they are virtually nonexistent. Miracle fuel additives or crankcase additives simply don't exist, except in the minds of snake oil salesmen and gullible motorists. There are chemical products that help clean fuel systems, dirty carburetors, and fuel injectors, and there are oil additives that can increase oil viscosity. But there isn't anything that comes in a can that can take the place of or eliminate the need for a real tune-up.

You should also be aware of the fact that a tune-up isn't a cure-all for what might be wrong with your engine, nor can it prevent problems from ever developing. It is a necessary part of preventive maintenance, and it can sometimes be a good remedy for minor ailments such as hard starting, missing, stalling, and rough idling. Don't expect a do-it-yourself or even a professional tune-up to make a worn out engine run like new.

A tune-up can only restore what's been lost. If new spark plugs and a few adjustments don't eliminate a performance problem, chances are, more ex-

Fig. 7-1. The tune-up isn't dead yet. There are still a number of items that require periodic checking, replacement, and adjustment.

tensive repairs are needed. Refer to Chapter 10 for diagnostic help.

THE ESSENTIALS OF A TUNE-UP

Fall is the traditional time for tune-ups, because winter is the hardest season of the year on an automobile as far as starting and driving are concerned. A fall tune-up, therefore, can improve starting and help ensure trouble-free performance during this season.

The basic tools needed for a tune-up include a timing light, a spark plug socket, a feeler gauge or spark plug gap gauge, a tachometer, a screwdriver, and a compression gauge. The following list of items is what, in my opinion, every tune-up should include—whether you do the job yourself or have it done by a professional mechanic.

Spark Plugs

One item that still requires periodic replacement is the spark plugs. In the days before electronic ignitions and unleaded gas, spark plugs usually needed to be changed every 12,000 to 15,000 miles. Today spark plugs can easily last 30,000 to 40,000 miles. Unleaded gas doesn't contain lead, which was one of the leading causes of plug fouling in older engines that burned regular gasoline.

Spark plugs wear for two reasons. The center electrode in the plug erodes and becomes rounded on the end instead of flat with sharp corners. This increases the voltage required to fire the plug, which can lead to hard starting and misfiring under load. Electrodes can be filed flat and regapped to extend plug life, but most people find it easier to simply replace the plug with a new one. Spark plugs also accumulate deposits on the white ceramic insulator that surrounds the center electrode. Spark plugs are self-cleaning to some extent because the plug usually runs hot enough to burn off the harmful deposits. In time, however, deposits can build up and provide a pathway to short the firing voltage away from the electrode. When this happens, the spark plug is said to be "fouled," and it won't fire. The result is a steady miss and a significant loss of power and fuel economy. You might not notice the loss of power caused by a fouled plug in a big V8, but it certainly won't escape detection in a small displacement four- or six-cylinder engine (Fig. 7-2).

Compression

When the plugs are out of the engine, it's a good idea to check compression. A compression check won't make your engine run any better, but it can tell you a great deal about your engine's condition. An engine must have a certain amount of compression in each of its cylinders to run properly. If the readings are low, it means the piston rings, cylinders, and/or valves are worn and are not holding pressure the way they should. If you sell the car now, you can avoid the cost of a valve job or overhaul.

A compression check can also be used to diagnose a problem cylinder. A blown head gasket or a bad valve will leak pressure, resulting in almost no compression. In most cases, such a cylinder will be dead in spite of how well the ignition system and spark plugs perform. So if you have an engine with a bad miss, and changing the plugs doesn't help, you'd better run a compression check to see if it has a bad cylinder (Fig. 7-3).

Distributor Cap, Rotor, and Plug Wires

The condition of the spark plug wires, distributor cap, and rotor should be carefully checked when the spark plugs are replaced. It isn't necessary to replace any of these items unless they are worn or damaged.

The distributor cap routes high-voltage electricity from the coil to each of the spark plugs. It should be replaced if it has any hairline cracks in it, or if the terminals are worn or corroded. Light corrosion can be scraped off the ends of the terminals inside the distributor cap with a screwdriver or small knife (Fig. 7-4).

Some people install a new rotor regardless of what the old one looks like. The rotor doesn't need to be replaced unless it's cracked or shows wear or corrosion on the metal tip (Fig. 7-5).

The spark plug wires should be replaced if the insulation is cracked, burned, or chafed, or if the

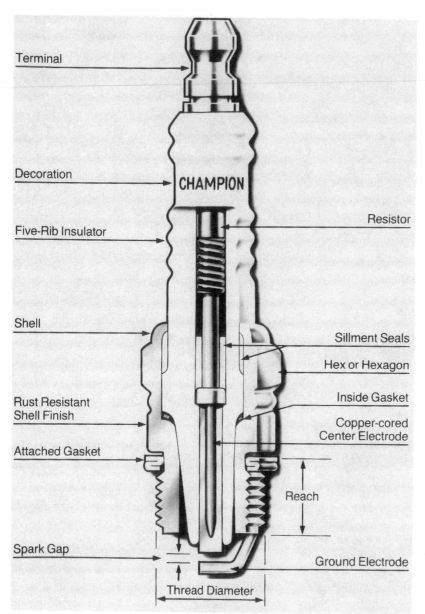

Terminal

Decoration

Five-Rib Insulator

Shell

Rust Resistant
Shell Finish

Attached Gasket

Spark Gap

Thread Diameter

CHAMPION

Resistor

Sillment Seals

Hex or Hexagon

Inside Gasket

Copper-cored
Center Electrode

Reach

Ground Electrode

Fig. 7-2. The internal parts of a spark plug. (Courtesy of Champion Spark Plug Company.)

terminals fit poorly around the spark plugs or into the distributor cap. One way to check the spark plug wires is to observe the engine compartment after dark while the engine is running *Caution:* Keep a safe distance away from the fan and pulleys. If the wires are leaking voltage, you'll often see little sparks or flashes of light around the spark plugs or between the wires and the engine. Some-

times you can hear a snapping sound that is caused by the spark shorting through a crack in the wiring.

Some types of carbon core wiring deteriorate over time due to heat and flexing. This increases the wire's internal resistance and eventually causes the spark plugs to misfire. If you suspect bad wiring, check the individual wires (engine off!) with an ohmmeter. Replace any that are found to have

Fig. 7-3. Compression is a good diagnostic check on your engine's health.

Fig. 7-4. The rotor should be replaced if it is worn or cracked.

more than 5000 ohms per inch resistance. If plug wires need to be replaced, change one wire at a time to keep from mixing up the firing order.

Ignition Timing

Ignition timing should always be checked, even on electronic ignition systems. Even though the base timing setting shouldn't change, there's no guarantee the timing was correctly set initially (Fig. 7-6).

To check the timing, you'll need a timing light and the basic timing specifications. Always use the tune-up specifications listed on the underhood emis-

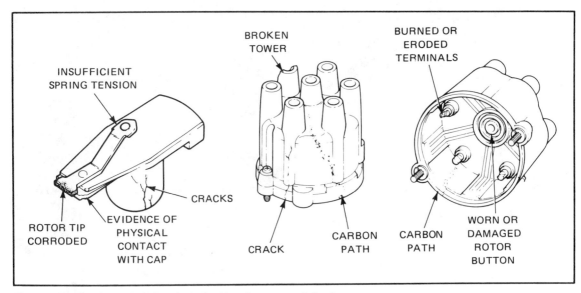

Fig. 7-5. Here's what to look for when checking the rotor and distributor.

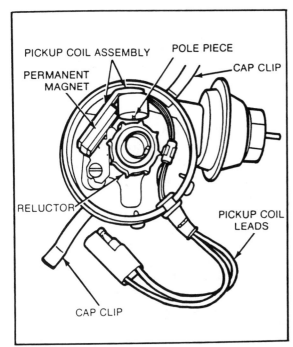

Fig. 7-6. There is not much to wear out inside a distributor with electronic ignition. (Courtesy of Chrysler Corporation.)

sions decal. Those specifications are far more accurate than those that you'll find listed in a typical tune-up manual.

Overadvanced ignition timing is a common cause of detonation or pinging during acceleration. Retarded timing can cause a loss of power and fuel economy. Ignition timing doesn't remain static, however. It changes as the engine revs up, slows down, and is put under varying degrees of load. The higher the engine *rpm* (revolutions per minute), the more timing advance it needs to burn the fuel properly. Under a light load, fuel economy can be increased by advancing the timing even further. Under a heavy load, however, the timing must be retarded to prevent detonation. Older distributors used a combination of centrifugal flyweights and a vacuum diaphragm to control timing advance and retard. Most computerized engine control systems, on the other hand, control advance and retard electronically via input from various engine sensors.

There is nothing to adjust with respect to timing advance and retard, but it should be checked to confirm that the ignition system is performing

properly. Timing advance can be checked by simply revving up the engine to see if the marks illuminated by your timing light appear to change. If they don't, you'd better seek the services of a professional mechanic who knows how to fix the problem.

Idle Speed

You can skip this check if your engine is equipped with computerized idle speed control (not to be confused with cruise control). If there's an idle speed adjustment screw on the throttle linkage, you should use a tachometer to compare the idle speed to the specifications listed on the underhood tune-up decal.

Idle speed is an important item to check, especially in vehicles equipped with automatic transmissions. Too high an idle speed can cause the vehicle to creep at a stop light while too low a speed can cause it to stall (Fig. 7-7).

There are actually two idle speed adjustments: fast and slow. Fast idle speed occurs when the engine is first started. A higher idle speed is provided to keep the engine from stalling while it warms up.

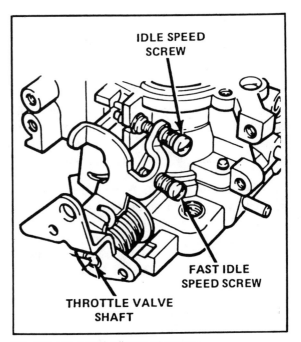

Fig. 7-7. Idle speed adjustment screws.

On an engine equipped with a carburetor, this is usually accomplished by a cam plate on the throttle linkage connected to the carburetor choke. The fast idle speed is set with the linkage resting on the highest cam position. Once the engine warms up, it idles at a slower speed. This is set with the choke cam in the lowest or disengaged position.

On many vehicles there is also an *idle stop* adjustment. A little solenoid on the carburetor linkage holds the throttle open slightly as long as the ignition is on. When the key is turned off, the solenoid collapses causing the throttle to snap shut. This cuts off the air supply to the engine and prevents dieseling (run-on). If the idle stop isn't adjusted correctly, a hot engine can continue to run and chug after the key has been turned off. Readjusting the idle stop will eliminate the problem.

Emission Control Components

No tune-up is complete without an inspection of the engine's emission control devices to make certain they are working correctly. A check should include each of the following:

- ☐ PCV valve and filter.
- ☐ EGR valve.
- ☐ Vapor canister.
- ☐ Air pump.

Fuel Filter

It doesn't take any longer to replace a fuel filter than it does to check one, so most people simply replace it as part of a tune-up. A new fuel filter isn't a necessary part of every tune-up, but because you're working on the car anyway, why not change the filter while you're at it? The recommended service interval is to change the filter yearly, which means changing it more often than when you do a tune-up. You can test a fuel filter for clogging by blowing through it. A good filter should offer little or no resistance. Replacement procedures are detailed in Chapter 5.

Air Filter

A new air filter isn't absolutely necessary, but like a fuel filter, changing it during the tune-up makes sense to save time and trouble. The recommended service interval for changing the air filter is yearly (or as needed in dusty areas), which means you'll be replacing the filter more often than when you do a tune-up. Replacement procedures are covered in Chapter 5.

Valve Lash Adjustment

Many import engines have mechanical rather than hydraulic, valve lifters. This type of lifter requires periodic readjustment to maintain the proper amount of valve lash in the engine. Most import car manufacturers recommend checking and resetting the lash every 24,000 to 30,000 miles. Failure to do so can result in premature valve failure and the need for a costly valve job. Setting valve lash can be complicated on many engines, so you might want to seek the services of a professional mechanic for this job (Fig. 7-8).

Maintenance and Safety Check

A tune-up should include a once-over maintenance and safety inspection as described in Chapter 6 (see Table 6-1). Checking fluid levels, various mechan-

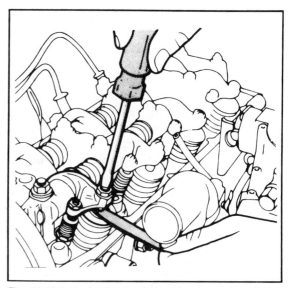

Fig. 7-8. Valve lash adjustment should not be neglected. But it is usually only necessary on import engines with mechanical lifters. (Courtesy of Chrysler Corporation.)

ical components, and safety items can lessen the chances of an unexpected breakdown while contributing to safe and trouble-free driving.

CHANGING SPARK PLUGS

Replacement spark plugs are readily available at all auto parts stores and many other retail outlets. You can find out what kind of plugs your car uses by either looking at the underhood tune-up decal or by looking up your vehicle and engine on the spark plug reference chart in the store. Spark plug manufacturers have greatly consolidated the number of different kinds of plugs in recent years. The introduction of copper core spark plugs (that have a much wider heat range than older style plugs) means one spark plug can satisfy the needs of many different applications.

What brand of spark plugs should you use in your engine? It really doesn't make much difference as long as the plug is listed as fitting your vehicle. In spite of all the hype, one manufacturer's plug is much the same as another's. A Bosch spark plug will perform just as well in a General Motors car as an AC brand plug will in an import. Cross reference charts in the back of spark plug catalogs can help you find the right number when comparing different brands.

One type of spark plug that is worth noting is the *platinum-tip* plug. These are premium-grade spark plugs that offer significantly longer life (up to 60,000 miles). They do cost more than ordinary spark plugs, but they're worth the money if you want a plug that's going to last forever.

Tools Needed. Spark plug socket wrench; feeler gauge or plug gap gauge; a rag and/or a length of plastic tubing.

Parts Needed. New set of spark plugs; tube of antiseize compound (aluminum head engines only).

How Often. Every 30,000 miles.

Location. The spark plugs are located in your engine's cylinder head. The easiest way to find them is to follow the spark plug wires from the distributor cap.

What To Do. Spark plugs are most easily changed when cold. The plugs are sometimes lo-cated in hard-to-reach recessed areas, so waiting until the engine is cold means you won't burn your fingers.

1. With the engine off, locate the spark plugs and pull the wires off the plugs. The easiest way to remove the wires is to grab the heavy boot that fits around the plug and twist as you pull. Don't jerk on the wire itself or you're likely to damage it. You can leave the wire dangling near the plug, but if it's close to the next plug, there's always a chance of getting the wires mixed up when you're ready to put them back. This can be avoided by wrapping a piece of masking tape around each wire and numbering the wire.

2. Wipe any grease or dirt away from the plug so that it doesn't fall into the engine once the plug is removed. If you can't reach it with a rag, use a length of plastic tubing like a straw to blow away the dirt.

3. Slip your socket wrench over the spark plug and remove it by turning the wrench counterclockwise. If the plug is in a hard-to-reach area, it might be necessary to use a swivel extension and/or to crawl under the car for better access.

If the plug doesn't budge, you might be in for trouble; sometimes carbon deposits will jam the plug threads. Using a larger wrench might be the answer; but be very careful not to break the plug. Twisting the plug at an angle will almost always break the ceramic insulator. On aluminum cylinder heads, stripped threads are a common problem, especially if the last person who changed the plugs overtightened them. Heat and penetrating oil applied around the base of the plug can help loosen a stubborn plug. If the plug strips the threads in the cylinder head, the threads will have to be repaired. This is done by drilling out the plug hole and installing a thread repair insert. If done carefully, the head doesn't have to be removed from the engine.

4. As you remove the plugs, line them up in sequence on the fender, air cleaner, your workbench, or whatever for inspection. Reading the

plugs will tell you a great deal about what is happening inside your engine. The ceramic insulator in the firing end of the plug should have a light brown to grey color if everything is operating properly (Fig. 7-9). Heavy, black deposits are carbon which indicate a rich fuel condition. This can be the result of short-trip driving where the engine never gets a chance to completely warm up. It can also be caused by a sticking or misadjusted carburetor or an overrich fuel mixture. Black, oily deposits are definitely bad news because it means your engine is burning oil (from worn valve guides, valve guide seals, piston rings, or cylinders). A yellow, glazed, or melted appearance means too much heat. A lean fuel mixture, vacuum leak, overadvanced ignition timing, or a cooling problem might be responsible.

5. Gap the new plugs before they're installed. New spark plugs are supposed to be pregapped at the factory; but with all the consolidation that's taken place, the factory gap might not be right for your engine. The spark gap requirements can be found on your underhood tune-up decal, in most spark plug catalogs, or a good shop manual.

The gap is measured by sliding a feeler gauge or plug gauge of the appropriate size between the electrodes on the end of the plug (Fig. 7-10). If the gap is too wide, gently tap on the end electrode to narrow the gap until the proper gauge just fits. If the gap is too narrow, gently bend the outer electrode away from the plug until the gap is correct.

Fig. 7-10. Plug gap can be checked by inserting a feeler gauge or wire gauge between the electrodes.

6. On engines with aluminum cylinder heads, a small drop of "anti-seize" compound should be placed on the spark plug threads before they are installed. This will make the plugs easier to remove the next time and reduce the likelihood of damaging the hole threads (Fig. 7-11).

7. Hand thread the plugs into their respective holes, then tighten with your wrench. Do not overtighten the spark plugs; as long as they are snug, they won't go anyplace. Overtightening the plugs on an aluminum cylinder head will almost always strip the threads in the plug hole.

8. Reconnect the spark plug wires.

9. Note the mileage at which you changed the plugs and the type of plugs used in your maintenance record.

CHECKING COMPRESSION

The best time to check compression is while the spark plugs are removed.

Tools Needed. Compression gauge; remote starter switch (makes the job easier, but it isn't absolutely necessary).

How Often. Every tune-up.

Location. Compression is checked at the spark plug holes.

What To Do. If you have a remote starter switch, connect it to the starter solenoid. A remote starter switch makes checking compression a one-person job. If you don't have a switch, you'll need a helper to crank the engine while you hold and/or read the compression gauge.

Fig. 7-9. Reading the spark plugs can help you spot problems. This is how a normal plug should look after many miles of use.

Fig. 7-11. Aluminum heads should be protected by applying antiseize compound to spark plug threads before installation.

1. Remove the high-voltage coil wire from the center of the distributor cap and ground it to the engine block. This will prevent the engine from starting while it's being cranked. Be sure to ground it so the voltage will have someplace to go; otherwise it might damage the electronic ignition.

2. Block the throttle wide open or have your helper hold the gas pedal to the floor. This is necessary for the engine to take in a full amount of air for each cylinder.

3. With the spark plugs removed, install your compression gauge into one of the plug holes. Quality gauges have threaded fittings that screw into the plug hole while lesser-quality gauges use a one-size-fits-all tapered rubber extension that must be held in place.

4. Now you're ready to check compression. Crank the engine over several times and note the reading on the gauge; write it down so you don't forget it. Then proceed on to the next cylinder and repeat until you've obtained readings for all the cylinders. Don't be alarmed if you hear a loud pop-ping noise while cranking; it means you aren't holding your compression gauge firmly enough in the spark plug hole. The gauge must be tight if you're going to get an accurate reading.

A healthy engine should have compression readings in excess of 100 to 140 psi. The readings should also vary no more than 10 percent cylinder to cylinder. If all the readings are low, it indicates advanced engine wear. A valve job and/or overhaul will soon be needed. You can tell if low compression is due to worn rings or valves by squirting oil into the cylinders and repeating the test. If the readings are no different, compression is being lost through the valves and a valve job is in order. If the readings go up 10 to 20 psi, worn rings are at fault and an overhaul is needed.

An extremely low or zero reading in any one cylinder indicates a dead cylinder. A bad valve is the most likely problem. An extremely low or zero reading between two adjacent cylinders usually means a blown head gasket. If all cylinders show little or no compression (and the engine won't start), a broken timing belt or chain is the culprit.

5. Note the compression readings in your maintenance record, then remove the compression gauge and remote starter switch (if used), reconnect the coil wire, and close the throttle.

CHECKING/ADJUSTING IGNITION TIMING

Timing is checked by using a *strobe light* (your timing light) to illuminate and align timing marks on the engine. Every time the spark plug fires, it flashes the light and illuminates the timing marks. By turning the distributor slightly one way or the other, the marks appear to move. The basic idea, therefore, is to line up the marks so that the right number of degrees of ignition timing is achieved.

On many engines this is a simple procedure. But on some, particularly those with computerized engine controls and electronic spark timing, special procedures complicate the task. You might want to have a professional mechanic check the timing for you.

Tools Needed. Timing light; wrench for loosening the bolt at the base of the distributor.

How Often. When the engine is tuned up or when a timing problem is suspected. A symptom of over-advanced timing is detonation (spark knock or pinging) during acceleration. Retarded timing will often cause a loss in performance and fuel economy.

Location. The timing marks will be found on either the crankshaft pulley or harmonic balancer or on the flywheel (Fig 7-12). The location of the number one engine cylinder can be found on Fig. 7-13.

What To Do. Look up the timing specifications for your engine on the underhood tune-up decal. It will be given as a fixed number of degrees before or after top dead center. Follow any special timing instructions given on the decal.

1. With the engine off, connect your timing light to the number one spark plug wire (refer to Fig. 7-13). If the timing light has power leads, connect them to the battery.

2. To make the timing marks more readable, wipe away any grease and highlight the appropriate marks with a piece of chalk or a dab of white paint (white typewriter correction fluid works fine and is easy to apply).

3. On engines with vacuum advance distributors, most applications require the hose to be disconnected from the distributor and temporarily plugged; a golf tee works great for this purpose. If the distributor has two vacuum hoses, disconnect them both (and note which one goes where so you can reconnect them correctly).

On General Motors applications with electronic spark timing, disconnect the four-wire computer connector from the distributor cap. On most Ford and GM engines with computerized engine controls, the computer must be put into the self-

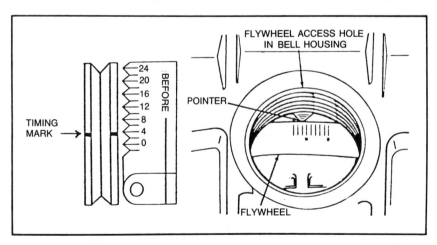

Fig. 7-12. Timing marks.

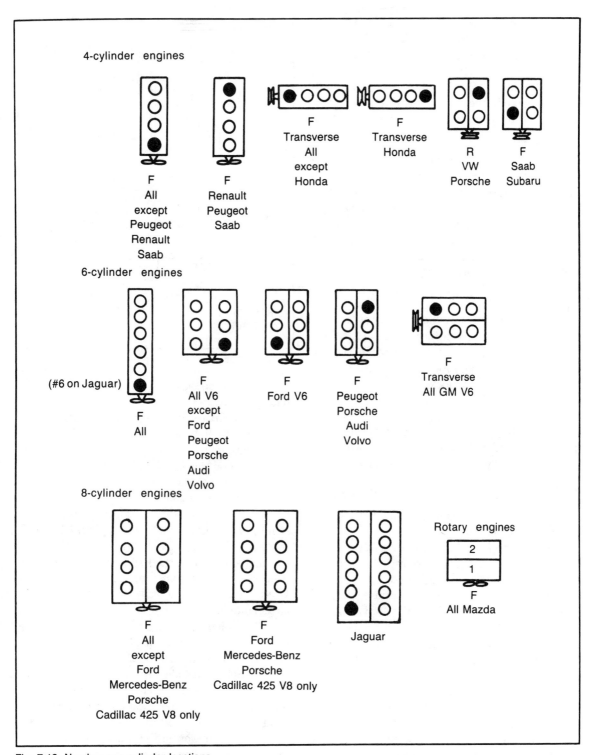

Fig. 7-13. Number one cylinder locations.

diagnostic mode to fix base timing. This is done by jumping and/or grounding the diagnostic connector under the dash or under the hood. The procedure varies from model to model, so refer to a shop manual for details. On Chrysler applications with spark computers, the throttle switch on the carburetor must be grounded before checking base timing.

4. Start the engine and let it come to a normal slow idle. The engine should be at normal operating temperature for an accurate timing reading. This means you might have to warm up the engine prior to making the timing check.

5. Aim your timing light at the timing marks to see if the marks indicate the specified number of degrees. If the marks align, you're finished. If not, go on to the next step.

6. Loosen the lock bolt at the base of the distributor and slowly turn the distributor a small amount. If the lines get further apart, turn the distributor in the opposite direction. Move the distributor back and forth until you get the marks aligned. Then tighten down the lock bolt and recheck the timing to make sure it didn't change—sometimes it will when the bolt is tightened (Fig. 7-14).

7. Changing the timing affects idle speed. If the engine seems to be idling faster or slower than before, you'll have to reset the idle speed.

CHECKING/ADJUSTING IDLE SPEED

If your engine has computer-controlled idle speed, you can skip this job.

Tools Needed. Tachometer; screwdriver.

How Often. At tune-up or as needed to correct an idle problem. The idle speed will usually change when ignition timing is readjusted. It will also require adjustment if the carburetor is replaced or rebuilt.

Location. The idle speed adjustment screw is located on the throttle linkage (Fig 7-7). On some engines, there are separate screws for fast idle (when cold), slow idle (when warm), and idle stop (when the engine is turned off).

What To Do. Fast idle should be set with the engine cold. Slow idle should be set with the engine at normal operating temperature.

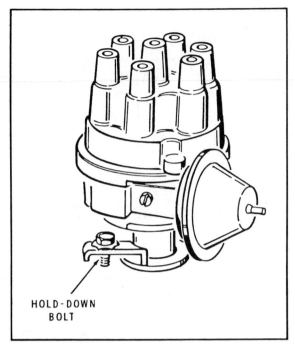

HOLD-DOWN BOLT

Fig. 7-14. Distributor hold-down bolt.

1. Look up the idle speed specifications on the underhood tune-up decal.

2. Locate the idle speed adjustment screw(s). If the throttle linkage has several screws and you don't know which is which, you can sometimes find an illustration that labels the screws in a service manual. The fast idle screw is usually the one that rests on a stepped cam (Fig. 7-15). The slow idle screw will rest against a flat tab on the throttle assembly or against a round solenoid (Fig. 7-16). This is often an idle stop solenoid that closes the throttle completely when the key is turned off to prevent dieseling. On some applications, it is an *idle kicker* solenoid that increases idle speed when the air conditioner is running.

3. With the ignition off, connect your tachometer to the negative (–) lead on the ignition coil, or to the "TACH" lead on the distributor cap.

4. Set the fast idle first. With the engine cold, start the engine and note the initial idle speed. If it doesn't match the specifications, turn the adjustment screw on the throttle linkage until you achieve the desired rpm—or until it idles best (no stalling or racing). Sometimes you have to improvise on the

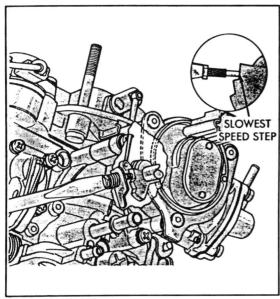

Fig. 7-15. Fast idle adjustment screen and cam. (Courtesy of Chrysler Corporation.)

factory specifications to get a good fast idle when the engine is cold. You have to make this adjustment quickly, because as the engine starts to warm up, the idle speed will automatically decrease.

5. Once the engine has reached normal operating temperature, set the slow idle speed to the desired specifications. Make sure the carburetor choke is wide open and that the fast idle cam is in the lowest position or disengaged.

6. If the engine has an idle stop solenoid, turn the engine off, then adjust the screw so the throttle is completely closed.

7. If the engine has an idle kicker solenoid, turn on the air conditioning while the engine is running and adjust the idle to the desired rpm.

INSPECTING EMISSION CONTROLS

Tools Needed. None.
How Often. Every tune-up.
Location. See below.
What To Do. See below.

PCV Valve and Filter

The *Positive Crankcase Ventilation* (PCV) valve is a thumb-sized device usually located on the valve cover and connected to the carburetor or intake manifold by a large rubber hose. The PCV system draws fresh air through the engine's crankcase to flush out moisture and reburn harmful vapors. If the valve becomes plugged, it can cause a rapid buildup of sludge inside the engine.

The PCV valve can be checked two ways. If

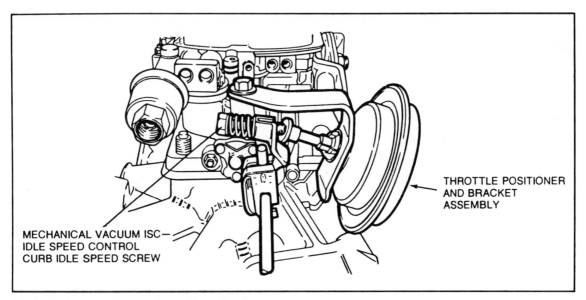

Fig. 7-16. Idle screw with throttle position solenoid.

it rattles when shaken, it's probably good. You should also feel vacuum if you pull it out of the valve cover while the engine is idling and place your finger over the open end of the valve. If it doesn't rattle or appears to be plugged, replace it (Figs. 7-17 and 7-18).

Some engines have a small PCV filter inside the air cleaner that filters the air entering the crankcase. The filter should be changed every 30,000 miles or as needed if found to be dirty (Fig. 7-19).

EGR Valve

The *Exhaust Gas Recirculation* (EGR) valve is located on the intake manifold. It can be identified by the round metal diaphragm housing on top with an attached vacuum hose. The EGR valve recirculates a small amount of exhaust from the exhaust manifold back into the intake manifold to dilute the incoming air/fuel mixture. This lowers combustion temperatures and reduces the formation of oxides

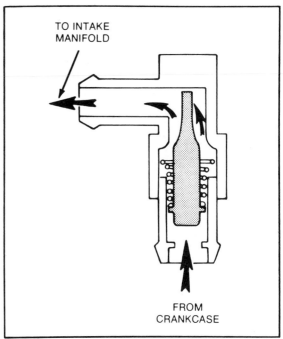

TO INTAKE MANIFOLD

FROM CRANKCASE

Fig. 7-18. Intake vacuum draws crankcase vapors through the PCV valve and back into the engine for reburning.

of nitrogen (NOX), a harmful air pollutant. The system is designed only to work once the engine reaches normal operating temperature and is running at speeds above idle (Fig. 7-20).

EGR problems fall into one of two categories: valves that don't open and valves that fail to close. If the diaphragm inside the EGR valve leaks or if the vacuum hose to the valve is plugged or disconnected, combustion temperatures will rise because the valve won't open. The result is often detonation (spark knock or pinging) during acceleration. If the valve sticks open (usually due to carbon deposits building up on the base of the valve), it will remain open at idle and/or when the engine is cold causing a rough running condition or a hesitation stumble when you step on the gas. In other words, it has the same effect on performance as a big vacuum leak.

To check the valve, the engine should be warmed up to operating temperature, then revved and held at 2000 rpm. You can assume the valve is working if the stem moves up and down. Unfortunately, this isn't always easy to see because of

Fig. 7-17. The PCV valve is usually found in the valve cover. It should pass vacuum with the engine idling and rattle when shaken when the engine is off.

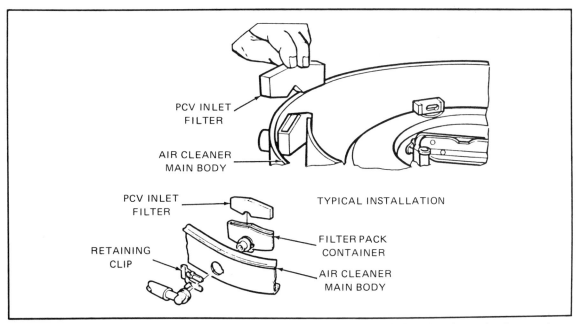

Fig. 7-19. Many vehicles have a PCV filter located inside the air cleaner housing. It should be changed at the same intervals as the air cleaner.

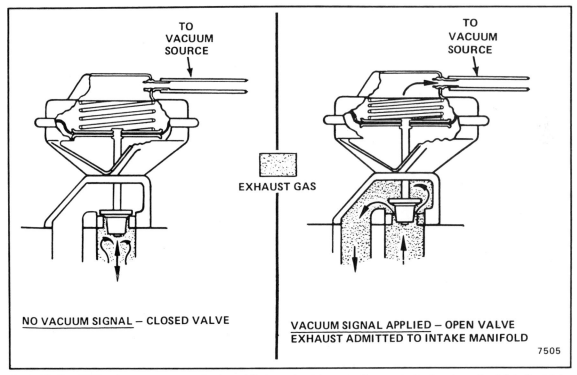

7505

Fig. 7-20. The EGR valve opens at speeds above idle to recirculate a small amount of exhaust gas back into the intake manifold. This reduces the formation of oxides of nitrogen, a major air pollutant. (Courtesy of General Motors Corporation.)

the valve's location on some engines. A small mirror on an extension handle and/or a trouble light will help your observations. An EGR valve can also be checked with a hand vacuum pump, but many won't open when vacuum is applied, unless there is also a certain amount of back pressure in the exhaust system. That's why the engine has to be revved to make the valve work.

A sticky EGR valve can sometimes be cleaned by removing and wire brushing the carbon deposits off the end of the valve. Solvent can be used, but be careful not to get any in the diaphragm housing (solvent attacks rubber). If the valve still sticks or fails to work, replace it with a new valve. If the vehicle is less than five years old or has less than 50,000 miles on it, take it back to the new car dealer for free replacement. The EGR valve is covered under the mandatory 5 year/50,000 mile emissions warranty on all 1981 and later model cars.

Vapor Canister

The *vapor canister* is an evaporative emission control device that traps and stores fuel vapors from the carburetor and fuel tank to prevent them from entering the atmosphere. The canister is mounted in the engine compartment and is attached to the fuel system with numerous hoses. Most require no

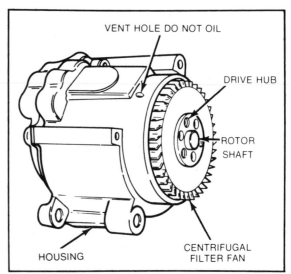

Fig. 7-22. A typical air pump. (Courtesy of Chrysler Corporation.)

service except to ensure that the hoses are tight (Fig. 7-21).

A few of the early GM units use a replaceable filter on the bottom of the canister that does require periodic replacement. Check your owner's manual for maintenance recommendations.

Air Pump

The air pump works in conjunction with the catalytic converter to burn harmful exhaust pollutants out of the exhaust. The air pump pumps air into the exhaust manifold so that the catalytic converter will have the extra oxygen it needs to reburn the pollutants. On 1981 and later cars, the pump also routes air directly to the converter once the engine warms up (Fig. 7-22).

The air pump requires no maintenance except to make sure its drive belt is properly adjusted. Squealing or scraping noises from the pump usually mean it has suffered internal damage and must be replaced. Sometimes a bad pump will seize and snap the V-belt. The pump is a factory-sealed assembly and cannot be rebuilt by a do-it-yourselfer. Like the other emissions control components, it is covered by the government-mandated 5 year/50,000 mile emissions warranty on all 1981 and newer passenger cars.

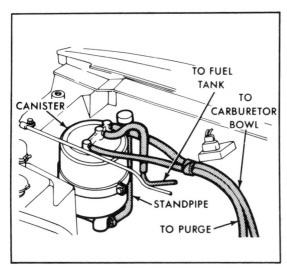

Fig. 7-21. The evaporative emissions vapor canister stores gasoline fumes from the fuel system when the vehicle isn't running.

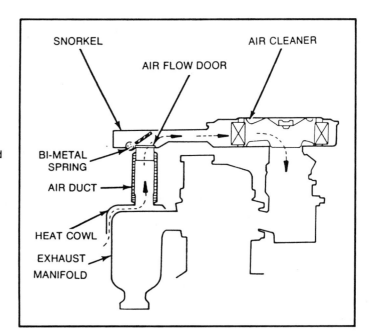

Fig. 7-23. The basic elements of the heated air intake system.

SNORKEL
AIR FLOW DOOR
AIR CLEANER
BI-METAL SPRING
AIR DUCT
HEAT COWL
EXHAUST MANIFOLD

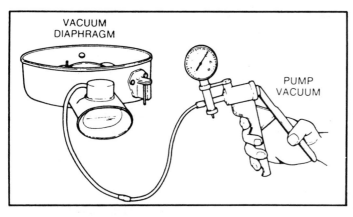

VACUUM DIAPHRAGM
PUMP VACUUM

Fig. 7-24. Checking the vacuum diaphragm that works the air flow control door with a hand-held vacuum pump.

Heated Air Intake System

The heated air intake system delivers warm air to the carburetor or fuel injection throttle body when the engine is cold to speed engine warm-up and to aid fuel vaporization. An air flow control door in the air cleaner snorkel closes off outside air when the engine is cold. A temperature sensor inside the air cleaner controls vacuum to the air flow door motor. As the engine warms up, the door opens and admits outside air.

If the door remains open at all times, the engine will warm-up slowly and might hesitate or stumble when cold. If the door remains shut, the air will be too hot, causing possible detonation during hot weather (Fig. 7-23).

To check the heated air intake system, make certain the air duct that connects the air snorkel and stove around the exhaust manifold is intact. The door should be closed when the engine is first started and then opened fully once the engine is warm. If the door fails to move, the vacuum motor can be checked with a hand-held vacuum pump. If it doesn't move when vacuum is applied (or fails to hold vacuum), the diaphragm is ruptured and the motor needs to be replaced (Fig. 7-24).

Chapter 8

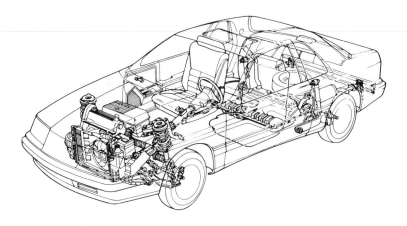

Winterizing

For anyone who lives north of the Sunbelt, winterizing is an annual ritual that should be completed a month or so before the onslaught of winter. For most motorists this means October or early November.

Cold weather is especially hard on vehicles. When temperatures plunge, oil thickens, battery cranking power drops, gasoline vaporizes much more slowly, liquids freeze, rubber becomes hard and brittle, and engines are harder to start and run less efficiently than they do at warmer temperatures. If a vehicle has starting problems or stalls or hesitates during warm weather, cold weather will only makes things worse. The wise do-it-yourselfer, therefore, will ensure his or her vehicle is thoroughly prepared (and repaired if need be) *before* Mother Nature delivers her blows.

The two most important items to consider when winterizing your vehicle are protecting the cooling system against freezing and making sure your engine will start reliably. Water freezes at 32 degrees Fahrenheit (0 degrees Celsius). When water turns to ice, its volume expands about 10 per-

cent. If the cooling system does not contain enough antifreeze, the coolant will freeze, expand, and most likely split the radiator open, push out the freeze plugs in the engine, and possibly even crack the engine block. To prevent such calamities from occurring, the strength of the antifreeze should always be checked well in advance of cold weather. The procedure for doing this is described later in this chapter.

As for cold weather starting, your engine faces three problems simultaneously. As temperatures drop the viscosity of engine oil increases. The lower the temperature drops, the thicker the oil becomes. Thicker oil creates more friction and drag, so the engine becomes progressively harder to crank. At the same time, however, lower temperatures rob the battery of its cranking power.

Low temperatures slow down chemical reactions inside the battery that create electrical current. At zero degrees Fahrenheit, your battery has only about 40 percent of the cranking power it normally has at 80 degrees. If the battery doesn't have enough reserve capacity (meaning it is too small for the car), there will not be enough cranking amps to overcome increased resistance of the oil to crank the engine. The same is true for an old battery that has lost some of its power or one that has been allowed to run down. The engine might start fine as long as temperatures are mild, but the first time the thermometer drops, the battery won't have enough power to start the engine.

The third problem your engine must overcome is that of sluggish fuel vaporization. The colder the temperature, the slower gasoline vaporizes inside your engine. Gasoline must be in the vapor state before it will burn, otherwise it just puddles and floods the engine, making it impossible to start. Refiners change the chemical makeup of gasoline during winter months to increase its volatility so it will vaporize more easily at low temperatures. But when the first cold spell hits, most service stations are still selling summer grade fuel. The result is a lot of service calls to start flooded engines.

Engines equipped with fuel injection are less sensitive to fuel vaporization problems because the fuel is sprayed into the engine as a mist. Engines with carburetors, on the other hand, are very vulnerable to cold weather fuel problems, especially if the choke is not adjusted correctly. An engine that is out of tune or one that has accumulated a lot of miles and has low compression will also experience hard starting, because the engine is less able to ignite the fuel mixture.

HOW TO ENJOY TROUBLE-FREE WINTER DRIVING

The basics of winterizing are summarized in Table 8-1. The following suggestions can also help prepare your vehicle for the hardships of winter driving, and hopefully reduce the likelihood of having trouble:

□ Include a tune-up as part of your winterizing routine.

□ Clean and regap your spark plugs or install new plugs to make your engine easier to start. New spark plugs can reduce the drain on your ignition system by as much as 50 percent (refer to Chapter 7).

□ Clean and retighten the battery terminals and cables.

□ Check the condition and charge of the battery. If the battery is more than four years old, now might be a good time to replace it. If the battery has a built-in charge indicator and the green dot isn't visible, it needs recharging (see Chapter 11).

□ Check the drive belt that turns the alternator to make certain it is tight and is not slipping (see Chapter 11).

□ If your engine has a carburetor, spray carburetor cleaner on the automatic choke linkage and check the operation of the choke. The choke should be closed when the engine is cold and open fully once the engine is warm.

□ Check the operation of the air preheating system. Inside the air cleaner snorkel or ductwork is a control flap. A temperature-sensitive thermostat inside the air cleaner regulates vacuum to the control flap diaphragm (refer to Fig. 7-23 in Chapter 7). When the engine is cold, the flap should be closed to outside air. This allows heated air from around the exhaust manifold to be drawn up behind the flap and into the engine to help vaporize cold fuel and to speed engine warm-up. As the engine begins to warm up, the control flap opens and allows unheated air to enter the engine. If the control flap is not working, or if the ductwork between the flap and exhaust manifold is loose or missing, the engine will draw in cold air when it doesn't need it. The result can be cold stalling and hesitation, and slow warm-up.

□ Spray the distributor cap and spark plug wires with a moisture-repelling or waterproof spray (ignition system sealer, WD-40, or silicone all work fine).

□ Add a can of fuel system deicer in the gas tank at least once a month to prevent the accumulation of moisture. Water can collect in the fuel line and freeze, blocking the flow of fuel.

□ Consider buying a larger capacity battery for additional cold starting power. Batteries are rated according to their cold cranking amp capacity; buy the one with the highest numerical rating.

□ Consider installing a 110-volt plug-in electric battery heater. The heating pad sits under the

Antifreeze—should be sufficient to provide freezing protection down to −34 degrees F, requiring a 50/50 mixture of antifreeze and water.

Battery—should have sufficient cold cranking amps and reserve capacity to handle the anticipated starting requirements of the engine, should be fully charged, be in good condition, and be free from corroded or loose terminal connections.

Battery cables—must be tight and free from corrosion. Check both the battery ends and the starter and ground connections.

Engine—ignition system and carburetion must be in good working condition and properly tuned. New spark plugs are recommended to ease starting. The oil should be clean and of the correct viscosity.

Exhaust system—should be carefully inspected for leaks. Check for leaks while the engine is running.

Heater and defroster—should be in good working condition. Low heat output can be caused by a defective or too low temperature engine thermostat, low coolant, obstructions in the heater core or heater inlet, a defective heater control valve, or air flow door.

Wiper blades—winter blades are highly recommended to resist ice build-up.

Washer fluid—washer reservoir should be filled with premix or water and concentrate to protect against freezing.

Door locks and latches—both should be sprayed with moisture-repelling lubricants to keep ice from freezing locks and latches shut.

Doors, trunks, and hatchbacks—to prevent freezing, weatherstripping around the doors, trunk and hatchback should be waxed or sprayed with silicone to prevent sticking.

Body and wheels—a coating of wax should be applied to protect against corrosion.

Trunk—winter survival gear should be onboard in case of an emergency. Other useful items include jumper cables, a shovel, and other aids for getting unstuck.

Glove box—should contain an ice scraper, an extra pair of gloves, a rag for wiping the inside of the windows, a flashlight (that plugs into the cigarette lighter), etc.

Tires—use snow tires or all-season tires to aid traction. Chains provide the best traction in deep snow but require mounting and dismounting. Tires should have adequate tread, worn tires provide poor traction.

Fuel tank—add a can of fuel system deicer once a month to keep moisture out of fuel lines to prevent gasline freeze. Diesel owners should switch to a winter blended fuel and install a fuel system heater if their vehicle isn't so equipped.

Table 8-1. Winterizing Checklist.

battery and boosts its output at low temperatures.

☐ Consider installing a 110-volt electric engine heater. A warm engine is easier to crank than a cold one, and a warm engine vaporizes fuel much more easily than a cold engine. The best kind of block heater to buy is one that heats the coolant. The heater can be plugged in at night to keep a warm engine warm, or it can be used to heat a cold engine by plugging it in several hours prior to starting. Dipstick oil heaters usually don't create enough heat to be of much help.

☐ Switch to a lower viscosity oil for winter driving. Instead of using a 10W-30 or 10W-40 oil, change to a 5W-30 or 5W-20 motor oil. The thinner oil will be significantly easier to crank in cold

weather, and you might also notice a slight increase in fuel mileage. If you choose 5W-20, be sure to replace it with a heavier viscosity oil before summer, because 5W-20 oil might not provide adequate lubrication for sustained high-speed driving during hot weather.

For Safer Driving

Here are some suggestions for improved winter visibility and safety:

☐ Check the operation of your heater, defroster, and rear window defogger before cold weather arrives.

☐ Clean the inside of the windows with an ammonia-based cleaner. This can help reduce window fogging when the weather gets cold.

☐ Consider installing a rear window defogger if your vehicle isn't equipped with one. A defogger is no substitute for scraping ice off the windows, but it can prevent the formation of ice while driving. Aftermarket rear window defogger kits are not expensive and are easy to install. A typical kit consists of metallic tape that is applied to the window (some kits have a clear plastic sheet with the heating wires embedded in the plastic), wiring, and a dash-mounted control switch. Average installation time is about one hour.

☐ Install winter windshield wiper blades. These blades have a rubber covering around the blade frame to keep ice out. Ice can build up inside ordinary blades and cause them to skip and streak.

☐ Use washer antifreeze in the windshield washer reservoir to prevent freezing. Some "pre-mixed" washer fluids are watered down and do not provide the freezing protection claimed on the label. If the pre-mixed fluid freezes, it can sometimes be thawed by adding washer concentrate (which is hard to find in auto parts stores because pre-mix dominates the market), or by adding a small amount of rubbing alcohol.

☐ Install snow tires or all-season tires on the drive wheels for improved traction. Snow tires go on the back of rear-wheel-drive vehicles, on the front of front-wheel-drive vehicles, or on all four wheels of a four-wheel-drive vehicle. *Do not* lower tire pressure in an attempt to improve traction. It will not make any difference and there is a very real possibility of ruining the tire if it is driven at high speed (Fig. 8-1).

☐ Add a bag of sand to the trunk—not as a traction aid, but to help get you unstuck in case you bury a wheel in ice or snow. Old newspapers, rubber tire mats, or traction mats (special plastic or metal mesh mats designed just for this purpose) can also help you get going.

☐ To keep from being frozen out of your car, lubricate all the door locks with a moisture-repellant spray (WD-40 or silicone, for example). Do not use oil because oil thickens at low temperature and also attracts dirt. This can gum up locks and make them stick. Weather strips around the doors, trunk, or tailgate should also be sprayed with silicone or waxed to keep them from sticking. Freezing rain can form a cement-like bond between cold rubber and steel making a door, trunk, or tailgate impossible to open.

Fig. 8-1. Winter driving is always easier with snow tires or all-season tires. (Courtesy of Chrysler Corporation.)

If you are frozen out of your vehicle, try squirting lock antifreeze into the keyhole. Using a cigarette lighter to heat the lock (be careful not to burn the paint or your fingers) can also thaw a frozen lock. Another trick is to use a hair drier to blow hot air on the door handle, lock, or weather stripping around the door. A heat lamp also works, but it's slow. Be extremely careful with extension cords in wet snow because of the shock hazard; use only an extension cord approved for outdoor use with a grounded plug.

☐ Inspect the exhaust system to make sure there are no leaks. Carbon monoxide is a silent killer; it has no odor and no color. Winter is especially dangerous because the windows are usually shut and the motor might be left idling for extended periods of time to keep the vehicle warm. You can protect yourself from the dangers of carbon monoxide poisoning by hanging a carbon monoxide detector (which resembles an air freshener) inside your vehicle. If the detector changes color, it means carbon monoxide is seeping into the passenger compartment. If you can not find the leak in the exhaust system, you better take it to a garage and have the problem fixed before it is too late.

☐ Carry winter "survival gear" in the trunk. This includes such items as a small shovel (an old army surplus or Boy Scout folding shovel works fine); a blanket to keep warm in case you are stranded; a set of jumper cables; a bag of sand; extra pairs of boots and gloves; and some energy food such as candy bars or nuts.

For Body Protection

To help preserve your vehicle's body against the ravages of winter and salt-encrusted roads, consider the following:

☐ Wax the body to seal it against moisture and salt corrosion. Pay special attention to protecting aluminum wheels and bumpers. Aluminum is extremely vulnerable to salt corrosion and one winter can turn a set of expensive wheels into pitted eyesores. Bare metal can be sprayed with clear urethane or paint to preserve the finish (special paints

are available for this purpose). A coating of wax should then be applied to the wheels to complete the protection.

☐ Undercoat the chassis and/or rustproof the entire vehicle to protect it against rust and corrosion (see Chapter 9).

☐ Seal any water leaks around windows or doors. The primary cause of rusted floor pans is water leaking into the passenger compartment around loose or cracked weather stripping. Silicone caulk and/or windshield sealer works great for sealing leaks.

☐ Buy your vehicle a good set of "winter" floor mats. Such mats are waterproof and contain a lip around the edge to prevent melted ice and snow from seeping into the carpet. If the floor does become wet from tracked-in snow, remove the mats and dry out the carpet by leaving the windows cracked open and driving with the heater on.

COLD STARTING TIPS

You've cranked the engine repeatedly and it won't start. What do you do now? Doing nothing is probably best, go back inside, sit down, and have a cup of coffee. Then come back out and try it again in 15 minutes or so. This rest time accomplishes several things: it gives the battery a little time to recoup its energies; it gives the gasoline, which has likely flooded the engine, some time to evaporate; and it gives the starter (and you) a chance to cool off.

Flooding

There are two mistakes that are commonly made when you run into starting problems. The first is giving the engine too much gas. Stomping furiously on the gas pedal in hopes of pumping the engine to life will only succeed in flooding it. A cold engine needs a little extra gas to start, but it does not need to be drowned. Once fuel starts to puddle in the engine, all hopes of starting are lost, and the only thing you can do is to let the engine sit and wait it out. Eventually, the fuel will evaporate and you can try again.

On fuel injected cars, the worst thing you can do is to jump in and pump the gas pedal. Most electronic fuel injection systems are designed to go into a "clear flood" mode when the pedal is floored. This temporarily shuts off the fuel supply so excess fuel can be pumped out of the cylinders while the engine cranks. This technique can be used as intended if the engine is flooded, but when initially starting a fuel injected engine, keep your foot off the gas.

For severe cases of flooding (where the spark plugs are wet), the engine can be dried out by removing the spark plugs, holding the throttle wide open (do not pump it), and cranking the engine. Dry off the spark plugs and replace them, then try to start the engine. Another trick that can help dry out a flooded engine is to use a hair drier to blow hot air down the throat of the carburetor. Remove the air cleaner and prop open the choke and throttle. The warm air will help evaporate the fuel and warm the engine.

Heating the intake manifold with a propane torch is another solution that can help a flooded engine in cold weather. This procedure is *not* recommended because of the dangers involved. Extreme care must be used to keep the flame away from the carburetor, fuel lines, rubber hoses, and wiring. There is also a danger of a backfire explosion up through the carburetor if the fuel vapors are accidentally ignited.

What about using starting fluid? Ether starting fluid is highly volatile and vaporizes when gasoline does not. If used *sparingly,* it can help a flooded engine start. A one- or two-second squirt down the carburetor throat is all that is needed (the choke and throttle should be held open while spraying). The tendency is to get carried away and use too much, however, which can lead to backfiring through the carburetor. Never spray starting fluid into the carburetor while cranking, and always keep your face and hands away from the engine while someone is attempting to start it.

Diesel Problems

Starting fluid is sometimes used to light the fire in a diesel engine, because diesels can be really sluggish when it comes to cold weather starting. Diesel engines rely primarily on compression to heat and ignite the fuel, so when temperatures drop, starting can be a problem. Using ether or gasoline as a starting aid in a diesel can damage the engine, because the fuel burns much to rapidly. It is similar to giving a hammer blow to something that is accustomed to a gentle push. Hot air from a hair dryer directed into the intake manifold is a much safer technique for starting a cold engine.

The most common cold weather starting problem with diesels, however, is fuel waxing. Diesel fuel is available in different grades. Using summer grade fuel in winter can lead to problems, because the fuel starts to gel when temperatures drop to around 40 degrees. Once the fuel freezes up, you can forget about starting. The only cure is to push the vehicle into a heated garage to thaw it out. Fuel waxing can be avoided by switching to winter grade blends that have a lower *cloud* point (the temperature at which the fuel gels or turns to wax). Various fuel tank additives are also available to help prevent freezing.

Dead Battery

The other mistake people usually make is to keep grinding the starter long after any hope of starting has passed. Excessive cranking only succeeds in running down the battery. The battery does not have as much reserve capacity when the temperature is low, so it does not take much cranking to use up those precious amps. Once the battery is dead, there is no hope of getting the engine started. Now you have to either jump start the battery, or recharge it. Bringing a low battery inside can help restore some of its capacity, but if it has been worn down by repeated cranking, it will have to be recharged.

The complete procedure for jump starting is described in Chapter 11, but to summarize, connect the positive (red) jumper cable to the positive terminal of both batteries, then connect one end of the negative (black) cable to the negative post on the good battery, and make the final connection *not* to the negative post on the dead battery, but to a good metal ground in the engine compartment. This keeps any sparks away from the battery and reduces the chance of blowing up the dead battery.

Do not try to start the engine immediately. Run the engine on the vehicle with a good battery for five or ten minutes to pump some life into the old battery. Then try to start the engine. If it does not start after 15 to 20 seconds of cranking, stop and wait a few minutes before trying again. Excessive cranking can ruin the starter, wear down the good battery, and overload the charging system in the other vehicle.

If you are trying to recharge a dead battery with a portable charger, give the battery plenty of time. Most home chargers do not put out enough amperage to quickly charge a battery. A six-amp charger can take hours to bring a battery up to the point at which it will crank the engine, and then the battery still needs more charging to bring it up to full capacity. The best advice is to pay a few extra dollars for a high-output charger, one that puts out a minimum of 10 amps and preferably 20 or 30 amps. If the charger has a "boost" feature, you might even be able to use it to start the car. Again, the boost feature on a typical home charger does not put out that many amps. It works best if the battery is at least partially charged, and then only for brief periods of cranking. Prolonged cranking will overload the unit and either trip its circuit breaker or burn it out.

If the engine still cranks slowly even with a jump start or fully charged battery, it probably means the oil is too thick. A heat lamp placed under the engine can help heat up the oil, as can plugging in the engine block heater or a dipstick oil heater.

TESTING ANTIFREEZE STRENGTH

Tools Needed. Antifreeze tester.
How Often. Every fall before winter arrives.
Location. Test the strength of the antifreeze in the radiator, not in the cooling system reserve tank.
What To Do. *Do not* attempt to open the radiator cap if the engine is warm. Wait until it has cooled completely.

1. Remove the radiator cap from the radiator.
2. Insert the antifreeze tester and siphon a

small amount of coolant into the tester. Some testers use floating balls (Fig. 8-2), a weighted float, or a pivot float to indicate the amount of antifreeze in the coolant. Follow the directions provided with the tester to determine the correct reading.

A 50/50 mixture of antifreeze and water will provide freezing protection down to −34 degrees Fahrenheit. Maximum protection can be achieved by using a 70-percent antifreeze mixture. Do not use straight antifreeze, because it does not work as well as a mixture of antifreeze and water.

3. If there is insufficient antifreeze in the cooling system, open the radiator drain (located at the bottom of the radiator) and drain out a quart or two of coolant. Then close the drain and add straight antifreeze to the radiator. Retest the strength of the coolant after the engine has been driven and allowed to cool.

Fig. 8-2. Antifreeze tester.

4. Make a note of the date and mileage in your maintenance record for future reference.

MOUNTING SNOW TIRES

Tools Needed. Jack; lug wrench or torque wrench; screwdriver.

How Often. Before the first snowfall of each winter.

Location. Snow tires are mounted on the drive wheels. For rear-wheel drive, mount them on the back wheels. For front-wheel drive, mount them up front. For four-wheel drive, put them on all four wheels.

What To Do. You cannot mount the snow tires unless the tires are first mounted on rims. Tires can be taken off and on rims using a large screwdriver and a hammer, but it is hard work and it is very easy to tear up the lip along the tire's sealing surface. The best advice is to buy an extra set of rims for your car or truck and have the snow tires permanently mounted by a professional mechanic on these rims so that you can change them yourself. A pair of snow tires that are only used for winter driving can last for years. Having the snow tires on their own rims also saves the wear and tear of dismounting your regular tires in the fall and then remounting them in the spring.

1. Set the parking brake and put the transmission in gear (manual) or park (automatic).

2. Remove the hubcap by prying it loose with a screwdriver.

3. Loosen each lug nut about half a turn while the wheel and the weight of the vehicle are still on the ground.

4. Raise the wheel off the ground by jacking up the body. Use a safety stand to help support the vehicle.

5. Remove the lug nuts and take the wheel off. Then roll the snow tire into position and carefully lift it onto the lugs. Avoid putting your hands, feet, or arms under the tire or between the tire and fender in case the jack slips.

6. Install and hand tighten the lug nuts.

7. Lower the jack so that the wheel touches the ground and some of the vehicle's weight is on the wheel. Then finish tightening the lug nuts in an alternating star pattern or cross pattern to about 80 foot/pounds of torque. A power impact wrench should never be used to tighten lug nuts because it can make the nuts extremely difficult to remove, it can sometimes damage wheels, and it can warp brake rotors.

8. Replace the hubcap and check tire pressure before driving.

Chapter 9

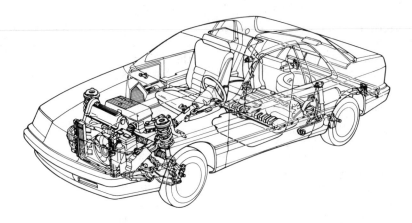

Preserving Your Car's Appearance

RUST NEVER SLEEPS

Rust is bad news. Besides being just plain ugly, rust often forces owners to get rid of vehicles that are otherwise mechanically sound. It eats holes in fenders, doors, and floors, weakens suspensions, and in time can transform even the stoutest hunk of metal into swiss cheese.

Why is rust such a problem? Because steel is chemically unstable. When man makes steel out of iron ore, oxygen is removed from the molten ore. This temporarily frees the iron for making steel, but almost immediately, chemical forces start to work to change it back. Iron and oxygen have a natural affinity for one another, and when they are allowed to come into contact, they recombine and form rust.

Rust is a one-way process. Once started, there's no way to reverse it. But there are a number of steps that can be taken to inhibit the process or, in some instances, to bring it to a temporary halt. But before telling you the secrets of rust prevention, let's examine some of the environmental factors that make rust such a problem.

Rust is the end product of an electrochemical reaction that transforms iron into *ferrous oxide*. The only ingredients required are iron and oxygen. Bare metal slowly rusts by picking up oxygen from the surrounding air. Add water and the rusting process shifts into high gear. The presence of water creates a miniature battery cell that pulls iron from the metal's surface and provides a pathway for oxygen to attack the steel. The result is a rapid buildup of iron oxide on the metal's surface and a rapid deterioration of the metal underneath.

If salt (sodium chloride) is added to the water, it makes the cell even more conductive. The result is a tenfold increase in corrosive activity. That is why rust-through is such a common problem in snowbelt states where road salt is used by the truck load.

Tests have shown that the most corrosive mixture is water with a two to six percent salt content, which happens to be the same concentration usually found on roads that have been salted to remove ice. One pound of salt will melt 46 pounds of ice and leave a two percent salt solution on the road. Add a little more salt and it makes puddles filled with highly corrosive three- to five-percent salt water. You can't escape salt corrosion by moving to the Sunbelt, either. For those who live near the ocean, rust can be a real problem because the concentration of ocean spray is about 3.5 percent salt!

When the weather turns unusually cold, road crews often add calcium chloride to help the road salt work at lower temperatures. This only makes the corrosion problem worse because calcium chloride picks up and holds moisture. As road spray and salt splash on the car and work their way into seams and crevices, calcium chloride enables the corrosive soup to continue eating away at the body even after the surface grime has dried. This kind of corrosion can destroy your car's sheetmetal nine times faster than just ordinary salt rust!

In highly industrialized areas, atmospheric pollution can be a significant factor, too. In fact, some people say it's worse than road salt because it also attacks the paint. The two main culprits here are ozone and sulfur dioxide, the latter of which is released into the atmosphere by burning high-sulfur content coal or oil. Sulfur dioxide combines with rain to form sulfurous or sulfuric acid (acid rain).

Temperature also plays a role in the rusting process. The warmer the temperature, the faster the chemical reaction proceeds. Believe it or not, a car that's been driven on salt-encrusted highways will rust faster when parked in a heated garage than if it is left outside or in an unheated garage.

Fighting Back

The use of galvanizing by vehicle manufacturers has increased in recent years as one means of preventing rust. *Galvanizing* is a thin coating of zinc on the sheetmetal. Zinc is more reactive than steel so it is "sacrificed" to protect the steel underneath. You will find galvanized steel used on many corrosion-prone lower body panels as well as the inner surfaces of fenders, doors, and deck lids.

Galvanized steel usually isn't used on the exterior of most body panels, because it's rough and doesn't produce a smooth finish when painted. Some manufacturers (such as Audi) are now galvanizing the entire body to protect it against rust.

The secret is using a very thin layer of electroplated zinc that leaves a smooth finish.

Another technique used by car makers to fight rust is *dip-priming*. The body shell is dipped in a huge tank of paint and is electrically charged to attract the paint into every corner and crevice. After final painting, the inner body surfaces are then sprayed with a waxy paraffin-based sealer.

To protect the exterior finish on lower body panels against stone chips that could open a pathway for rust, you'll find a flexible coating either over or under the paint. The coating cushions the paint against rocks and debris kicked up by the wheels, and lessens the likelihood of the paint being chipped.

The increased emphasis on fighting rust means today's new cars are better able to resist the ravages of rust than ever before. Cadillac, for example, has such confidence in its rust-prevention measures that it offers a five-year unlimited-mileage no-rust guarantee. In spite of the increased use of galvanized steel, more plastic, and factory-applied sealers, however many new vehicles can still benefit from the application of additional rust-prevention products.

Rustproofing Versus Undercoating

Rust has created nearly a billion-dollar industry for rustproofing and rust-treatment products in the United States. More than 3.5 million people will pay up to $200 this year to have their cars rustproofed either by new car dealers or aftermarket franchise outlets. Some people will choose to do their own rustproofing using various chemicals and products available through retailers and auto parts stores.

It is important to distinguish undercoating and rustproofing. *Undercoating* is spraying the underside of the car with a tarlike petroleum-based substance that protects the undercarriage against rust. Undercoating also helps to quiet road noise. Unfortunately, undercoating protects only about 12 percent of the rust-prone areas on a typical automobile.

Rustproofing, on the other hand, is applying a rust-inhibiting coating inside body panels, as well as underneath, and any place else that rust could pose a potential problem. This includes the insides of doors, fenders, inner fender panels, wheel wells, quarter panels, rocker panels, pillar posts, inside body seams, hood and deck lids, cowls, and even the backsides of the bumpers and body moldings.

The suppliers of various rustproofing compounds regard their formulas as proprietary secrets, and each claims certain advantages over their competitors. Some are solvent-based petroleum products while others are paraffin-based waxes. Some compounds form a water-resistant barrier while others actually bond to the surface. Some products include chemicals to help neutralize acids or existing rust; an important quality that can help prevent rust from being trapped beneath the coating.

Chip resistance and the ability to "self-heal" are two other very important characteristics claimed by some of the products on the market. The ability to self-heal, however, can be a double-edged sword. A compound must be able to creep slightly to fill in nicks or voids, yet at the same time be thick enough to prevent sagging and literally dripping off the vehicle. Another feature to look for is the ability to penetrate deep into body seams and to displace any existing moisture. Some can do this. Rustproofing compounds should also be nontoxic, non-conductive electrically, thermally stable, and fire resistant.

Another important difference between rustproofing products is the way in which they're applied. Some manufacturers of these products insist that the only way to effectively rustproof a car is to drill access holes to reach all of the hidden areas. Others say drilling holes promotes rust, therefore, the best way to apply it is through existing body access holes and openings.

I won't compare the relative merits of one product or application system to another. But you should be aware of the fact that all rustproofing compounds and systems are not alike, and for any given application, one product or method of application might offer certain advantages over another, which makes that product better for you.

Rustproofing doesn't last forever. Every rustproofing job should be checked periodically and touched up as needed. Road abrasion can wear away the protective coating in wheel wells, along lower body panels, or along rocker panels. If the damage isn't corrected, corrosion can find an easy path to the vulnerable metal underneath. That's why most rustproofing guarantees require the customer to return periodically for inspection and touch-up, and that's why you should do the same for your own vehicle if you do your own rustproofing.

How To Apply Rustproofing

One of the potential pitfalls of rustproofing is misapplication of the product. Figures 9-1 through 9-4 show where rustproofing should be applied. Whether you do the job yourself or have it done professionally, care must be taken *not* to spray rustproofing on any part of the vehicle where it could interfere with normal operation or servicing of the vehicle. This includes:

☐ Any part of the exhaust system, catalytic converter, or exhaust system heat shields.

☐ All electrical components including the battery, battery cables, starter, alternator, distributor, ignition wires, wiring harness, electronic modules, windshield wiper motor, power window motors inside door panels, power antenna motor inside fenders or trunk, radio speakers, and the windshield wiper motor.

☐ All brake components including the brake drums and rotors, calipers, and backing plates. Rustproofing on the brake linings can cause erratic braking.

☐ Transmission/transaxle shift linkages and breather vents, the speedometer cable, transmission/transaxle oil pan, the engine oil pan, rear axle/differential, radiator, belts and hoses, oil cooler, power steering pump, rack and pinion steering housing, or steering box.

☐ Any part of the cooling system such as the radiator, fan, or hoses.

☐ The energy absorbers behind the bumpers. Rustproofing here can interfere with the collapsing of the absorbers in an accident.

☐ Suspension components such as shock absorbers, MacPherson struts, and any rubber com-

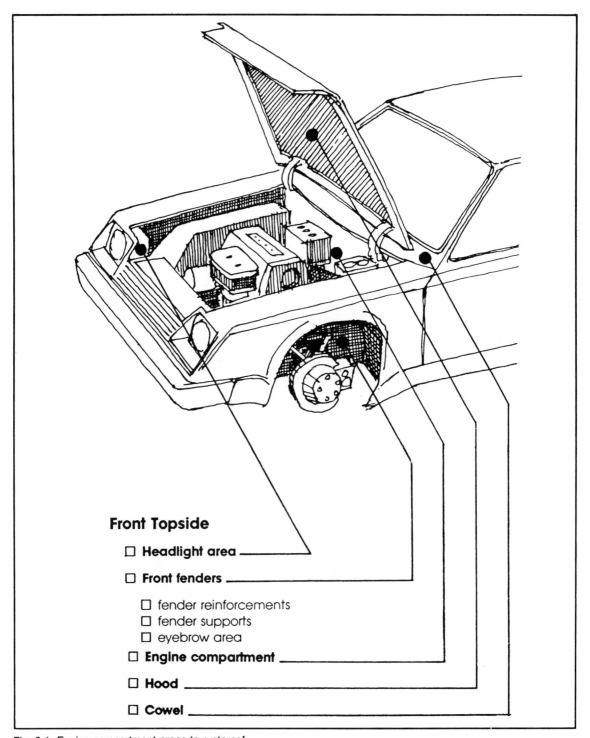

Front Topside

☐ **Headlight area**

☐ **Front fenders**

    ☐ fender reinforcements
    ☐ fender supports
    ☐ eyebrow area

☐ **Engine compartment**

☐ **Hood**

☐ **Cowel**

Fig. 9-1. Engine compartment areas to rustproof.

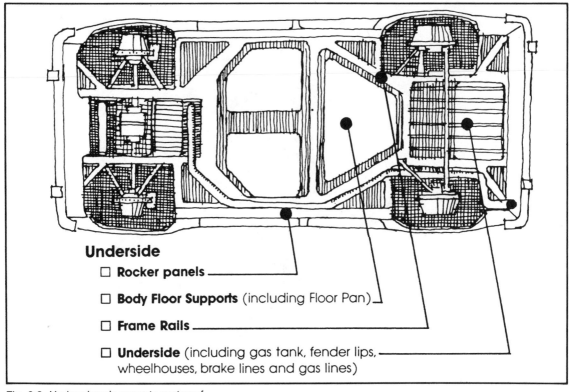

Underside

☐ **Rocker panels**

☐ **Body Floor Supports** (including Floor Pan)

☐ **Frame Rails**

☐ **Underside** (including gas tank, fender lips, wheelhouses, brake lines and gas lines)

Fig. 9-2. Under-chassis areas to rustproof.

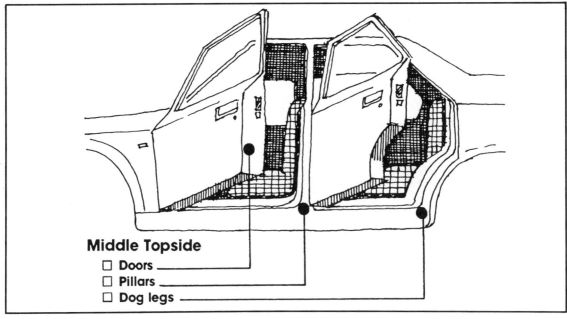

Middle Topside

☐ **Doors**
☐ **Pillars**
☐ **Dog legs**

Fig. 9-3. Door areas to rustproof.

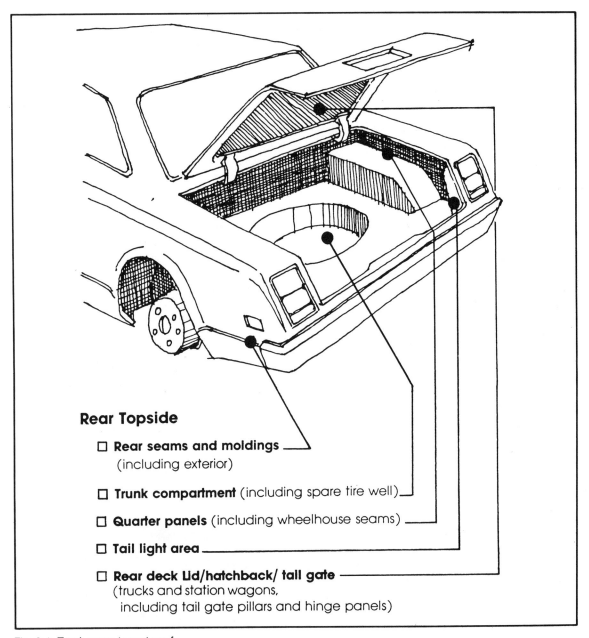

Rear Topside

- ☐ **Rear seams and moldings**
  (including exterior)

- ☐ **Trunk compartment** (including spare tire well)

- ☐ **Quarter panels** (including wheelhouse seams)

- ☐ **Tail light area**

- ☐ **Rear deck Lid/hatchback/ tail gate**
  (trucks and station wagons,
    including tail gate pillars and hinge panels)

Fig. 9-4. Trunk areas to rustproof.

ponents such as control arm bushings, grommets, etc.

☐ Fuel tank fittings, in-line fuel filters, and electric fuel pumps.

☐ Seat belt retractors.

☐ Door latch and window mechanisms.

Fighting Rust Electronically

One high-tech solution that has emerged in the war on rust is an electronic method of preventing corrosion. Rust is an electrochemical reaction that works similar to a battery. Water and salt form the electrolyte that completes the circuit. Oxygen assumes the role of the negative cathode and the car's body acts as the positive anode. The difference in electrical potential drives oxygen into the metal (to form rust) and pulls metal out (to form pits and at the same time expose more surface to the oxygen).

The same reaction can happen between dissimilar metals in the car's body, such as steel and aluminum. This is referred to as *galvanic* corrosion and the metal that is the most reactive—in this case aluminum—is the metal that corrodes.

One way to control this process is to use a sacrificial anode. Magnesium is more reactive than steel so if a sacrificial magnesium anode is used it can protect the rest of the car. This is also referred to as *cathodic protection.* All corrosion is focused on the small sacrificial anode. The idea isn't bad, but a simple bolt-on anode won't last forever and protection depends on maintaining good electrical contact with the rest of the car.

The same basic idea, however, can be taken one step further and used much more effectively with the help of electronics. One such product is called Rust Evader by Automotive Corrosion Control Company, Altoona, Pennsylvania

(814-944-8700). It sells for approximately $250 retail.

The Rust Evader system uses battery voltage to maintain an offsetting current throughout the vehicles body. By feeding direct current into the vehicle's body, the body becomes the cathode and is protected against corrosion. The electronic control circuit balances the current flow depending on the wetness of the body. The wetter the body (the lower the resistance), the higher the current flow. Maximum current drain is half a milliamp. This same technology is being used to protect bridges and pipelines against corrosion.

There are several interesting features about this approach worth mentioning. The first is that this method stops existing rust from spreading, which surface treatments can't always do. Second, the car owner can remove it when he trades cars, which can't be done with any other type of rust treatment. And third, the manufacturer claims it can protect a car indefinitely (Fig. 9-5).

Tips on DIY Rust Repairs

What makes rust such a problem is that once

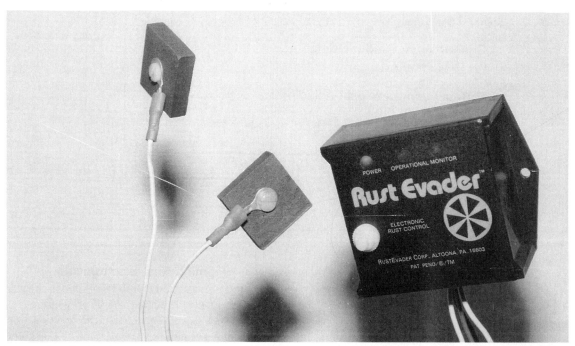

Fig. 9-5. Rust Evader electronic rust protection control module and body electrodes. (Courtesy of Rust Evader Corporation.)

started, it's nearly impossible to stop. Body shops can patch obvious damage, but few will guarantee such work and many are reluctant to take on such repair work. That means you often have to be your own doctor when it comes to treating rust.

What should you do when you discover rust on your car's exterior? The one thing you don't want to do is to simply paint over it. Painting over rust will only temporarily conceal the problem, but it certainly won't cure it. Sooner or later the concealed rust will bleed through, causing the newly applied paint to blister and peel. In fact, painting over rust can sometimes aggravate the problem by trapping moisture beneath the finish.

Before applying paint or primer, the first step is to remove as much rust as possible. Surface rust can be removed by grinding or sanding or by using a chemical rust-removing cleaner or gel. If sanding, use progressively finer grit abrasives to scour away the loose paint and rust until the metal is clean and smooth. Paint surrounding the rusted area should be sanded to a feathered edge so that the repair will be invisible when repainted.

It is also extremely important to find out what's causing the rust. Water leaks around window and body seams are the leading culprit of rust, eating from the inside out. To stop it, you have to find and fix the water leak. Windshield sealer works fine for

Fig. 9-7. Use a rust conversion chemical to convert existing rust into an inert black oxide. This will greatly prolong the life of any rust repair.

glass leaks and silicone caulk can be used to patch leaky weatherstripping.

Rust Conversion Treatments

Once all surface rust has been removed by sanding and/or chemical cleansing, a rust conversion treatment should be applied to the metal to transform any remaining rust into inert black oxide. The oxide forms a protective barrier that resists corrosion and helps to extend the life of the repair. This step isn't absolutely necessary, but if you want the repair to last, it is strongly recommended.

There are a variety of rust conversion treatments available. Although some treatments use different ingredients, all accomplish essentially the same result: they convert rust to a more chemically stable compound such as iron tannate or iron phosphate (Figs. 9-6 and 9-7).

Such treatments are easy to apply. After

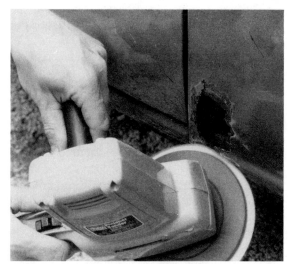

Fig. 9-6. Rust-damaged areas should be thoroughly sanded to remove all surface rust prior to patching.

removing the surface rust, all you do is brush the chemical onto the rusted area. Once applied, it begins to react with the rust and turn it black. Within 15 to 20 minutes the basic chemical reaction is complete, but you should wait 12 to 24 hours for a complete cure before painting.

Some treatments include epoxies that make them self-priming so you can paint right over them once they've cured. For the longest-lasting repair, however, the entire area should be primed with a top-quality zinc chromate primer/sealer before painting.

Filling Holes

For damaged areas that have rusted through, the metal surrounding the hole should be trimmed back until you find solid metal. It doesn't do any good to patch a hole unless there is solid metal to hold the patch. This should be done prior to applying a rust conversion treatment.

Some people think the way to patch a rust hole is to stuff it full of wadded-up newspapers or rags and then smear plastic body filler over it. Do it this way and you'll have problems. Newspapers and rags trap moisture, which encourages rust to reform behind the patch. If there's no reinforcement behind the patch, in time it will crack and break loose.

The best way to patch a hole is to first fill the cavity with urethane foam. The closed-cell foam forms a moisture-proof barrier behind the hole while creating a firm foundation. It can be easily shaped once hard to restore the original contours of the body.

Another alternative is to seal the back (not the front) of the hole with fiberglass cloth. The damaged area must be sanded down to bare metal on both sides so the patch will have a good surface on which to adhere. Saturate the cloth with epoxy, apply it to the back side of the hole, and allow it to harden (you can speed up the curing time by applying heat from an infrared light). Once the patch has hardened, the hole can be filled and leveled with plastic body filler, sanded smooth, primed, and painted. Buffing with rubbing compound will help blend the repainted area into the surrounding body panel. As a finishing touch, a coat of wax is recommended to seal the new paint against air and moisture.

THE TRUTH ABOUT WAXES AND POLISHES

Wax doesn't last forever; neither do "lifetime" sealers. How long a wax or sealer lasts depends on the environment. The more rain, snow, sleet, salt, sun, and industrial pollution the finish is exposed to, the shorter its life. For a garaged vehicle, the finish can hold up for about a year before it needs rewaxing or polishing. For a vehicle that's kept outdoors, the finish will need to be redone in about six months.

How well does wax actually protect the finish? Not that well. Wax is water repellant so it can help protect the body against moisture and rust. Wax is especially protective against moisture and rust on aluminum wheels, bumpers and trim.

The main benefit that wax provides, besides moisture resistance, is shine. If you want your paint job to shine, then wax it regularly. The benefits of a wax job are mostly aesthetic, but good looks enhance beauty and resale value. There are probably as many different types of wax on the market today as there are vehicles. Paste wax that requires a lot of rubbing and buffing has generally been replaced by liquid waxes that combine both cleaning agents and wax in one bottle.

Cleaners are mild abrasives that scour off the top layer of oxidized paint to reveal the bright paint underneath. A can of rubbing compound is the ultimate cleaner for restoring life to dull, faded paint. Cleaners are fine for older or weathered vehicles, but they are not recommended for new cars or vehicles with clear-coat paint jobs. The luster in a clear-coat paint is in the clear top coat. Rub it away and you'll lose the sheen.

For interior protection, various spray waxes are available to restore and protect dash boards, door panels, kick panels, and vinyl upholstery. For fabric interiors, Scotch Guarding is very good protection for keeping stains and moisture out of the material. No product, however, can protect an interior from sun fade; the only prevention for fading is to use window shades or to keep the vehicle garaged.

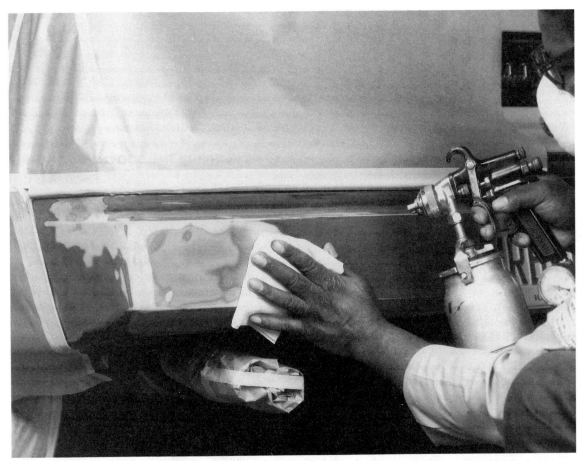

Fig. 9-8. Overspray is always a problem when painting, so mask off surrounding areas to prevent misting.

TOUCH-UP PAINTING MADE EASY

The best way to prevent rust from getting a foothold on the exterior of your vehicle is to touch up paint nicks and chips regularly. Regularly means as soon as they're discovered. If you notice a small nick or scrape while washing the car, make a mental note of it and try to touch it up as soon as possible. The longer you wait, the more time nature has to attack the wound. Moisture will work its way through the breech in the paint and start to eat away at the metal underneath. It doesn't take long for the surrounding paint to start to blister and peel.

Touch-up paint can be purchased in bottles or spray cans. The paint in bottles is thicker and is best for touching up small nicks and chips. Spray paint, on the other hand, goes on thinner for a smoother finish. It is best for restoring large areas such as rocker panels, fenders, doors, etc.

Matching the color is always a problem, even on a brand new car because of variations in paint batches and sun fading. The touch-up paint recommended for your car might not match exactly. Solid colors match better than pastels or metallics. Clear coat paint jobs can be especially difficult to match because the upper clear coat alters the color of the underlying paint slightly. When touch-up paint is used, it often looks dull or faded next to the original paint. Applying clear over the retouched area might help.

When touching up a small chip or nick, don't just dab on the touch-up paint and consider it fixed. If the nick has penetrated the primer layer underneath, the damaged area should be buffed lightly with steel wool, then primed before painting. Be careful not to buff the adjacent area because steel wool will dull the finish. If rust has gotten a foothold, scrape away any loose paint, sand down to the bare metal, then prime. Applying a rust conversion chemical can also help stop the rust from returning.

When spray painting, you'll get a much better finish if you use several light coats rather than one heavy coat. This method will also lessen the possibility of the paint running. If it does run, just wait a couple days and buff out the runs with rubbing compound.

Canned spray paint contains a high percentage of solvent, which means it dries fast but tends to mist. It is difficult to make an invisible repair because the paint dries before it has a chance to level out. When trying to touch up a small spot on a car hood or door, for example, the sprayed area will be very noticeable, even if the color matches perfectly, because of the difference in texture. Buffing with rubbing compound several days later can help blend the repainted area into the surrounding finish. Professional painters even recommend repainting the entire body panel, or at least painting to the nearest body seam or trim line to hide the repair.

One problem you're likely to run into when touch-up spray painting is paint incompatibility. There are different types of paint used on automotive finishes and some are not compatible with others. If lacquer is applied over enamel it will "lift" the enamel leaving a lumpy, wrinkled-looking finish. The touch-up paint in the spray can might not be compatible with your vehicle's paint, so always experiment, if possible, by painting a small, hidden area (inside the trunk, etc.). You can also avoid problems by using the same brand of primer as touch-up paint. Paint manufacturers usually make certain their primer is compatible with their touch-up paint, but you have no such guarantees if you use Brand X primer with Brand Z spray paint.

Another potential problem when spray painting is mist travel. It's amazing how far the wind can carry the tiny droplets of paint, especially when there's an item nearby you don't want paint on. Cover tires, glass, trim, bumpers, adjacent body panels, etc., with masking tape and old newspapers to save yourself the headache of trying to remove oversprayed paint. Steel wool will remove overspray from chrome bumpers, tires, and trim, and a good cleaning wax or rubbing compound will remove it from painted surfaces.

KEEPING THE BODY LUBED

The automobile body actually requires little in the way of lubrication, but certain items do require periodic attention to prevent problems from developing. Locks and latches should be sprayed periodically with a moisture-repelling lubricant such as graphite, WD-40, or silicone. Oil should not be used because it attracts dirt and can gum up mechanisms. Hood releases, truck latches, and seat adjusters can be kept lubricated with white lithium grease. Hood, trunk, and hatchback hinges can be lubricated with graphite, white lithium grease, silicone, or WD-40 to keep them from rusting and binding.

REPAIRING MINOR DENTS AND BODY DAMAGE

Repairs in this subheading fall into three categories: repairing metal, repairing fiberglass, and repairing plastic.

Fixing Metal

Small dents and dings can be fixed by pounding out the damage as best as possible and then restoring the original contours of the body with plastic body filler. If dents can be pounded out from behind, small holes can be drilled into the metal and a slide hammer used to pull the dent out from the front.

There are a few items to keep in mind about plastic body filler. For the filler to stick, the surface underneath has to be clean and free from paint. That means sanding the damaged area down to bare metal and then applying the filler. The other recommendation is to use as little filler as possible. Smearing on layer after layer of body filler to fill a dent is no substitute for straightening the metal as much as possible. The thicker the layer of filler, the more likely it is to crack and pull loose.

Plastic body filler comes with a creme hardener. Use the hardener sparingly, but don't forget it or the filler will remain soft forever. Use too much hardener and the filler will become rock hard before you can get it on the body. Always follow the directions provided with the product.

The best way to sand body filler is before it's rock hard. After the product has set up, it can be "shaved" into shape with a special body file. Then, progressively finer sandpaper can be used to smooth the filler. If you're using a power sander, be sure to wear a dust mask to keep the filler dust out of your nose and lungs.

A common mistake that's made when sanding is to use sandpaper that's too coarse. The paper leaves deep scratches that are hard to remove, and when painted, tend to exaggerate the rough finish even more. It might require several thin coats of filler to get a perfectly smooth finish, but taking your time is well worth the effort. When smooth, the repaired area should be primed before painting. Using a sandable primer can help blend the repaired area into the surrounding finish.

Fiberglass Repairs

Like sheetmetal repairs, fiberglass requires a smooth surface free from paint for maximum adhesion. The damaged area should be sanded to a feather edge; this should be done on both sides if a hole extends through the body panel. Be sure to wear a dust mask, gloves, and long sleeves because fiberglass can be very irritating.

Once the surface has been prepared, a piece of fiberglass cloth is laid over the hole and saturated with epoxy (epoxy requires mixing the hardener with the resin). The cloth should be thoroughly soaked so that no air bubbles show. Curing time is usually 30 to 45 minutes. Once cured, additional coats of fiberglass can be applied as needed. The damaged area can then be sanded down and finished with ordinary body filler until smooth.

Plastic Repairs

Some hard plastics can be repaired with fiberglass or ordinary body filler, but many plastics are too "slick" to provide good adhesion. Polyethylene and polypropylene are virtually impossible to repair except by hot air welding, a process better left to a professional mechanic with the right equipment and knowledge.

Soft bumpers and flexible body panels can usually be patched with special *flexible adhesives*. These products are like an epoxy in that a hardener is mixed with a resin. The only difference is that these adhesives remain flexible when cured, so they won't crack or peel loose from flexible body parts. The basic finishing procedure is the same as with fiberglass. You first have to sand down the damaged area to remove all the paint. Then the material is applied to the hole or crack, it is cured, and is lightly sanded until smooth.

When painting a flexible body panel, ordinary touch-up paint won't adhere well because it lacks the flex additive of the original finish. In time it will crack and peel loose. Special flex additives can be added to paint for repainting soft body parts, but such products are designed for professional body repairmen, not do-it-yourselfers. A few paint suppliers now offer flexible touch-up paint in spray cans, but it's hard to find.

Chapter 10

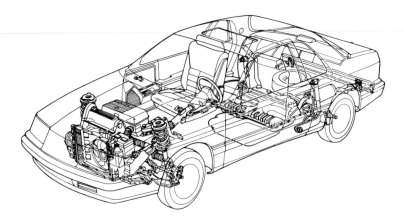

Troubleshooting Simplified

The system charts in this chapter can help you diagnose possible causes of unusual sounds, vibrations, and various driveability problems. The left column of each chart lists the symptoms. The dots to the right correspond to the possible causes listed along the top of each column. (Tables 10-1 through 10-10)

COMMENTS AND SUGGESTIONS

When diagnosing a problem, it's a good idea to look for the symptom on more than one chart. Let's say your vehicle experiences a high-speed vibration. If you look at the steering and suspension system chart, you'll find two possible causes listed, which are wheels and tires out of balance or worn shock absorbers. If you also look at the transmission and driveline troubleshooting chart, you'll also find an out-of-balance rear-wheel driveshaft listed as a possibility. How do you pinpoint the cause of your problem? By a process of elimination. If your vehicle is FWD, you can eliminate driveshaft vibrations. You can inspect the shocks by doing a bounce test to see if they are in good condition. That leaves the

wheels as the most likely cause.

The troubleshooting chart for engine problems is limited to basic complaints. Because of the complexity of today's computerized engine control systems that regulate fuel, ignition, and emissions, there's no way to include these systems in a simplified troubleshooting chart. The factory service manuals for late-model computer systems typically contain diagnostic sections that occupy several hundred pages. The danger in trying to condense this information is that it oversimplifies and encourages people to jump to conclusions without performing the necessary step-by-step diagnostic tests. A late-model engine with computerized engine controls can still lack power because of bad valves, but it can also lack power for dozens of other reasons related to the computer system. If you suspect a computer problem, find yourself a competent mechanic who is knowledgeable about computer diagnostics.

Additional troubleshooting help and service guidelines can be found under many of the terms listed in the glossary of this book.

Table 10-1. Troubleshooting the Engine.

Symptoms	Burned or worn valves	Worn piston rings	Worn valve guides	Oil leaks	Valves need adjustment	Valve sticking	Valve spring broken	Broken timing belt	Broken distributor drive	Broken engine mounts	Damaged main bearing	Damaged connecting rod bearing	Worn piston pins	Computer system fault
Engine lacks power	●	●												●
Poor fuel mileage	●	●												●
Excessive oil use		●	●	●										
Fumes from engine		●												
Light clicking noise					●	●	●							
Rough operation						●	●							●
Engine won't run								●	●					
Engine shakes										●				
Heavy thudding											●			
Sharp metallic knock												●	●	
Check engine light on														●

Table 10-2. Troubleshooting the Fuel System.

Symptoms	Faulty automatic choke	Low fuel pump pressure	Faulty carburetor adjustment	Fuel line hot—vapor lock	Dirt or water in fuel	Clogged fuel filter	Dirty carburetor	Clogged air cleaner	Faulty accelerating pump	Binding accelerator linkage	High fuel pump pressure	Sticking needle valve
Hard starting when cold	●											
Hard starting when hot	●		●									
Engine stalls	●		●	●		●						
Smoky exhaust (black)	●		●			●	●				●	●
Poor gasoline mileage	●		●			●	●				●	●
Engine 'starves' at high speed		●	●	●	●	●						
Rough idle	●		●		●	●					●	●
Engine stumbles on acceleration			●			●			●	●		
Flooded carburetor	●		●			●	●				●	●
Engine backfires		●	●		●	●						

Table 10-3. Troubleshooting the Emission Control System.

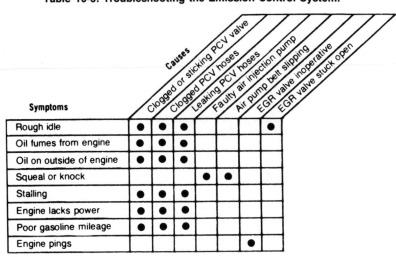

Symptoms	Clogged or sticking PCV valve	Clogged PCV hoses	Leaking PCV hoses	Faulty air injection pump	Air pump belt slipping	EGR valve inoperative	EGR valve stuck open
Rough idle	●	●	●				●
Oil fumes from engine	●	●	●				
Oil on outside of engine	●	●	●				
Squeal or knock				●	●		
Stalling	●	●	●				
Engine lacks power	●	●	●				
Poor gasoline mileage	●	●	●				
Engine pings						●	

Table 10-4. Troubleshooting the Cooling System.

Symptoms	Low coolant level	Cooling system clogged	Loose or broken V-belt	Thermostat stuck closed	Thermostat stuck open	Debris on radiator	Faulty water pump	Collapsed water hose	Leaking cyl. head gasket	Late ignition timing	Heater core clogged	Faulty temperature control	Low refrigerant charge	Loose or broken drive belt	Faulty compressor clutch	Debris on condenser	Electric cooling fan inoperative	Fan thermostat defective
Engine overheats	●	●	●	●		●	●	●	●	●							●	●
Engine warms up slowly					●													
Insufficient heat					●						●	●						
Insufficient air-conditioning												●	●	●		●		
No air-conditioning													●	●	●			

Table 10-5. Troubleshooting the Exhaust System.

Symptoms	Hole in muffler or exhaust system	Tail pipe bent or clogged	Exhaust pipe or muffler clogged	Leaking tail pipe	Loose pipe or muffler	Pipe touching frame or body	Loose tubes inside muffler	Catalytic converter clogged
Loud exhaust	●							
Hissing exhaust		●						
Fumes under car	●			●				
Rattles					●	●	●	
Vibration						●		
Engine lacks power		●	●					●
Engine overheats		●	●					●

Table 10-6. Troubleshooting the Transmission and Driveline System.

Symptoms	Clutch needs adjustment	Clutch disc worn	Transmission low on lubricant	Incorrect grade of lubricant	Shift linkage out of adjustment	Low fluid level	Bands need adjustment	Control valve sticking	Throttle linkage needs adjustment	Leaking seals or gaskets	Worn CV joints (FWD only)	Bad U-joint	Unbalanced RWD driveshaft	Broken transmission mounts
Clutch slips	●	●												
Hard shifting (manual)	●		●	●	●									
Gears clash (manual)	●		●	●	●									
Automatic transmission slips						●	●	●						
Automatic doesn't shift properly						●	●	●	●					
Transmission low on fluid										●				
Rough engagement of drive or reverse								●						
Clicking noise while turning											●			
Vibration at high speed												●	●	
Clunk when auto trans put in gear												●	●	●
Clutch chatters when engaged	●													

Table 10-7. Troubleshooting the Starting, Ignition, and Electrical System.

Symptoms	Battery discharged	Loose or broken cables	Faulty starter or solenoid	Faulty ignition switch	Faulty neutral switch	Spark plugs fouled	Improper spark plug gap	Faulty coil	Damaged dist. cap or rotor	Damaged ignition cables	Incorrect spark timing	Alternator belt slipping	Faulty voltage regulator	Low regulator setting	Faulty alternator	Battery worn out	Corroded battery terminals
Starter won't operate	●	●	●	●	●											●	
Starter turns, engine won't start			●			●	●	●	●	●	●						
Engine misfires						●	●	●	●	●							
Engine cuts out at high speed						●	●	●	●	●							
Engine knocks or pings											●						
Engine lacks power						●	●	●	●	●							
Engine idles roughly						●	●		●								
Battery frequently discharged												●	●	●	●	●	●
Alternator does not charge												●	●		●		

Table 10-8. Troubleshooting Lighting and Safety Devices.

Symptoms	Battery discharged	Bulb burned out	Faulty wiring	Fuse blown	Faulty flasher unit	Faulty wiper motor	Faulty wiper linkage	Faulty wiper park switch	Fluid low in reservoir	Tubing disconnected	Clogged nozzle	Faulty washer pump	Faulty stop light switch	Short circuit in wiring
Lights very dim	●													
One light doesn't work		●	●	●										
Turn signals flash on only one side		●	●											
Turn signals do not flash			●	●	●									
Windshield wipers don't work			●	●		●	●							
Windshield wipers don't park								●						
Windshield washers don't work									●	●	●	●		
Stop lights don't work		●	●	●										
Stop lights stay on			●										●	
Headlights flash on and off														●

Table 10-9. Troubleshooting the Steering and Suspension System.

Symptoms	Low or uneven tire pressure	Steering linkage dry	Front end out of alignment	Suspension arms damaged	Ball joints binding	Sagging springs	Power steering belt slipping	Power steering fluid low	Loose front wheel bearings	Worn ball joints	Loose steering linkage	Maladjusted steering gear	Worn shock absorbers	Wheels and tires out of balance	Upper strut bushings bad
Hard steering	●	●	●	●	●	●	●	●				●			●
Car pulls to one side	●		●	●		●			●	●	●	●			
Car wanders from side to side	●		●			●			●	●	●	●	●		
Uneven tire wear	●		●	●					●	●	●		●	●	
Front wheel shimmy									●	●	●				
High-speed vibration													●	●	
Car not level				●		●									
Heavy thumps on rough roads				●		●				●			●		
Play or looseness in steering									●	●	●	●			
Rattle in steering gear												●			
Thump from front end				●						●					

Table 10-10. Troubleshooting the Braking System.

Symptoms	Low fluid level	Air in hydraulic system	Brakes need adjustment	Brake fade due to overheating	Grease or fluid on linings	Linings glazed	Wet brakes	Faulty vacuum booster	Linkage binding	Weak flexible hoses	Loose or worn wheel bearings	Loose or worn front end parts	Front wheels out of alignment	Loose disc brake caliper	Warped brake disc	Eccentric brake drum	Faulty wheel cylinder	Faulty master cylinder	Weak or broken retracting springs	Scored brake drums	Dirt in brake mechanism	Clogged or kinked brake lines
Play in pedal	●	●	●						●								●	●				
Hard pedal				●	●	●	●	●	●								●	●				●
Spongy pedal	●	●							●													
Pedal sinks to floor	●																●	●				
Pedal vibrates		●							●	●					●	●						
Brakes grab				●															●			
Brakes drag		●					●										●	●				●
Brakes pull		●		●		●					●	●	●	●			●		●			●
Erratic braking		●		●							●	●		●	●	●			●			
Squeal or chatter		●				●									●	●				●		

Chapter 11

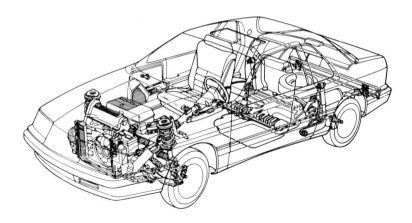

Easy Repairs

This section describes the step-by-step procedures for some typical light repair jobs you can do. The procedures described are generic in that they are written to apply to the broadest category of vehicles possible. In some instances, one step or two might have to be taken out of sequence to satisfy the needs of your particular vehicle.

Under each heading you'll find a listing of the tools needed or recommended, the necessary replacement parts (where applicable), general comments or suggestions as to when such repairs might be necessary, a general description of where the repair site is located on your vehicle, and finally, the step-by-step procedures for repairing or replacing the item.

The instructions in this book should be all you need to complete the basic repairs. But if you do need additional guidance, refer to a good repair manual.

Before starting a repair, read the instructions first so you will know exactly what is involved. This will also help you clarify in your own mind the steps that will be necessary to complete the task. If you don't understand the terminology or have questions, refer to the Glossary.

REPLACING A MUFFLER AND TAIL PIPE

Tools Required. Jack, safety stands, wrenches, hacksaw, muffler chisel, hammer, safety glasses.

Parts Needed. Replacement exhaust pipe or muffler; pipe clamps.

How Often. When exhaust leaks or noise are noticed.

Location. The components in a typical exhaust system are shown in Figure 11-1. The pipe that runs from the exhaust manifold on the engine to the catalytic converter is called the *headpipe*. The pipe after the converter is the *exhaust pipe,* and the pipe after the muffler is the *tail pipe.* Some vehicles use a second muffler called a *resonator* for additional sound control. Most original equipment exhaust systems are welded together rather than clamped. This means you'll have to saw or chisel the pipes apart to replace a faulty component.

What To Do. First determine the nature of

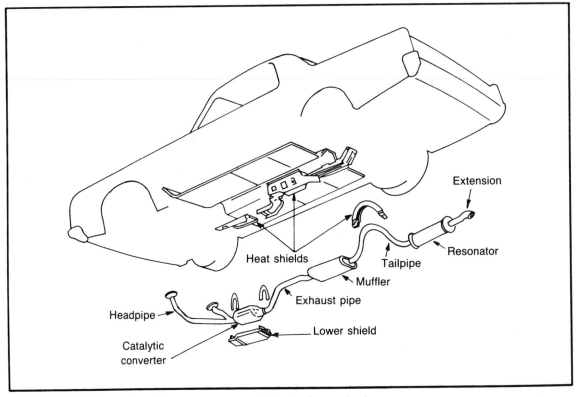

Fig. 11-1. Exhaust system components. (Courtesy of Chrysler Corporation.)

the problem by carefully inspecting the exhaust system from end to end. Most leaks occur at pipe connections or at tight bends in the pipe. Mufflers rust through at the pipe connections and along end and side seams (Fig. 11-2). Converters tend to rot off only at pipe connections.

1. With the vehicle parked on level ground, set the parking brake and place the transmission in park (automatic) or gear (manual). Also block the wheels.

2. Raise whichever end of the vehicle is necessary to gain access to the faulty exhaust component and support the vehicle on safety stands.

3. It might be necessary to support part of the exhaust system while removing a rusted pipe or muffler. Use a short piece of wire to prevent the pipes from dropping.

4. Remove any clamps holding the pipe or muffler. Old clamps should be discarded and new

ones installed when components are replaced. The bolts will likely be rusted solid. If they can't be freed with penetrating oil and heat from a propane torch, you will have to twist, saw, or chisel them off (Fig. 11-3).

Don't waste your time trying to separate a corroded pipe joint. Once an exhaust system accumulates many miles, the connections become permanently rusted together. Heat and penetrating oil are useless and the only way to separate two pipes at a connection is to split the outer pipe open with a muffler chisel. This obviously ruins the outer pipe connection, but by sawing off the damaged end and using a reducer coupling, the old pipe can be reconnected to the new one.

If the exhaust system is the original that came on the vehicle, or if the system has been "Midasized" (Midas welds pipes and mufflers in place), you will have to hacksaw the pipes apart. A flexible hacksaw blade is recommended to prevent blade

Fig. 11-2. Mufflers tend to rust out along the end seams and pipe connections.

breakage. If there isn't enough elbow room to saw the pipes completely in two, saw the pipe as far as you can from underneath, then pull it down to gain additional clearance. Bending the pipe back and forth repeatedly after it has been partially sawed can help break it apart. Professional mechanics don't have these problems because they use an acetylene torch to simply cut away the old clamps and pipes. It's fast and easy, but most do-it-yourselfers don't have access to acetylene torches.

5. Install the new pipe or muffler by slipping each end into position. Pay attention to any markings on the muffler that indicate which direction to install it (installing it backwards could in-

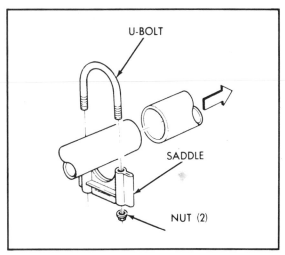

Fig. 11-3. Exhaust clamp. (Courtesy of Chrysler Corporation.)

pounded into the pipe to expand or reduce the diameter of the pipe. Either tool can usually be rented at an auto parts store.

6. The secret to getting rattle-free repair is to carefully position the pipes before tightening the clamps. Wiggle the pipes around until they align properly and nothing touches the suspension or underside of the vehicle. Make sure the exhaust system allows adequate room for the fuel tank, suspension travel, and ground clearance. Then mount the new pipe clamps and tighten firmly.

7. Lower the vehicle and start the engine. Rev the engine and listen for exhaust leaks or rattles. Readjust and/or retighten the pipes if needed.

8. After the vehicle has been driven a few hundred miles, retighten the clamps.

crease back pressure and reduce sound control). Make certain all pipe connections are shoved together as tight as possible. If you have to pound them together, use a rubber hammer to avoid denting the pipes.

Sometimes a replacement pipe coupling will be slightly dented or deformed, which prevents it from slipping together. A special tool called a *pipe expander* or *muffler cone* can be inserted into the end of the pipe to restore its shape (Fig. 11-4). A pipe expander pushes out as you tighten a bolt to reshape or expand the pipe. A muffler cone is

REPLACING A LEAKY WATER PUMP

Tools Required. Wrenches, pliers, screwdriver, scraper, funnel, bucket.

Parts Needed. Replacement water pump; water pump gasket; gasket sealer (or RTV silicone sealer to form your own gasket); possibly antifreeze and water (if the coolant also needs changing).

How Often. When coolant is observed to be leaking around the water pump shaft, when noise is heard from the pump, and/or when wobbling or freeplay is noticed in the pump shaft.

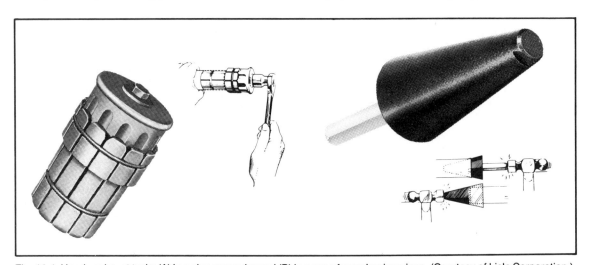

Fig. 11-4. Handy exhaust tools: (A) is a pipe expander and (B) is a cone for reshaping pipes. (Courtesy of Lisle Corporation.)

Location. The water pump on most engines is located on the front of the engine and is driven by a V-belt from the crankshaft pulley or by the timing belt. On a few front-wheel-drive vehicles with transverse-mounted engines, the pump can be located at the rear of the block (on Mitsubishi 2.6 liter four-cylinder engines, for example) or offset to one side at the front of the block (Fig. 11-5).

What To Do. First determine that the pump is defective. If any leaks are observed around the pump shaft, the pump is bad and must be replaced. Removing the V-belt and spinning the pump pulley by hand will tell you if there is any roughness in the pump bearings. Also try wiggling the pulley or fan (if mounted on the pump pulley). If you feel looseness in the pump shaft, the pump needs to be replaced.

Sometimes a water pump will fail internally. The impeller that pushes the coolant through the system can separate from the pump shaft or wear down (a process called *cavitation*). If the engine overheats and the thermostat, coolant level, and fan appear to be working correctly, try feeling the upper radiator hose to determine if coolant is moving through the system when the engine is hot. No movement means the pump isn't working. Sometimes a clogged radiator or collapsed lower radiator hose can cause the same kind of trouble.

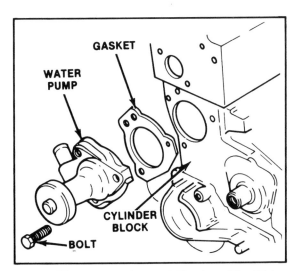

Fig. 11-5. Water pump replacement. (Courtesy of *Ford Motor-craft Shop Tips*, Vol. 19, No. 2.)

To Replace a Defective Water pump:

1. Drain the cooling system by placing a bucket under the radiator drain plug and opening the plug. Wait until the engine has cooled before opening the radiator cap.

2. To gain access to the pump, it might be necessary to remove the fan shroud from the radiator, the fan, and various drive belts. The shroud is usually held in place by a couple of bolts or screws at the top or side of the radiator. The fan will have four long bolts running through the pump pulley. The bolts do not have to come completely out to remove the fan, just far enough to clear the pulley, then the fan can be pulled loose from the pump pulley. Corrosion will sometimes hold an aluminum fan extension in place, so you might have to tap it loose with a rubber hammer.

3. Remove the pump V-belt by loosening the adjustment bolts on whatever other accessory the belt drives (alternator, A/C compressor, air pump or power steering pump). Do not try to twist or force a belt off a pulley; it will damage the belt.

On overhead cam four-cylinder engines that drive the water pump off the rubber timing belt, the timing belt cover must be removed to get to the belt. Locate the belt *tensioner* (a little pulley that holds the belt tight) and loosen the adjustment bolt to relieve tension. Do *not* remove the belt unless it's absolutely necessary to replace the pump, otherwise you'll be faced with the added task of realigning the camshaft timing marks.

4. Disconnect the hoses from the water pump. When the lower hose is disconnected, coolant might gush out of the engine block, so have your bucket handy.

5. Unbolt the water pump and remove the pump. *Caution:* On General Motors front-wheel-drive V6 engines, the water pump bolts extend through the timing cover to hold the cover in place. If guide pins are not used to hold the cover in place, it might break the seal and result in an oil leak.

6. Scrape away all the old gasket material from the pump mating surface, then wipe it dry.

7. Apply gasket sealer to both sides of the new pump gasket and position the gasket on either the replacement pump or the engine. If you are us-

127

ing RTV silicone caulk instead of a gasket, apply a 1/8-inch bead of sealer along the pump mating surface and all around the bolt holes and water passages. Be careful not to smear the sealer during installation.

8. Mount the new pump on the engine, and install and tighten the bolts. Note: coat the threads of any bolt that extends into the water jacket with gasket sealer or pipe dope to prevent leaks.

9. Replace all the components you had to remove in reverse order. Make sure the belts are properly tensioned.

10. Refill the cooling system, start the engine, and check for leaks.

CHANGING A DEFECTIVE THERMOSTAT

Tools Required. Wrench, pliers, funnel, bucket.

Parts Needed. New thermostat; thermostat gasket; gasket sealer (or RTV silicone sealer in place of a gasket).

How Often. When the engine is overheating because the thermostat is sticking shut, if it is not reaching normal operating temperature because the thermostat is stuck open, or to install a warmer- or cooler-rated thermostat.

Location. The thermostat is located inside a housing where the upper radiator hose connects to the engine (Figs. 11-6 and 11-7).

What To Do. To check the thermostat, remove the radiator cap and start the engine while it is cold. Looking inside the radiator you should see no movement of coolant. After the engine has run for five minutes or so, the upper radiator hose should start to feel hot signaling that the thermostat has opened and the coolant is now circulating through the system. Inside the radiator you should also see coolant movement. If there is no movement

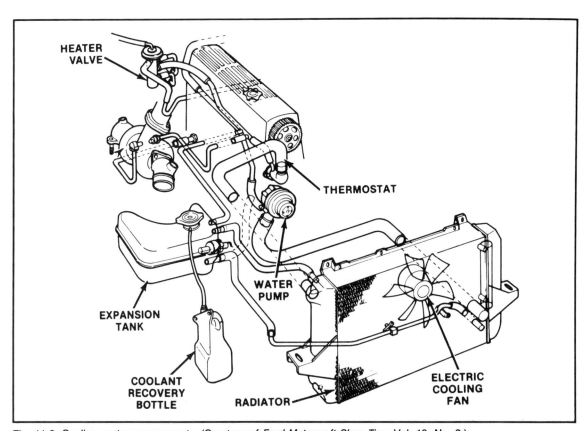

Fig. 11-6. Cooling system components. (Courtesy of *Ford Motorcraft Shop Tips,* Vol. 19, No. 2.)

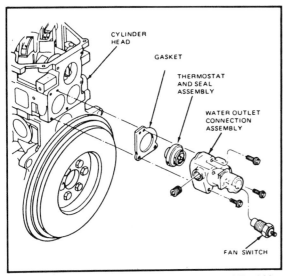

CYLINDER HEAD
GASKET
THERMOSTAT AND SEAL ASSEMBLY
WATER OUTLET CONNECTION ASSEMBLY
FAN SWITCH

Fig. 11-7. Thermostat replacement. (Courtesy of Ford Motor Company.)

and the engine starts to overheat, or if there is flow immediately upon starting a cold engine, the thermostat is defective and should be replaced.

A suspicious thermostat can also be tested by removing it from the engine and dropping it into a bucket of near boiling water. It should be closed when cold, opened once it hits the hot water, then closed again after it's been removed and allowed to cool.

To Replace the Thermostat:

1. Drain some coolant out of the cooling system. You do not have to completely empty the radiator. Drain only enough coolant so the level is below that of the thermostat.

2. Remove the two bolts that hold the thermostat housing to the engine, then pull the housing loose. There is no need to disconnect the upper radiator hose unless it makes the housing difficult to remove.

3. Note the position of the thermostat in the housing (which side faces up), then remove the thermostat. Test it in hot water, if necessary, to confirm whether it is defective.

4. Scrape all the old gasket material from both the housing and engine mating surfaces. Position the new thermostat in the housing or engine

with the heat-sensing element *toward* the engine.

5. Apply a coat of gasket sealer to both sides of a new gasket, then position the gasket and reinstall the housing. If using RTV silicone sealer, run a 1/8-inch bead of sealer along the mating surface of either the engine or housing.

6. Tighten the housing bolts. Do not apply too much torque because the cast aluminum housing can be easily cracked.

7. Refill the cooling system, start the engine and run it at fast idle until the new thermostat opens and coolant starts to flow. Replace the radiator cap, let the system build up pressure, and check for leaks.

FIXING A COOLANT LEAK

Tools Required. None.

Parts Required: Tube of cooling system sealer or a tube of radiator epoxy.

How Often. Leaks should be plugged as soon as they are discovered to prevent loss of coolant and overheating.

Location. Coolant can leak from just about anywhere in the cooling system. The most vulnerable parts are the hoses and water pump. Leaky water pumps and hoses cannot be fixed with stop-leak additives, They must be replaced.

External leaks are the easiest to notice because they leave puddles under the vehicle. Leaks often occur at the freeze plugs on the side of the engine block, at the water pump, thermostat housing, intake manifold or head gasket, and at the radiator. Pinhole leaks in any of these components can usually be plugged by adding a can of sealer to the cooling system. Large leaks are more difficult to seal.

Unless a radiator leak was caused by an outside puncture or vibration cracking, it usually indicates advanced corrosion within the radiator. A sealer might plug the leak, but sooner or later the radiator will have to be recored (new center section installed) or replaced.

Internal coolant leaks are harder to diagnose because they do not leave puddles or other visible clues. A low coolant level with no visible leakage might be a sign of such a problem. A weak radiator pressure cap can also allow coolant loss, so try replacing the cap. Internal leaks can be diagnosed with a pressure tester that applies pressure to the system. The same equipment can be used to test the radiator cap.

Internal leaks occur in the engine or radiator. Coolant can be lost through leaks in the head gasket, cracks in the cylinder head or engine block, or through the intake manifold gasket. Because antifreeze and oil do not mix, a coolant leak into the engine can cause extensive damage to piston rings, cylinders, and bearings. On most vehicles with automatic transmissions, an oil cooler for the transmission fluid is located inside one end of the radiator. If the cooler develops a leak, coolant can enter the transmission fluid lines and contaminate the fluid. This can ruin a transmission. Internal leaks, like external leaks, often respond to cooling

system sealers. Because of the serious nature of the leak, the cause should be investigated and repaired.

What To Do. To temporarily plug a small leak in the cooling system, open the radiator cap (when the engine is cold) and pour in a can of sealer. Follow the product directions.

To repair a small leak in a radiator, first drain the radiator. Clean away all paint, dirt, or grease from the leaky area with a wire brush or sandpaper. If it's an aluminum radiator, use a stainless steel wire brush. Leaks can be sealed in copper/brass radiators by soldering. You will need a propane torch or a soldering iron to get the radiator hot enough to accept the solder. An electric hand soldering gun doesn't produce enough heat for this kind of work.

To patch a hole in an aluminum radiator, you will have to use epoxy because aluminum can't be

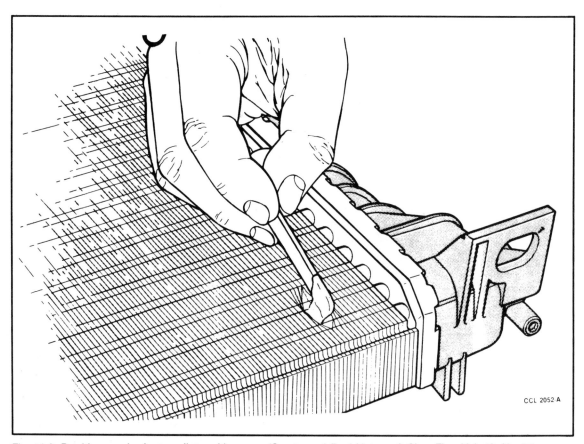

Fig. 11-8. Patching an aluminum radiator with epoxy. (Courtesy of *Ford Motorcraft Shop Tips*, Vol. 19, No. 2.)

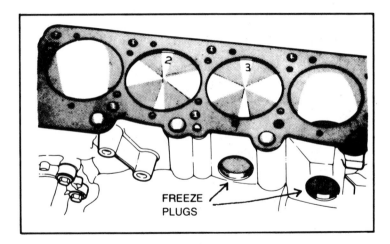

Fig. 11-9. Freeze plugs are located along the side of the engine block. (Courtesy of Chrysler Corporation.)

FREEZE PLUGS

soldered. After cleaning the damaged area, mix the epoxy and use it to fill the hole. Allow the epoxy to cure before refilling the system (usually half an hour) (Fig. 11-8).

For repairing a leaky freeze plug, you'll need a hammer and drift (or large screwdriver). The hardest part of the job is getting at the freeze plug, because on many engines the plugs are not visible and are difficult to reach. Use the hammer and drift or screwdriver to drive the plug out of its hole.

Pounding in on one side of the plug will usually cause the other side to pop out. The plug can then be pried from its hole. Clean the hole, then apply a liberal coating of sealer to the sides of the hole and new plug and drive in the new plug. Make certain the plug goes in straight or it won't seal. One type of replacement plug uses an expandable rubber grommet to seal the hole. All you do is position the plug in the hole and tighten a bolt (Figs. 11-9, 11-10, and 11-11).

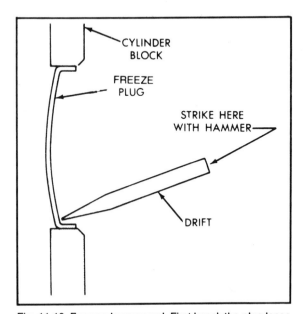

CYLINDER BLOCK

FREEZE PLUG

STRIKE HERE WITH HAMMER

DRIFT

Fig. 11-10. Freeze plug removal. First knock the plug loose with a drift by pounding in at the bottom or side. (Courtesy of Chrysler Corporation.)

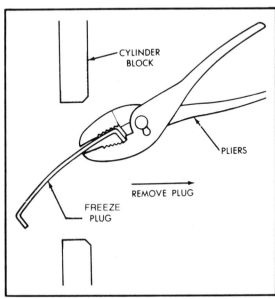

CYLINDER BLOCK

PLIERS

REMOVE PLUG

FREEZE PLUG

Fig. 11-11. As one side of the freeze plug tips in, the other side should tip out making removal easy. (Courtesy of Chrysler Corporation.)

REPLACING A RADIATOR OR HEATER HOSE

Tools Required. Screwdriver, pliers, razor blade or knife, bucket, funnel.

Parts Needed. New radiator hose; new clamps; antifreeze, if the cooling system is low or needs changing.

How Often. Hoses should be replaced if found to be leaking, mushy, brittle, cracked, or chafed.

Location. Two radiator hoses connect the radiator to the engine: an upper hose and a lower hose. The upper is usually the easier of the two to replace. Depending on the application, the vehicle might have two or more heater hoses. Front-wheel-drive engines in particular seem to have an abundance of hoses to route coolant to the radiator core. On some vehicles, the heater supply and return hoses are all the same diameter; on others, one hose may be slightly larger or smaller.

What To Do. This job is best done with the engine cold.

1. Drain the radiator. Open the radiator drain plug and drain the coolant into your bucket. Loosen the clamps on the hose to be replaced. *Caution:* if the lower radiator hose is being replaced, coolant will probably gush out of the engine as soon as the hose is disconnected. Have your bucket handy.

2. Pull the old hose off its fittings. Hoses tend to corrode in place and not pull loose easily. It helps to twist the hose while pulling. If that fails, use a razor blade or knife to slit the hose.

3. Clean the corrosion off the hose fittings before installing the new hose. If replacing a radiator hose, note which end goes where. On many vehicles the hose has different diameters at each end. With heater hoses, cut the new hose to the same length as the old. If you need more length to prevent chafing, add a few inches. Slide the hose clamps onto the new hose, then slide the new hose into place. Do not use grease or gasket sealer between the hose and its fittings.

4. Tighten the clamps. Do not overtighten as doing so can cut the rubber. Refill the cooling system, start and run the engine while adding coolant to get all the air out of the system, then replace the radiator cap and check for leaks.

REPLACING A DRIVE BELT

Tools Required. Wrenches, large screwdriver, pry bar or breaker bar.

Parts Needed. New drive belt. To make sure you get the right replacement belt, it helps to take the old belt to the parts store and compare both width and length.

How Often. Belts should be replaced if frayed, heavily cracked, or otherwise damaged. Belts can also be replaced as a preventive maintenance measure every three to four years.

Location. The drive belts are on the front of the engine and are used to drive various engine accessories (water pump, alternator, power steering pump, air pump, and air conditioning compressor) (Fig. 11-12).

What To Do. To replace a *serpentine* belt (a flat rubber belt that "snakes" around the front of the engine to drive all the accessories), all you have to do is find the automatic belt tensioner and pry it back to relieve tension. This can be done with a half-inch drive breaker bar or large screwdriver. If the routing of the belt is not included on the underhood tune-up decal, pay close attention to which way the belt runs as you replace it.

To replace a conventional V-belt, just loosen the accessory pivot bolts and adjustment bolt to relieve belt tension. Once the bolts are loose, push the accessory toward the engine to create enough slack to slip the belt off the pulleys. If the belt you want to replace is behind other belts. You will have to remove the outer belts first. Slip the new belt into the appropriate pulley grooves, pry out on the accessory, and tighten the pivot and adjusting bolts while maintaining tension. A belt is correctly tensioned if it deflects about half an inch when pushed down firmly midway between the two furthest pulleys. Overtightening a belt so it's as tight as a banjo string shortens the life of the belt and puts added stress on accessory shaft bearings.

When prying out on an accessory to tension a belt, use the leverage lugs on the bracket or pry against the bracket itself if possible. Never pry on a power steering pump because the thin metal housing can be damaged. Be extremely careful when prying against the aluminum housing on an alter-

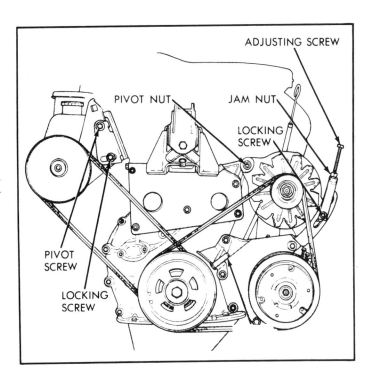

Fig. 11-12. Drive belt pulleys, pivots, and adjustment points. (Courtesy of Chrysler Corporation.)

nator, air pump, or air conditioning compressor or you are liable to damage the casting.

When you've finished installing the belt, make a note of the date and mileage in your maintenance record for future reference (Figs. 11-13 and 11-14).

INSPECTING AND
REPLACING SHOCK ABSORBERS

Tools Required. Wrenches, lug wrench (if removing the wheel is necessary to reach the shocks), spring compressor (if replacing most struts), jack, safety stands.

Parts Needed. A pair of replacement shocks or struts.

How Often. The shocks should be inspected as part of a regular maintenance checkup, when greasing the chassis (or when doing any other kind of under-vehicle work), or when ride quality seems to be deteriorating. They should be replaced if found to be worn or leaking fluid.

Location. Shock absorbers or struts are at every wheel on the suspension. Bolts at both the top and bottom hold the shock or strut in place.

What To Do. To inspect shocks, the bounce

test is hard to beat. Push down on the bumper at one corner of the vehicle and rock the vehicle up and down, then let go. A good shock should stop

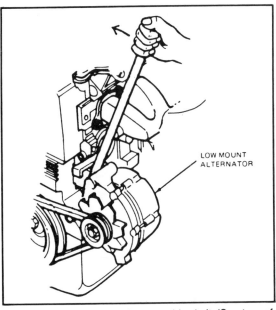

Fig. 11-13. Tightening an alternator drive belt. (Courtesy of Ford Motor Company.)

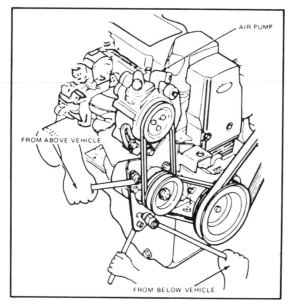

Fig. 11-14. To tighten the belts on some accessories, special lugs might be provided. (Courtesy of Ford Motor Company.)

the bouncing immediately. If it looks as if you've discovered perpetual motion, the shock on the nearest wheel is bad and needs to be replaced. Repeat the test for each corner of the vehicle.

Symptoms of worn shocks include a bouncy ride, wheel hob and vibration after hitting bumps, bottoming over bumps, and sometimes a cupped-wear pattern on the tires. Most shocks weep a small amount of fluid, but if a visual inspection finds a

shock coated with oil, the seals are probably shot and the shock needs to be replaced.

To Replace Front Shocks:

1. Set the parking brake, and place the transmission in park (automatic) or gear (manual). Block the rear wheels to prevent the vehicle from rolling. On some vehicles, it may be necessary to remove the front wheels to get to the shocks. If this is the case, pry off the hubcap, loosen the lug nuts, then raise the vehicle and remove the front wheels.

2. Raise the front of the vehicle and support it on safety stands. Make sure the stands are positioned so they won't interfere with shock replacement.

3. Unbolt the upper and lower shock mounts. To reach the upper bolts, it might be necessary to work from above through access holes in the inner fender panels. The bolts will usually be rusted tight, so if penetrating oil and heat from a propane torch fail to loosen them, plan on hacksawing or chiseling off the fasteners.

4. Position the rubber bushings on the new shock, then slip it into place and install the upper mounting hardware first to hold it in place. Then connect the lower end and tighten the fasteners. The fasteners should be snug, but not so tight as to squash the rubber bushings out of shape.

5. Make a note of the date and mileage at which the shocks were replaced in your maintenance record (Figs. 11-15 and 11-16).

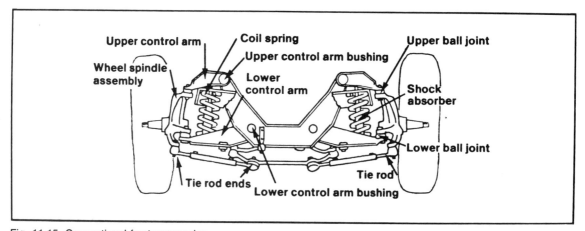

Fig. 11-15. Conventional front suspension.

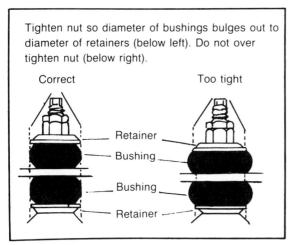

Tighten nut so diameter of bushings bulges out to diameter of retainers (below left). Do not over tighten nut (below right).

Correct   Too tight

Retainer

Bushing

Bushing

Retainer

Fig. 11-16. Shock absorber bushing installation.

To Replace Rear Shocks:

1. On front-wheel-drive vehicles, put the transmission in Park (automatic) or gear (manual). On rear-wheel-drive vehicles, the front wheels must be blocked to prevent the car from rolling once the rear end has been raised.

2. Removing the rear wheels isn't usually necessary, but if there's no other way to reach the upper shock mounts, pop off the hub cap and loosen the rear lug nuts. Then raise the car and take off the wheels (Fig. 11-17).

3. Raise the back of the car and position your safety stands under the rear axle or control arms. This is absolutely necessary on vehicles with coil spring rear suspensions, because once the shocks are removed the axle can drop down, allowing the springs to fall out (which is how you change the rear springs) (Fig. 11-18).

4. Unbolt the shock from its upper and lower mountings and remove the shock. On some vehicles, the upper shock mounts can only be reached through access holes in the trunk or luggage compartment. Install the rubber bushings on the new shocks, then position each new shock on its mounts, install the remaining mounting hardware, and tighten the fasteners.

5. Make a note of the date and mileage at which the shocks were replaced in your maintenance record.

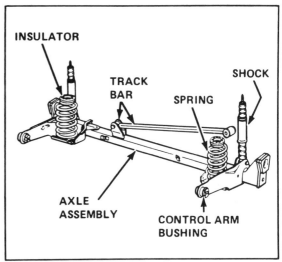

Fig. 11-17. Typical rear suspension on a front-wheel-drive vehicle.

REPLACING A MACPHERSON STRUT

Replacing a MacPherson strut might be beyond the abilities of some do-it-yourselfers. On many vehicles, coil springs are used around the struts to support the vehicle. To disassemble the strut, a spring compressor must be used. A compressor can usually be rented, but it must be used correctly so the spring doesn't slip out of its grip. The brake lines have to be disconnected on some applications

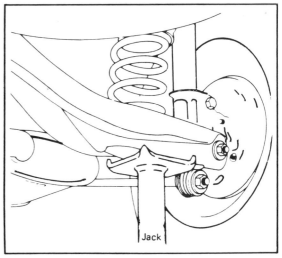

Fig. 11-18. Support the axle or lower control arm when removing the rear shocks.

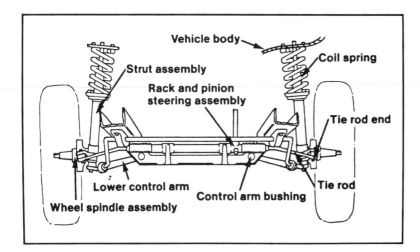

Fig. 11-19. MacPherson strut front suspension.

to remove the strut, which means you'll have to bleed the brakes afterward to get the air bubbles out of the lines. On many vehicles, the front wheels also have to be realigned following strut replacement. This is something a do-it-yourselfer cannot do very accurately, so it might be better to let a professional mechanic handle the entire job (Fig. 11-19).

Struts fall into two broad categories: rebuildable and non-rebuildable. A *rebuildable* strut is one that has a removable nut on the strut housing. Once the nut has been removed, the strut can be disassembled and a new shock cartridge installed. As a rule, all import struts, with the exception of Honda, are rebuildable (Fig. 11-20). *Non-rebuildable* struts are those with welded housings. They are

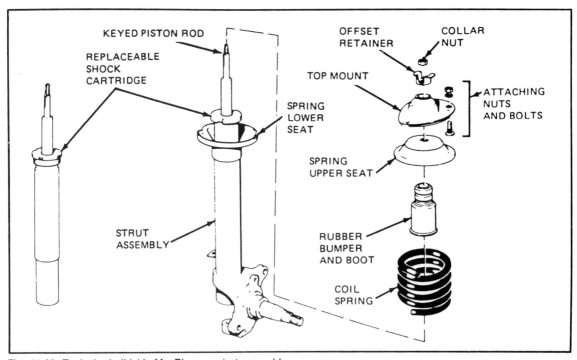

Fig. 11-20. Typical rebuildable MacPherson strut assembly.

sealed shut, so there is no way to rebuild them. The entire strut assembly (minus the spring and upper mounting hardware) must be replaced if the unit goes bad. This is the type of strut found on most American-built cars.

Tools Required. Wrenches, jack, safety stands, lug wrench, spring compressor (most applications), pry bar, brake bleeder wrench (some applications), pipe wrench.

Parts Needed. Pair of replacement struts or strut cartridges.

How Often. The struts should be inspected as part of a maintenance checkup, when greasing the chassis, or when ride quality seems to be deteriorating. They should be replaced if found to be leaking or if the vehicle fails a bounce test.

Location. MacPherson struts are an integral part of the suspension. They are not a hang-on item like an ordinary shock absorber, so removal is a bit more complicated. The upper end of each strut attaches to a bearing plate inside a tower on the inner fender panel. The lower end of the strut attaches to the steering knuckle or is an integral part of the front wheel spindle, depending on the application.

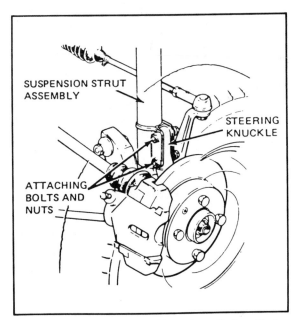

Fig. 11-21. Lower strut mount with camber adjustment bolts. (Courtesy of Chrysler Corporation.)

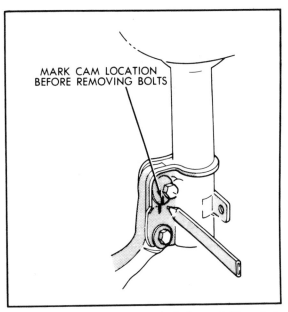

Fig. 11-22. Mark the camber bolts before unbolting strut.

What To Do.

1. Set the parking brake and place the transmission in park (automatic) or gear (manual). Raise the vehicle and support it on safety stands so the front suspension hangs free. In other words, place the safety stands under the center crossmember or subframe so the lower control arms hang down.

2. If the lower end of the strut can be unbolted from the steering knuckle, use a piece of chalk to mark the approximate locations of the bolts (Figs. 11-21 and 11-22). These bolts determine wheel alignment, so you can eliminate the need to realign the wheels if, and only if, the original struts can be rebuilt and the bolts are returned to their original positions. If the strut is non-rebuildable and is replaced, the geometry of the new strut might vary from that of the old strut, requiring the wheels to be realigned. If the strut cartridge can be replaced without having to remove the strut from the car, this step can be skipped.

3. On some vehicles the upper strut mount is movable and is also used to adjust wheel alignment. If the mounting holes are elongated to provide adjustment, mark the relative position of the upper mount with chalk so you can realign the strut during installation. Again, if a new strut is used, the

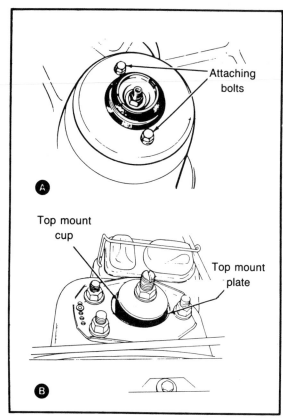

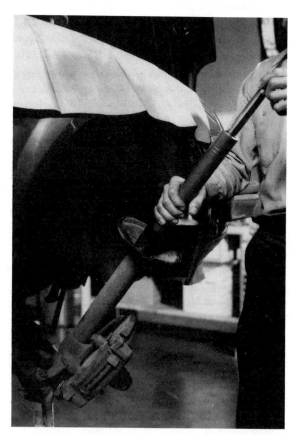

Fig. 11-23. Typical upper strut mounts.

old alignment marks will probably be of little value (Fig. 11-23).

4. Go to the top of the strut and *loosen but do not remove* the large piston rod nut. One or two turns should be sufficient. You will need a hex wrench or locking pliers to hold the strut shaft while you loosen the nut. These nuts are often put on with considerable torque, so plenty of muscle might be needed to break it loose. The reason for not removing the nut is because it holds the entire strut assembly together. Take it off and there will be nothing to hold the coil spring in place.

5. On many import cars with rebuildable struts it is often possible to disassemble the strut without having to completely remove it from the vehicle (Fig. 11-24). Once the upper end is unbolted from the strut tower, the suspension can be pushed down and the strut swung out from under the fender. A spring compressor can then be used to

disassemble the strut for cartridge replacement. If this is the case, skip the next step.

6. Unbolt the lower end of the strut from the steering knuckle. It will probably be necessary to pry the strut out of the knuckle. If the strut is part of the steering spindle, the front wheel, brake caliper, rotor, and hub must be removed and the lower ball joint separated from the control arm to allow complete strut removal. The brake hose might also have to be disconnected from the strut.

7. Unbolt the upper mounting plate from the strut tower in the inner fender panel, but leave the big center nut in place, for the time being, to hold the strut assembly together.

8. With the strut out of the vehicle or swung out from under the fender, install the spring compressor and squeeze the spring until pressure is off

Fig. 11-24. On some vehicles the strut doesn't have to be removed for rebuilding. Just push the suspension down and tilt the strut out from under the fender for disassembly.

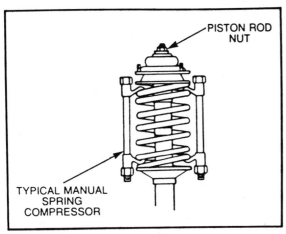

Fig. 11-25. Spring compressor.

the upper mounting plate (Fig. 11-25). Make sure the spring compressor has a good grip on the spring and won't slip, then remove the large nut from the top of the strut rod. You can now disassemble the upper hardware from the strut. Pay close attention to the order of disassembly so you can reassemble the parts correctly.

9. If the strut is the rebuildable variety, use a pipe wrench to remove the large nut from the top of the housing (Fig. 11-26). Then pull out the old shock cartridge or wet elements from inside. Drain out the old oil and save about a shot glass full for reuse; use automatic transmission fluid if all the old fluid is gone.

10. Drop a new cartridge into the strut housing, pour the fluid from the shot glass in around the cartridge until the fluid level is within an inch or two of the top. The fluid helps cool the strut by transferring heat from the cartridge to the housing. Don't fill the housing all the way to the top because the fluid needs room to expand when it gets hot.

11. Install a new housing nut on the strut (provided with the cartridge), then reassemble the strut assembly. Don't release the spring compressor until the upper mounting plate is in place and the large center nut has been tightened.

12. Replace the strut in the vehicle (or shove the upper end back under the fender), realign any alignment marks on the upper and lower mounts (if the same strut housing is being reused), and torque all fasteners firmly in place.

13. If the suspension is adjustable and a new strut housing was installed (which is the case with most American-built cars), the front wheels will need to be realigned.

14. If the brake line had to be opened to disconnect it from the strut, the brakes must be bled to remove all air bubbles from the lines.

15. Make a note of the date and mileage at which the struts were replaced in your maintenance record for future reference.

INSPECTING RACK AND PINION STEERING

Tools Required. None.

How Often. The steering gear should be inspected as part of a regular maintenance checkup, when lubricating the chassis, or when steering-related problems are noticed such as wander, noise or harshness.

Location. The rack and pinion steering housing is mounted on the crossmember of many vehicles and on the firewall of others. The unit is connected to the steering column by a flexible coupling (which should also be checked for looseness or corrosion), and is held in place by clamps or bolts through rubber grommets.

What To Do. Have a friend rock the steering wheel back and forth while the front wheels are

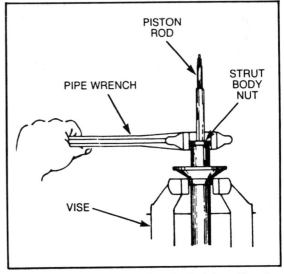

Fig. 11-26. Removing the strut housing body nut with a pipe wrench.

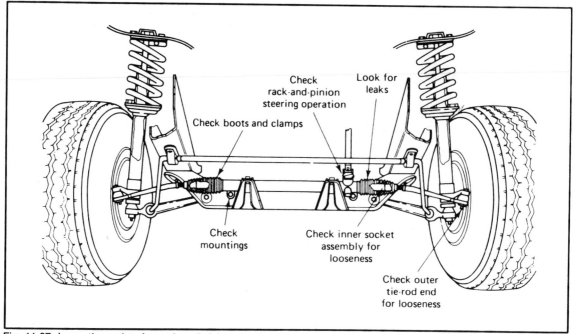

Fig. 11-27. Inspection points for rack and pinion steering.

on the ground. Having the wheels on the ground loads the steering linkage and is more likely to reveal any looseness in the system. Look under the hood or under the vehicle and watch the rack and steering linkage for any looseness. If the rack moves with respect to the firewall, or if any of the linkage connections appear to be loose, repairs are in order. The inspection points are illustrated in Fig. 11-27.

Outer tie rod ends are simple to replace (Fig. 11-28). Counting the number of threads that show on the tie rod and measuring the distance between the front and back edge of the front tires with respect to one another can eliminate the need to realign the front wheels when a new tie rod is installed (otherwise "toe" alignment must be reset). Worn inner tie rods are a different matter. This requires removing the entire steering unit from the car for disassembly and repair. This job is better left to a professional.

Any movement between the steering housing and chassis while the steering is being rocked means the rubber mounting bushings or grommets have shrunk, split, or deteriorated. These can some-

times be replaced without having to remove the rack from the chassis. Another item to watch for with rack and pinion steering is the condition of the rubber bellows on both ends of the steering gear. These must be tight and free from cracks to protect the steering gear from dirt and moisture. If split or damaged, the bellows should be replaced immediately to save the steering gear from damage. You can do this yourself by disconnecting the outer tie rod from the steering arm, unscrewing the tie rod end, and slipping off the old bellows.

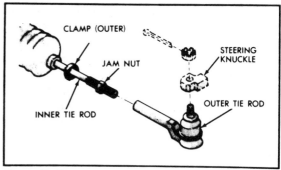

Fig. 11-28. Tie rod end replacement. (Courtesy of Chrysler Corporation.)

140

On vehicles with power steering squeeze the rubber bellows to see if the steering seals are leaking fluid. If they "squish" plan on a steering overhaul soon. Rebuilding power racks is a difficult procedure even for a highly experienced mechanic. Most simply replace a leaky rack with a new or remanufactured unit.

CHANGING A FLAT TIRE

Tools Required. Jack, lug wrench (or preferably a torque wrench), safety stand (recommended). For a roadside emergency, reflectors or safety flares are recommended.

Parts Needed. A spare tire. *Caution:* many vehicles have "temporary" rather than full-size spare tires (to save weight and space). If your spare tire is a temporary, it should only be used in an emergency to get you to the nearest service facility. Temporary spares are not designed for high-speed driving (limit speeds to under 45 mph) nor are they capable of long-distance travel (most recommend a maximum distance of 50 miles or less). Temporary spares are also of a much smaller size than the other tires on your vehicle, so they can have an adverse effect on handling, steering, and braking.

How Often. A tire should be changed when it won't hold air. If you know you have a slow leak, it is a good idea to change it and/or have it repaired before taking any long trips to save yourself the hassle of changing it along side the road somewhere—which invariably happens in the rain and at night.

Location. Hopefully, there's a spare tire full of air in the trunk or luggage compartment of your car, or if you have a van or pickup, under the cargo compartment. Hopefully, there is also a complete jack and a lug wrench. Some temporary spares are the folding variety, which means they have to be inflated with a pressurized canister. If your car has one of these, hopefully, you'll also find a fully charged canister. If you lack any of the above, hopefully, you'll have a quarter to call for a service truck.

What To Do.

1. With the vehicle parked on level ground, set the parking brake and put the transmission in park (automatic) or gear (manual). If the tire is being changed along the highway, turn your emergency flashers on.

2. Remove the spare tire and jack from the trunk or storage compartment. Pop off the hubcap with the lug wrench or a screwdriver. Then loosen each lug nut half a turn. The weight of the vehicle will help hold the wheel while you loosen the nuts. If you try to loosen the nuts once the wheel has been raised, the wheel will probably turn or you'll tip the vehicle off the jack.

3. Raise the vehicle with the jack until the wheel is about an inch or so off the ground. A bumper jack will have a hook or tang that grips the bottom of the bumper or fits into a slot in the bumper. A scissor jack lifts the vehicle from underneath. There is usually a small *locator pin* or notch under the side of the car to position the jack (Fig. 11-29).

4. Finish removing the lug nuts, then remove the wheel. Mount the spare tire on the hub and finger-tighten the lug nuts. Keep your hands, arms, and feet out from under the tire and out from be-

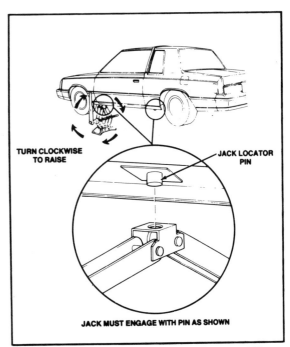

TURN CLOCKWISE TO RAISE

JACK LOCATOR PIN

JACK MUST ENGAGE WITH PIN AS SHOWN

Fig. 11-29. Lift points with a scissor jack. (Courtesy of Chrysler Corporation.)

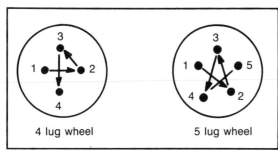

Fig. 11-30. Wheel lug tightening patterns.

tween the tire and fender (in case the jack slips while you're changing the tire).

5. Lower the car to the ground, then finish tightening the lug nuts as shown in Fig. 11-30. Tightness will vary, but 60 to 70 foot/pounds of torque is generally about right for most cars and light trucks.

6. Replace the hubcap, then put the flat tire, lug wrench, and jack back in the trunk or storage compartment. Take the flat tire to a nearby service facility to have it repaired.

Note: A small puncture in the tire tread can be easily patched or plugged, but a puncture or split in the sidewall can't. That doesn't mean the tire is no good. Installing a tube inside a tubeless tire can often salvage a tire with sidewall damage as long as the sidewall damage isn't too extensive.

ROTATING THE TIRES

Tire rotation is a means of extending the life of your tires by evening out the wear. If your vehicle has a full-size spare, it should be included in the rotation to increase tire life 20 percent.

On front-wheel-drive vehicles, there is some disagreement as to whether rotation saves rubber. The back tires on a FWD car can sometimes last 60,000, 70,000, or even 80,000 miles. The front tires, however, wear out much faster than those on a rear-wheel-drive car, because they have the added burden of driving the vehicle as well as steering it. Tire life can be as little as 30,000 to 40,000 miles. Rotating the tires will spread the wear out to all the tires. But what is the least expensive— to replace only the front tires at 40,000 miles or to

replace all the tires at 50,000 miles? That is for you to decide.

Tools Required. Jack, lug wrench (or torque wrench), *four,* safety stands. The entire vehicle must be raised off the ground to rotate all four tires.

How Often. Every 15,000 to 20,000 miles.
What To Do.

1. Pop off all the hubcaps, then loosen all the lug nuts half a turn.

2. Raise all four wheels off the ground and position a safety jack under each corner of the vehicle to support it.

3. Now remove each wheel and place it on the ground next to the hub from which it was removed. If your vehicle has a full-size spare and you're including the spare in the rotation pattern, take it out of the trunk and lay it on the ground.

4. Now rotate the tires. Both front wheels should be remounted on the back (same side). Both back tires should be mounted on the opposite side on the front. This is called an "X" rotation. The front wheels go to the back and the back ones change sides and go to the front. If the spare is included in the rotation, use this scheme: mount the spare tire on the left front (drivers's side) hub; put the right rear (passenger's side) tire in the trunk;

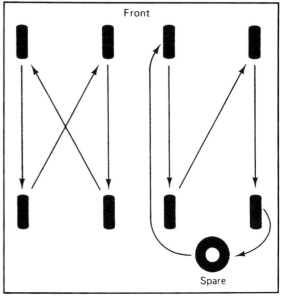

Fig. 11-31. Tire rotation patterns with and without the spare.

the right front tire moves to the rear (same side); and the left rear tires crosses over to the right front.

5. Finger-tighten all the lug nuts, then lower the vehicle to the ground and finish tightening all the nuts. Replace the hubcaps and put the jack and lug wrench back in the trunk or storage compartment.

6. Make a note of the mileage at which you rotated the tires in your maintenance record for future reference (Fig. 11-31).

REPLACING A BATTERY

Tools Required. Voltmeter or hydrometer for checking charge, wrench, pliers, screwdriver, cable puller, and gloves (for replacement).

Parts Needed. A new battery of equal or greater capacity than the battery being replaced.

How Often. The charge level of the battery should be checked as part of a general maintenance check if the alternator warning light comes on or if the engine is sluggish to crank. A low battery can be recharged, but a worn battery must be replaced.

Location. The battery is usually located in the front of the engine compartment, but on some vehicles it might be hung underneath, under the back seat, or in the trunk or storage compartment.

What To Do. To inspect a battery, first note its external appearance. If it has crud all over the top and the posts are corroded, clean it. A mixture of baking soda and water is good for scrubbing off the outside, but don't let any of the mixture get into the battery because it will neutralize the acid. If you find any cracks in the battery case (and the case appears to be leaking acid), the battery can sometimes be salvaged by patching the crack with silicone sealer.

Water level is extremely important. Checking the water level is covered in Chapter 5, but to summarize, the level must be kept above the cell plates or the plates will dry out and lose their ability to produce electricity—even when water is added later. Add only distilled water to the battery. Sealed-top batteries don't allow water, to be added so if the level is low, it means the battery is nearing the end of its useful life (it can also signal overcharging by the alternator).

Load Test:

The best way to check a battery's condition is with a load test. A load test applies a heavy drain on the battery to see if it can deliver adequate current. It is an excellent means of determining whether the battery is getting old and needs to be replaced. A load test normally requires special test equipment (a carbon pile) to place a controlled load on the battery. After the load has drained some of the battery's current, a voltage reading is taken to see how far the battery has dropped. Some retail automotive service centers (like Sears, Wards, or K-Mart) will often test a battery at no charge but you can approximate your own load test by doing the following:

1. The battery must be at least 75 percent charged before doing a load test. If the battery is low, recharge it first.

2. Disconnect the high-voltage coil wire from the distributor cap and ground it on the engine block. This will prevent the engine from starting while you crank it.

3. Connect a voltmeter to the battery posts, then crank the engine for 15 seconds (this loads the battery) while observing the voltage reading. If the voltage output of the battery remains about 9.6 volts, the battery still has plenty of life. But if it drops below 9.6 volts, it's getting old and will need replaced soon.

Checking Battery Charge

There are several ways to determine whether or not a battery is fully charged. One method of checking battery charge is with a hydrometer reading. If the battery has removable caps, a hydrometer can be inserted into each cell to take a sample of the cell acid. A hydrometer tests the density or *specific gravity* of the water and acid mixture inside the battery. The higher the specific gravity reading, the higher the concentration of acid and the higher the state of charge. A fully charged battery should read 1.265 or higher at 80 degrees Fahrenheit (you have to compensate the readings for variations in temperature by adding 0.004 for each 10 degrees above 80 or subtracting 0.004 for each 10 degrees below 80). Cell readings should not vary

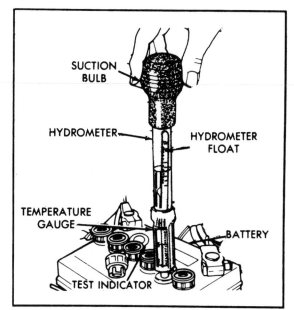

Fig. 11-32. Checking battery charge with a hydrometer. (Courtesy of Chrysler Corporation.)

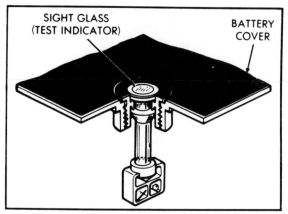

Fig. 11-33. A built-in battery hydrometer. (Courtesy of Chrysler Corporation.)

more than .050 from cell to cell, and if the readings are 1.225 or lower (75% charged) the battery should be recharged (Fig. 11-32).

On some sealed-top batteries, a built-in hydrometer is provided for determining battery charge (Fig. 11-33). If a green dot is visible in the window, it means the battery is at least 75 percent charged. If the circle appears black or dark, it means the battery needs to be recharged. If the window appears yellow or clear, it means the water level inside the battery has dropped below the charge indicator and that the battery will need to be replaced (Fig. 11-34). Do not try to recharge a battery with a low water level, the danger of explosion is too great.

A third method of determining battery charge is with a voltmeter (Table 11-1). If the voltage reading is low (ignition and all accessories must be off when taking the reading), the battery should be recharged.

Battery Replacement:

If a battery is aged, won't hold a charge, or lacks sufficient capacity to start the engine relia-

bly in cold weather, it needs to be replaced. To replace the battery:

1. Disconnect both battery cables from the battery posts or side terminals. The cable clamps will be difficult to remove from the posts, so use a puller or insert a regular screwdriver into the clamp to pry it open. Do not pry against the top of the battery or jerk on the cables, because doing so can sometimes break off the battery posts. Make sure the ignition switch and all accessories are off before you disconnect the battery. If a cable is disconnected while the key is on, it creates a *voltage spike* in the electrical system that could fry a microchip in the electronics.

Note: When the battery is disconnected, all electronic devices in the vehicle will lose their memory and will need to be reset.

2. Disconnect the clamp that holds the battery in place. In some vehicles, you might also have

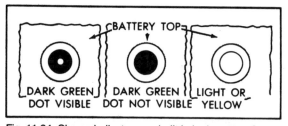

Fig. 11-34. Charge indicator on a built-in hydrometer. Green means the battery is at least 75% charged, dark means it needs recharging, light or yellow means low water level. (Courtesy of Chrysler Corporation.)

Table 11-1. Determining Battery Charge with a Voltmeter.

Charge Level	Specific Gravity	Battery Voltage
100%	1.265	12.7
75%	1.225	12.4
50%	1.190	12.2
25%	1.155	12.0

to remove a fender brace or ductwork before you can extract the battery from its tray. Put on gloves to protect your hands, grasp the battery by its corners or bottom (not sides), and carefully lift the battery off its tray. Squeezing the side of plastic case batteries can sometimes force liquid out of the battery. Be careful because the battery is filled with a mixture of water and acid. If you spill acid on your skin, it can burn or blister (flush with cold water and/or neutralize with baking soda). If you get acid on your clothes, the next time they're washed holes will magically appear. It is a good idea to use a battery carrying strap or handle.

3. While the battery is out of the vehicle, clean the battery tray with baking soda and water

to remove any corrosion or residue. If the tray is metal, you might want to spray it with paint or a rubberized undercoating to help protect it against corrosion.

4. Install the replacement battery by following the above steps in reverse order (Fig. 11-35).

RECHARGING A BATTERY

Tools Required. Wrench, battery charger, battery cable puller.

How Often. Recharge the battery if it is found to be less than 75% charged.

Location. The battery is usually located in the front of the engine compartment, but on some vehicles it can be hung underneath, under the back seat, or in the trunk or storage compartment.

What To Do.

1. To protect your vehicle's electrical system and electronic components, disconnect one or both battery cables from the battery. Make sure the ignition switch and all accessories are off before you disconnect the battery.

2. If the battery caps are removable, remove

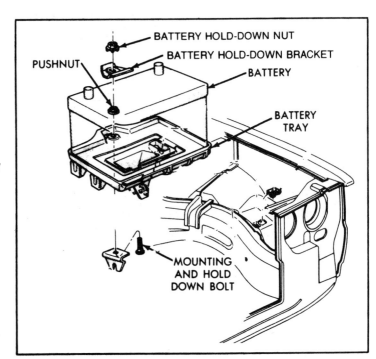

Fig. 11-35. Battery replacement. (Courtesy of Ford Motor Company.)

the caps so the battery can more easily vent hydrogen gas while charging.

3. Connect the positive charger lead to the positive (+) battery post, and the negative charger lead to the negative (−) battery post. Do not plug in the charger until the battery connections have been made.

4. If your charger has a 6-volt/12-volt selector switch, set it at 12-volts for a car or light truck battery (unless the vehicle is an antique and has a 6-volt system), then plug in the charger and turn it on.

How long it takes the battery to recharge depends on the output of your charger and how far the battery was run down. A 6-amp charger, for example, can take 12 hours or more to completely recharge a dead battery.

Most do-it-yourself battery chargers have *automatic taper charging rates,* which means the charger gradually reduces the charging rate as the battery approaches full charge. The battery will be fully charged when the charge rate on the meter drops to a constant minimum value. You can also check the state of charge by taking a hydrometer reading, by checking the built-in charge indicator in the top of the battery (if it has one), or by disconnecting the charger and taking a digital voltage reading.

While the battery is charging it will bubble hydrogen gas. Do not smoke near a charging battery and keep clear anything that produces an open flame or sparks. If the battery is brought indoors for charging, it should be recharged in an open area with adequate ventilation to prevent a build-up of hydrogen gas.

SAFELY JUMP STARTING A DEAD BATTERY

Tools Required. Jumper cables, protective eye covering.

How Often. When the engine fails to crank because of a low or dead battery.

Location. The battery is usually located in the front of the engine compartment, but on some vehicles it can be hung underneath, under the back seat, or in the trunk or storage compartment.

What To Do. *Caution:* batteries give off explosive hydrogen gas. Keep cigarettes, sparks, and open flames away from the battery at all times. A spark can cause the battery to explode. Avoid leaning directly over the battery while making jumper connections and wear eye protection.

1. Open the hood on your vehicle and pull the vehicle that is going to give you a jump as close as possible to your vehicle so the jumper cables will reach. The vehicles must not touch.

2. Make sure both vehicles have compatible batteries (jump a 12-volt battery with another 12-volt battery only—not a 24- or 6-volt). *Caution:* On late model vehicles with computerized engine controls, do not attempt to jump start with a booster charger that puts out over 16 volts. Excessive voltage can damage the electronics.

3. Determine which battery terminals are positive (+) and negative (−). The negative battery cable will attach to a ground such as the engine block or an accessory mounting bracket. The negative cable might also be made from uninsulated braided wire. The positive cable attaches to the starter or starter solenoid switch (which is located on the inner fender of some vehicles). Battery cables are sometimes color-coded (positive is red, negative is black), but you can't always rely on this, because many cables are not color coded (both might be black, for example) or the original cables might have been replaced. This step is extremely important because if you accidentally reverse the battery connections, you can damage the charging system and/or melt the jumper cables.

4. On batteries with removable caps, open the caps and look inside (use a flashlight if necessary) to see that the water is not frozen. *Never* use a match or cigarette lighter. Do not attempt to jump start a frozen battery. On sealed-top batteries, check the charge indicator to make sure it is not yellow or clear. This means the water level is too low inside the battery. Jump starting is not recommended. Replace the battery.

5. Connect the jumper cables as follows: the red cable to the positive (+) terminal on the good battery and the black cable to the negative (−) ter-

minal on the good battery; then connect the other end of the red cable to the positive terminal on the dead battery. *Do not* connect the black cable directly to the negative post on the dead battery (Fig. 11-36). The final jumper cable connection will likely spark when you make it. Make the final connection to a good ground such as the engine block, an accessory mounting bracket, the frame, or even the bumper. This will keep the spark away from the battery and greatly lessen the chance of a battery explosion.

6. DO NOT try to start the engine immediately. Run the engine on the vehicle with the good battery at fast idle for 5 minutes or so to pump some life into the dead battery. Then try to start the engine. This will make starting much easier and it will prevent draining the good battery or overloading (and possibly damaging) the charging system on the other vehicle.

If the engine fails to crank or cranks very slowly, it means the jumper cables are not making good connection. Try wiggling the jumper clamps to improve their contact. Don't crank the engine for more than 30 seconds without pausing a minute or two to let the starter cool off. Continuous cranking is very hard on the starter and it is possible to burn it out if cranked too long.

7. As soon as the engine starts, disconnect the jumper cables.

TESTING AND REPLACING AN ALTERNATOR

Tools Required. Voltmeter for testing, wrench, large screwdriver, and pliers for replacement.

Parts Needed. A replacement alternator (new or rebuilt) if the alternator is bad.

How Often. Charging system output should be tested whenever the alternator warning light glows, the charging gauge shows discharge, or the

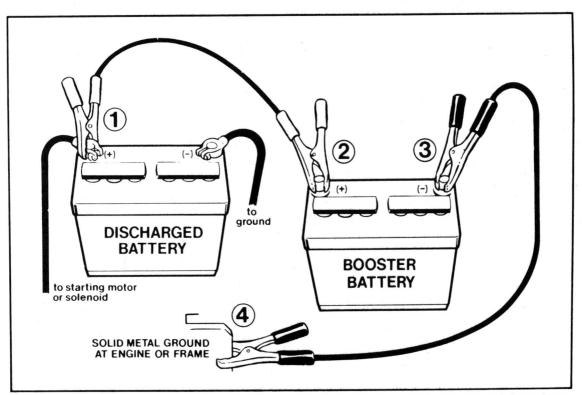

Fig. 11-36. Safe jump starting procedure. Attach the jumper cables in the sequence shown. (Courtesy of Chrysler Corporation.)

voltage gauge reads low. Dim headlights, a discharged or dead battery, and slow or sluggish cranking are other symptoms of possible alternator problems.

Location. The alternator is driven by a belt of the engine crankshaft pulley. It is a round aluminum housing with wires attached to the back and usually a finned pulley on front.

What To Do. Don't replace anything until you've checked charging system output first. A slipping drive belt can sometimes prevent the alternator from charging properly, as can a poor ground connection or corroded battery cables. In late model cars with solid state regulators, a poor ground at the regulator can result in overcharging.

Checking Charging System Output:

1. First check base battery voltage by taking a reading while the ignition and accessories are off. It should be approximately 12.4 volts or higher if the battery is at least 75% charged.

2. Turn the headlights on and leave them on for about a minute to drain some current out of the battery.

3. Then start the engine and immediately take a second voltage reading at the battery. If the charging system is working correctly, you should see a reading of 13.5 volts to 14.8 volts (the voltage will vary depending on the application). If the voltage reading is the same as before, the charging system is not working and the alternator or voltage regulator might be defective. If the voltage is higher than 14.8 volts, the voltage regulator is causing the alternator to overcharge the battery.

In many late-model vehicles (General Motors, Ford, and many imports), the voltage regulator is incorporated into the alternator, so if either is bad the alternator must be replaced. On applications where the two are separate, alternator output can be checked by *full fielding* the alternator. This procedure bypasses the voltage regulator and causes the alternator to put out its maximum current. This test is best performed by a professional with the proper equipment. If you suspect alternator problems, remove the unit and take it into an auto parts store. Many can bench test the unit for you to determine whether it is defective.

Alternator Replacement:

1. With the ignition and accessories off, disconnect the negative (−) ground cable from the battery.

2. Remove the wires from the back of the alternator. Note where each wire goes so you can reconnect them to the replacement alternator correctly (Fig. 11-37).

3. Loosen the alternator pivot and adjustment bolts to relieve tension on the drive belt. Then push the alternator toward the engine and remove the belt. On engines with serpentine belts, find the automatic belt tensioner and pry it back using a half-inch drive handle, pry bar, or large screwdriver to remove the belt. Remove the pivot and bracket bolts and remove the alternator.

4. When mounting the new alternator, install the pivot bolts first, then the bracket bolt. Slip the drive belt around the pulley, pull the alternator out to tension the belt, then tighten the pivot and bracket bolt.

5. Reconnect the wires to the back of the alternator, and then reconnect the battery cable. Start the engine and check charging voltage to confirm the new unit is working properly. It is not uncommon to find a defective rebuilt alternator. Most auto

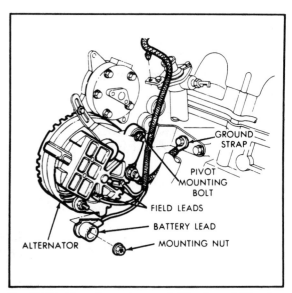

Fig. 11-37. Alternator replacement. (Courtesy of Chrysler Corporation.)

parts stores will not give a refund on electrical parts, but they should give an exchange.

Note: If the battery is dead or is very run down, it's a good idea to recharge the battery with a battery charger prior to starting the engine. This will reduce the initial load on the new alternator and better enable it to keep the battery properly charged.

REPLACING A STARTER

Tools Required. Wrenches, pliers, possibly a jack and safety stands.

Parts Needed. A replacement starter (new or rebuilt).

How Often. The starter should be replaced if a fully charged battery with clean terminals and good cable connections fails to crank the engine or cranks it very slowly.

Location. The starter is located at the back of the engine. The starter drive engages teeth on the flywheel when cranking the engine. The starter can be easy or extremely difficult to reach depending on the vehicle. In some instances, it might be necessary to disconnect an exhaust pipe, remove ductwork, unbolt a motor mount, or even raise the engine slightly to replace the starter.

What To Do. Before you condemn the starter, consider the following. If you hear a "whirring" noise but the engine does not crank, it means the starter is spinning but is not engaging the flywheel. The starter drive or solenoid that pushes the drive forward to engage the flywheel might be defective. Missing teeth on the flywheel can also prevent the starter from cranking the engine. If the starter only "clicks," it might indicate a low battery or a loose or corroded battery cable connection. Check battery charge and condition first.

If nothing happens when you turn the key, it might mean there is a defect in the ignition switch, ignition wiring, or solenoid. With the key on, use a jumper wire to try shorting the positive battery cable to the solenoid starter connection. If the starter now cranks, the problem is in the wiring circuit. If nothing happens, the solenoid fails to "click", it is probably defective. The starter is usually bad if it does nothing at all (even when

jumped), if it cranks very sluggishly, or if it makes grinding noises while cranking.

If you take the old starter to an auto parts store, they can often bench test it for you to see if it works. Or you can bench test it yourself by using battery jumper cables. Connect the negative cable to the starter housing and touch the positive cable to the positive connection on the starter motor. The motor should spin if it's good.

To Replace the Starter.

1. Disconnect the battery ground cable from the battery.

2. Unbolt and remove anything that obstructs access to the starter. In many instances, the starter can only be removed from under the car. This will require you to jack up the car (be sure to support it with safety stands).

3. Disconnect the wires from the starter motor paying careful attention to which wires go where.

4. Unbolt the starter. Most starters are held in place by either two or three bolts. Be careful as you remove the last bolt because the starter is heavy and it will fall. Put your hand under it to support it as the last bolt is removed. Then remove it from the vehicle (Fig. 11-38).

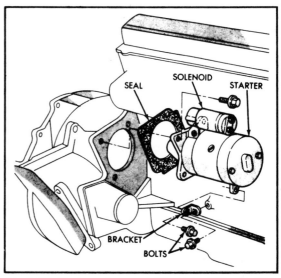

Fig. 11-38. Starter replacement. (Courtesy of Chrysler Corporation.)

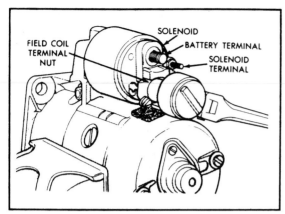

Fig. 11-39. Replacing a defective starter solenoid. Note: only some starters have a solenoid mounted as shown. (Courtesy of Chrysler Corporation.)

☐ While the starter is out wipe away any grease or dirt that has accumulated around the starter hole. If only the solenoid or starter drive is defective, either of these components can be replaced without having to replace the entire starter.

☐ Install the replacement starter following the above steps in reverse order (Figs. 11-39 and 11-40).

FIXING AN OIL LEAK

Cork/rubber gaskets tend to harden and shrink with heat and age. Inferior quality gaskets tend to be more brittle and short-lived than better quality gaskets, but even the best gaskets will eventually lose their ability to hold a seal. Many engines use

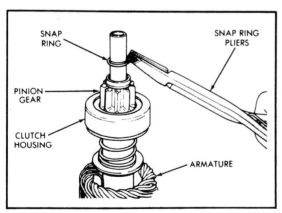

Fig. 11-40. If only the starter drive mechanism is faulty, it can be replaced separately. (Courtesy of Chrysler Corporation.)

beads of silicone rubber instead of gaskets to seal certain components. If properly applied, the material holds up as well as any gasket. But if the mating surface isn't perfectly clean, or if the sealer is put on too thin or too thick, leaks can develop. Rubber crankshaft seals eventually leak as a result of continued wear.

There are various crankcase additives that claim to fix leaks by causing gaskets and seals to swell. Such products give marginal benefits at best, and they cannot stop a leak through a cracked or broken gasket.

Tools Required. Wrenches, scraper, screwdriver, clean rag, gear puller (for front crankshaft seal), floor jack or engine hoist (for rear crankshaft seal).

Parts Needed. Replacement seal, gasket or a tube of RTV silicone sealer.

How Often. A leaky seal or gasket should be fixed as soon as discovered.

Location. Common leak points for engine oil include the valve cover gaskets, timing cover gasket, oil pan gasket, and front and rear crankshaft seals.

What To Do. To fix a leaky gasket, remove the cover or component over the gasket and scrape away all the old gasket debris from both mating surfaces. Wipe the surface clean with a rag. Then apply gasket sealer to both sides of the new gasket, position it, and reinstall the cover. The important point here is to tighten down the cover bolts evenly and to not overtighten them. If you put too much pressure on the gasket, you'll break it or force it out of position (Fig. 11-41).

To fix a leaky gasketless joint that is sealed with RTV silicone, remove the cover, scrape away all the old sealer, and wipe both mating surfaces clean. Replacement gaskets are made for many applications that originally used silicone sealer. You can go ahead and install a gasket, or you can apply a 1/8-inch bead of silicone (Fig. 11-42) on one mating surface (go around all bolt holes). Be careful not to smear the sealer during installation. Then replace the cover and tighten the bolts. It's a good idea to wait 30 minutes or so before starting the engine to give the silicone adequate time to cure.

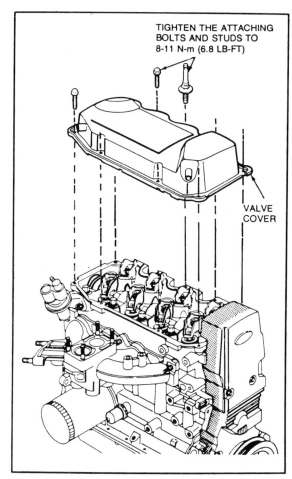

TIGHTEN THE ATTACHING
BOLTS AND STUDS TO
8-11 N-m (6.8 LB-FT)

VALVE
COVER

Fig. 11-41. Replacing a leaky valve cover gasket. (Courtesy of Ford Motor Company.)

On late model engines with oxygen sensors, you should use a low-volatile type of silicone. Ordinary silicone contains chemicals that can be drawn through the engine and sometimes foul the oxygen sensor.

To replace a leaky seal on the front of the crankshaft, you have to remove the crank pulley before you can pry out the seal. You will need a gear puller to get the crank pulley off. Don't pound on the pulley or you'll damage it. If the surface of the crankshaft is worn, slip-on repair sleeves are available to restore the surface. A special seal is usually required if a sleeve is used.

Leaky rear main oil seals are tough to replace, because it involves dropping the oil pan and unbolt-ing the rear main crankshaft support cap inside the engine. On some vehicles, the flywheel has to come off, which means pulling the transmission or engine. On most vehicles today, there isn't enough room to drop the oil pan unless the engine is unbolted from its mounts and jacked up. You might consider having a professional perform this task. Once the pan has been dropped and the rear main support cap removed, the upper portion of the rear seal can be removed by pushing it out with a small screw-driver or piece of wire. The new seal must be care-fully positioned, the rear main support cap replaced (and torqued to specifications), and the oil pan put back in place.

RELINING THE BRAKES

Relining brakes means replacing the worn drum shoes or disc brake pads with new or rebuilt parts. A complete brake job usually involves new linings, rebuilding or replacing the hydraulic components in the brakes (calipers and wheel cylinders), resur-facing the drums and rotors, replacing springs and other brake hardware, and finally, bleeding the brake lines.

In many instances, however, a vehicle doesn't require a complete brake job. If the hydraulic com-ponents are not leaking fluid and the drums and ro-tors appear to be in good condition, you can often get by with a simple relining.

Tools Required. wrenches, pliers, screw-driver or brake adjusting tool, jack, safety stands, lug wrench (or torque wrench), hammer, possibly a drum puller (for rear drum brakes).

Parts Needed. Replacement disc brake pads and/or drum brake shoes; tube of high-temperature brake grease; can of liquid brake parts cleaner; tube of antisqueal compound (for disc brake pads).

How Often. Brakes should be relined if the linings are worn within 1/16 inch of the rivet heads (riveted linings) or are thinner than 1/8 inch in thick-ness (bonded linings). If the linings are allowed to wear until there is metal-to-metal contact, it will damage the drum or rotor. Brake squeal does not mean the linings are worn and need to be replaced, unless it is a metallic scraping sound.

Location. On vehicles with disc brakes the

Fig. 11-42. Applying a 1/8-inch bead of silicone sealer to an engine cover.

pads are held in position by the calipers. To replace the pads the calipers usually have to be removed. Calipers can be removed with ordinary hand tools. On vehicles with drum brakes, the drums have to be removed to gain access to the shoes. This might require a drum puller if the drums fit tightly.

What To Do. Because of the tremendous variation in brake designs, you should refer to a shop manual for specific step-by-step disassembly and installation instructions. The brakes are a critical safety item on your vehicle and if improperly installed, they will not be able to stop the vehicle. If you feel the least bit uneasy about tackling a brake job you would better have the job performed by a competent mechanic.

Front Disc Brake Reline:

1. Set the parking brake and put the transmission in park (automatic) or gear (manual). Remove the hubcap and loosen the lug nuts on the wheel half a turn.

2. Raise the front of the vehicle and support it on safety stands, then remove the wheel.

3. The brake caliper will be held in place by a pair of bolts, screws or lock pins. Remove the

bolts, screws, or pins and drive out any retaining springs or clips that might also be used to secure the caliper (Fig. 11-43).

4. Lift the caliper off the rotor and remove the inner and outer pads (Fig. 11-44). It might be necessary to pry the pads back away from the rotor slightly with a screwdriver before the caliper will come off. There is no need to disconnect the brake hose from the caliper, but do not let the caliper hang by the hose, this can damage the hose. Lay the caliper on the suspension control arm or support it with a short piece of wire.

5. Carefully inspect the caliper for leaks around the piston seal. If no leaks are detected and the rubber dust seal is not cracked or loose, the caliper can be reused.

6. Inspect the condition of the rotor next. The rotor should be flat with no visible warpage (discolored streaks radiating outward often indicate high spots, check for flatness by laying a ruler across the face of the rotor). The rotor must also be free from heavy cracking, deep grooves, or scratches. If the surface is rough, the rotor should be removed and taken to an auto parts store for resurfacing on a brake lathe (if worn beyond limits,

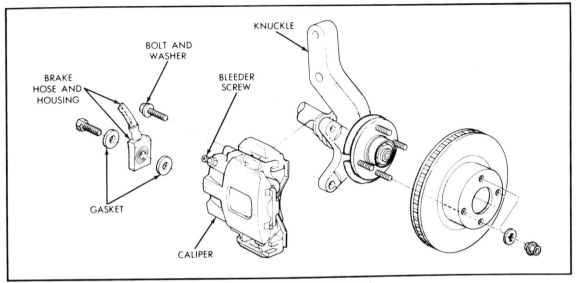

Fig. 11-43. Typical disc brake assembly. (Courtesy of Chrysler Corporation.)

however, the rotor will have to be replaced). If the surface is smooth, take some medium-grit sandpaper and swirl polish both faces. This will help seat the new pads and reduce squealing.

7. Install the new pads in the caliper, making certain you don't get the inner and outer pads mixed up if there is a difference. If the pads use retaining clips, bend the tangs to hold the pads se-

curely. Applying antisqueal compound to the backs of the pads (metal side, not friction side) can help reduce squealing.

8. Reposition the caliper and pads on the rotor and install the caliper mounting hardware. On vehicles with *floating* (self-centering) calipers, the point where the caliper slides on its mount as well as the mounting pins should be lubricated with high-

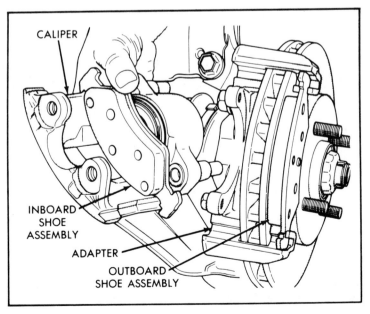

Fig. 11-44. Replacing the disc brake pads once the caliper has been removed. (Courtesy of Chrysler Corporation.)

temperature brake grease. New pins are recommended because the old pins are usually corroded.

9. Torque the caliper fasteners to the required specs, replace the wheel, lower the vehicle, and tighten the lug nuts.

10. Pump the brake pedal several times before driving to establish a firm pedal. Avoid panic stops for the first few hundred miles to prevent the new pads from glazing and squealing.

11. Make a note of the mileage at which the linings were replaced in your maintenance record for future reference.

Rear Drum Brake Reline:

1. Do not set the parking brake. This will lock the drum and make it impossible to remove. Leave the transmission in neutral and block the wheels to keep the vehicle from rolling.

2. Remove the hubcap, loosen the lug nuts on the rear wheels half a turn, then raise the back of the vehicle and support it on safety stands. Remove the rear wheels.

3. Remove the brake drums (Fig. 11-45). If the drums don't remove easily, try backing off the brake shoes by turning the adjuster star wheel inside the drum (turning the drum by hand will tell you if your adjustments are making the shoes tighter or looser). If the drum is stuck to the axle, penetrating oil and heat from a propane torch can loosen it, as can pounding on the face of the drum with a rubber (not metal) hammer. Never try to beat the drum off, because doing so will usually crack or chip the drum. If all else fails, use a drum puller.

4. Inspect the inside of the drum. If the drum is smooth and free from cracks, it can be reused. If the friction surface is scored or grooved, the drum should be taken to an auto parts store for resurfacing on a lathe.

5. Clean the drums and brakes with liquid brake cleaner. *Caution:* Brake linings contain asbestos. Breathing the dust can be hazardous, so don't blow off or vacuum dirty brakes. Use only an approved liquid cleaner.

6. Check the wheel cylinder for possible leaks. If none are detected and the rubber seals look

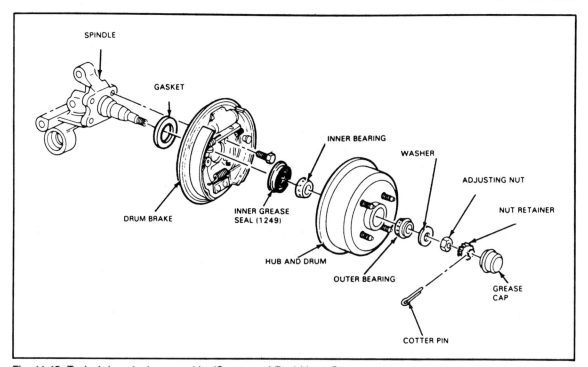

Fig. 11-45. Typical drum brake assembly. (Courtesy of Ford Motor Company.)

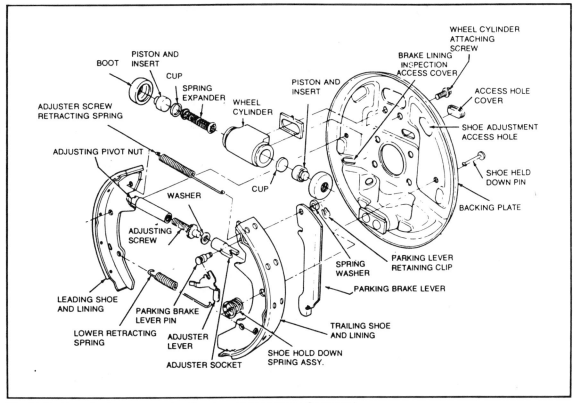

Fig. 11-46. Drum brake components. (Courtesy of Ford Motor Company.)

good, rebuilding or replacing the wheel cylinder should not be necessary.

7. Make a careful mental note (or make an actual sketch) of how the brake shoes and parts go together (Fig. 11-46). Pay special attention to the self-adjuster mechanism and parking brake levers. Do one wheel at a time to avoid mistakes (if you forget how it goes together, just look at the other wheel).

8. Disassemble the brakes. Using pliers to first release the spring clips that hold the shoes works best. Then you can slide the shoes off their pivot to relieve tension on the return springs (Fig. 11-47). Be careful not to overstretch springs or bend anything. Any brake hardware that is corroded should be replaced.

9. Apply high-temperature brake grease to the high points on the brake backing plate where the shoes ride. The self-adjuster star wheel should also be disassembled, cleaned, and greased.

10. Install the new shoes on the backing plate. Hook up the parking brake cable, then position the

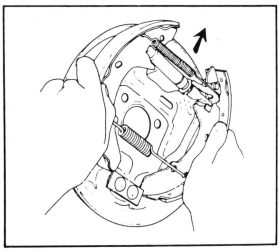

Fig. 11-47. Removing the brake shoes. (Courtesy of Ford Motor Company.)

155

self-adjuster mechanism and install the return springs.

11. Put the drum back on (you might have to back off the adjuster for the shoes to clear the drum), then readjust the brakes so a slight drag is felt when the drum is turned by hand.

12. It is highly recommended that the brakes be bled after relining to remove moisture-contaminated fluid and air bubbles from the system.

13. Put the wheel back on and lower the car. Pump the brake pedal several times, then go for a test drive.

14. Make a note of the mileage at which the brakes were relined in your maintenance record for future reference.

BLEEDING THE BRAKES

This is the process of removing old brake fluid and air bubbles from the brake system by pumping fresh fluid through the lines. Air bubbles are undesirable because they compress when pressure is applied resulting in a low or spongy-feeling pedal.

The brake system uses a special kind of alcohol-based hydraulic fluid. The fluid is *hydroscopic,* which means it tends to absorb moisture over time (never leave a can of brake fluid open for this reason). Moisture lowers the boiling point of the fluid and causes internal corrosion in the brake system. That is why the fluid should be replaced when brake repairs are made or every few years, whichever comes first. The best kind of brake fluid is silicone-based. It won't absorb moisture and doesn't require periodic replacement, but it costs several times as much as ordinary brake fluid.

Tools Required. Jack, safety stands, wrench to fit bleeder screw on calipers and wheel cylinders, short length of clear plastic tubing, clear glass jar.

Parts Needed. Can of fresh brake fluid (DOT 3 rating for passenger cars/light trucks).

How Often. Every two to three years, or when the brakes are relined.

Location. Bleeder screws are located on the backs of the disc brake calipers and drum brake wheel cylinders. *Caution:* bleeder screws are often corroded and break off when you try to loosen

them. They are quite small, so it doesn't take much effort to twist one off. If the screw doesn't loosen under light pressure, apply a small amount of penetrating oil around the base of the screw. If you do break one off, the caliper or wheel cylinder will have to be removed and drilled out to accept a new bleeder screw.

What To Do. The correct procedure for bleeding the brakes on most RWD vehicles is to start at the furthest wheel. Do the right rear brake first, then left rear brake, followed by the right front and left front brakes. On a FWD vehicle with a diagonally-split brake system, do the right rear then left front brake, followed by the left rear and right front brake.

1. Raise the vehicle and support it on safety stands. For RWD vehicles, raise the back end of the vehicle first. Bleed the rear brakes, then lower the back end and raise the front end to do the front brakes. In FWD vehicles, you'll have to raise and lower each end of the vehicle twice as you go from the right rear brake to the left front, followed by the left rear and right front brakes. In some instances, you might be able to reach the bleeder screws without having to raise the vehicle. Turning the front wheels out often provides enough room to reach the bleeder screws on the calipers.

2. Remove the lid or caps from the master cylinder. Be careful that no dirt, grease, or debris falls into the fluid reservoir.

3. Begin the bleeding process with the rear brake or brakes first.

4. Connect one end of the plastic tubing to the bleeder screw, and insert the other end of the tube into a glass jar about one-third full of brake fluid (this will prevent air bubbles from being siphoned back into the system once the bleeder screw is opened). The bleeder screw is a nipple-shaped screw that resembles a grease fitting. On drum brakes, it's usually located at the top on the back of the drum backing plate.

5. Carefully loosen the bleeder screw (go easy on the wrench or you'll break it off). Back it out about a turn and a half. This opens the hydraulic system.

6. Slowly depress the brake pedal to pump fluid through the system. As the old fluid is pumped out through the bleeder screw, it will usually be brown and dirty (an indication that the fluid is over-due for replacement). There might also be air bubbles, which you'll see in the plastic tubing. When you've pushed the brake pedal all the way to the floor, wait a few seconds then, let it up slowly. Continue pumping until clear fluid starts to flow through the line or until all the air bubbles are removed.

7. Check the fluid level periodically in the master cylinder to make sure it doesn't run out. Add fluid as needed during the bleeding procedure.

8. Close the bleeder screw once the line has been thoroughly bled, then move on to the next wheel and repeat the same process.

9. After all the lines have been bled, add fluid as needed to fill the master cylinder fluid reservoir, then replace the lid or caps.

10. Pump the brake pedal several times to make sure you have a firm pedal before driving the car. If the pedal is low, there might still be air in the lines. If this is the case, more bleeding is necessary to get all the air out. You should also recheck the bleeder screws to make sure they're all tight and none are leaking pressure.

RECHARGING THE AIR CONDITIONER

Tools Needed. Air conditioning recharging hose and valve kit, eye protection.

Parts Needed. One to three cans of Freon refrigerant.

How Often. Add Freon only when the system is low. A low system indicates a leak. All air conditioning systems leak a small amount of Freon, but if the system has lost its charge in less than a year, it indicates a significant leak. Recharging can make the system work temporarily, but eventually the new Freon will be lost unless the leak is repaired.

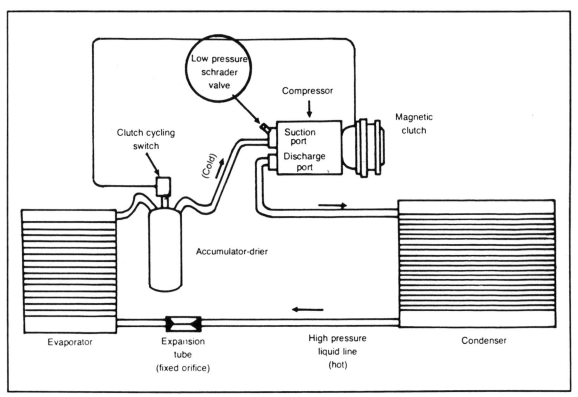

Fig. 11-48. The air conditioning system is recharged by feeding Freon vapor through the low pressure Schrader valve fitting. (Courtesy of Ford Motor Company.)

Do not overcharge the system. Adding too much Freon can reduce cooling efficiency and possibly damage the compressor.

You can tell when a system needs Freon by its reduced cooling output or by looking at the "sight-glass" on the receiver-drier (car manufacturers have unfortunately done away with this useful feature on many systems). If bubbles are visible in the sight-glass after the system has been running for five minutes, it indicates a low charge.

Location. Freon is added to the Schrader valve fitting on the low-pressure side of the system. This will be at the suction port on the compressor or a fitting on the suction line. You can tell the high-pressure line from the suction line by feeling the lines while the system is running. The high-pressure line is always hotter. *Caution:* Do not connect your recharge kit to the high-pressure side because the pressure could rupture the Freon can (Fig. 11-48).

What To Do. Make sure you've identified the suction line and located the proper fitting.

1. Start the engine and turn the air conditioner on high or maximum output.
2. Connect the recharging adapter valve to the can of Freon. Momentarily open the valve to blow any air or moisture out of the adapter hose (this is important to prevent air or moisture from entering the system). Screw the adapter hose onto the Schrader valve fitting on the suction line.

3. Open the valve on the can of Freon. Hold the can upright so only vapor enters the hose. For kits that tap into the side of the can, hold the can sideways so the vapor rises to the top and enters the hose. Holding the can in the wrong position can allow liquid to enter the hose, which could possibly damage the compressor.

4. Suction in the low-pressure side of the system will draw Freon vapor out of the can. When the can is empty, turn the valve off, and disconnect the adapter hose from the Schrader valve fitting.

5. Recheck the sight-glass or check the performance of the system. If it seems to need additional Freon, add another can. The maximum capacity of most systems is 2 1/2 to 4 cans of Freon the larger the vehicle, the larger the capacity of the system). If your efforts to recharge don't improve cooling output, take it to a professional mechanic for repairs. You should also have it checked for leaks if it doesn't hold a cooling charge for a full season.

Chapter 12

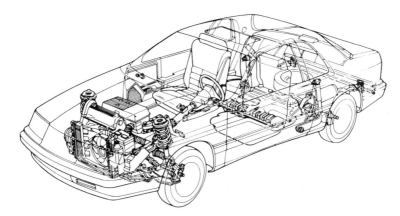

When You Need Professional Services

In spite of your desire to do most of your own maintenance and repairs, there will be times when you need the services of a professional. This chapter is included to help steer you clear of the "Mr. Badwrenches" of the world, and to hopefully get you better service and satisfaction for your repair dollar.

You have probably noticed that in describing some of the repair procedures in this book I have tried to warn you that some repairs are best handled by a professional mechanic. This includes complicated jobs such as troubleshooting a driveability problem on an engine with computerized controls. It also includes jobs for which most do-it-yourselfers lack the necessary tools and know-how, such as wheel alignment, overhauling an engine, or rebuilding a transmission. For jobs like these a professional mechanic is an absolute necessity (Fig. 12-1).

Other times the nature of the job makes doing it yourself less than appealing. Replacing an exhaust system, for example, is well within the abilities of most people. But if you do not want to spend half the day laying on your back sawing, pounding, and cursing, it is probably worth the few extra dollars a muffler shop would charge to install the sys-

tem in 20 minutes. Or let us say it is January, you live in Chicago, you do not have a garage, and your water pump goes out. You cannot put off the repair until spring, and the idea of standing out in the howling wind in 2 feet of snow to change the water pump gives you shivers just thinking about it. Who would not want to take their car to a professional mechanic under such circumstances?

Sometimes it's necessary and other times it is easier, more convenient, and less hassle to pay somebody else do the work. The quick-lube oil change outlets that have been springing up nationwide are a prime example of selling consumers convenience. All you do is pull in line and wait your turn. You pay $15 to $20 for a job you could do yourself for less than $7, but you do not have to get out of the car or even get your hands dirty. The same applies to muffler shops, brake shops, tire stores, tune-up shops, you name it.

HOW TO FIND
AND KEEP A GOOD MECHANIC

Let us say you are in need of the services of a mechanic for whatever reason. To whom do you

159

Fig. 12-1. The service bay has gone "high tech" right along with the changing technology under the hood. It often takes a diagnostic computer to determine what is wrong with the on-board computer—and that means you will need professional help to fix many of today's driveability problems.

go? There are thousands of mechanics and would be mechanics waiting to take your money. Whether you get your money's worth, however, will depend on the skill level of the person who does the work, the labor rate you are charged, the quality of the parts installed, and the promptness of the repair.

Mechanics are human beings, and like the people who work in any recognized profession, individual skill levels vary tremendously. There are extremely qualified people who can fix almost anything and fix it the first time. Then there are the "parts changers" who do not really understand the problems they are trying to solve. Their way of eliminating a problem is to replace first one component and then another until they eventually stumble upon the cure, or until the customer gets fed up and takes his or her vehicle someplace else. Even a good mechanic can make a mistake, but a hack mechanic will waste his customer's time and money on trial-and-error repair techniques.

What separates a good mechanic from a bad, therefore, is the ability to accurately diagnose the cause of a problem *before* repairs are made. That is the difference between repeated returns for subsequent repairs and getting your vehicle fixed right the first time. Misdiagnosis accounts for more "repair rip-offs" and misunderstandings than any conscious attempt to deceive or cheat the public.

A competent mechanic has the necessary training to cope with the problems he is likely to encounter. He will attend schools and shop clinics to upgrade his skills and to stay current with changing technology. In short, he will take his job and his responsibilities seriously and so will his employer.

How do you find a service facility that has competent mechanics? The following suggestions can help steer you to the right place.

Look for a service facility that displays the blue and white "Automotive Service Excellence" sign that says "We employ mechanics certified by the National Institute for Automotive Service Excellence."

The National Institute for Automotive Service Excellence—ASE (formerly NIASE)—is an indus-

160

try organization that certifies professional mechanics on a voluntary basis. Twice a year competency tests are offered to mechanics at testing centers nationwide. A mechanic has to correctly answer a high percentage (usually 70% or more) of the questions in a given category in order to receive certification in that repair specialty. The eight categories for cars and light trucks include engine repair, engine performance (tune-up), brakes, front end (suspension), electrical systems, heating and air conditioning, automatic transmission, and manual transmission/driveline. There are also equivalent categories for heavy-duty truck mechanics. Body repair mechanics can seek certification in painting/refinishing and body repair.

A mechanic who passes the test in any given category receives an ASE patch and certificate (look for the patch on his uniform and/or the certificate on the wall). Those who pass all eight automotive tests receive a special ASE patch with gold letters to signify their higher level of achievement.

The industry has tried to promote certification of professional mechanics as a means of preventing government licensing. Those who support voluntary certification say the tests are tougher and those who are certified are more likely to know what they are doing. Government licensing as a panacea for consumer complaints about repair rip-offs is no answer, because many mechanics would be licensed who are not competent (because of grandfather clauses and easier tests). Some cities have adopted shop licensing laws, but generally speaking, such laws have not reduced the number of returns and misrepairs.

Look for a service facility that promotes advanced training among its mechanics to keep their skills current. Automotive technology has undergone a tremendous revolution in the past decade, and there are a lot of working mechanics who do not know the first thing about computerized engine controls or electronic fuel injection. Their numbers are dwindling, but just because somebody is a mechanic does not make them an expert in things they have not been trained to service.

New car dealers usually send their top people to the automobile manufacturers' annual training schools to keep up with the new models, but they send only the top mechanics. The other mechanics do not receive as much training as a rule. If you take your car back to the dealer, it is possible the dealer will not assign the most qualified person to work on it.

Look for a service facility that is AAA (American Automobile Association) approved. AAA has an excellent certification and inspection program that requires a service outlet to maintain a high level of competency and to have certain types of repair equipment available. If a facility does not live up to the requirements, AAA will pull its seal of approval.

Look for independent repair garages that are members of a professional trade association such as ASA (Automotive Service Association). Trade associations tend to attract the cream of the crop, and are self-policing by expelling any member that fails to live up to the association's credo.

Look for service facilities that back their work with a written guarantee. The longer the guarantee, the more faith and confidence you can have in the repairs made.

Do not judge the competence level of a repair facility or its technicians by appearances. There is no assurance that a clean, neat shop with lots of shiny equipment and mechanics who look like Robert Redford is any better than some grease-pit garage staffed with Neanderthals. The proof is in the finished product, not in the polish.

Look for a repair facility with an outstanding reputation. Ignore any advertising claims or promises the shop might make, and listen instead to what your friends, relatives, or co-workers have to say. Word-of-mouth advertising is by far the best kind. So if you hear a name frequently mentioned as a place to go for repairs, heed the advice.

Look for a facility that specializes in the type of repairs you need. Specialists are often better equipped and educated to handle specific kinds of repairs (such as automatic transmissions, alignment, air conditioning, electrical work, import cars, etc.) than a shop that offers a wide range of services.

Do not equate high prices with high quality. True, some shops might command a higher labor rate because their mechanics are better and their services are in demand, but most shops simply charge what the traffic will bear. Paying a premium means nothing if you do not get your money's worth.

WHAT A PROFESSIONAL SHOULD DO FOR YOU

The ideal mechanic should do the following:

☐ Fix the problem correctly the first time.

☐ Give you a written estimate *before* he starts to work—and stick to it.

☐ Explain to you the nature of the problem and what's necessary to fix it.

☐ Appreciate your desire to have the problem fixed quickly so he does not tie up your vehicle needlessly.

☐ Replace only those parts he thinks really need to be replaced and advise you if he thinks other repairs might be necessary in the near future.

☐ Charge a fair price for his services.

☐ Give you a written guarantee for the work performed.

A mechanic and the service facility for which he works should never make you feel as if they are doing you a favor by working on your vehicle. Often you must make an appointment just to wait in line at some places. The service writer or advisor might be rude, the mechanic might not do all the items you instructed, and you might leave the shop with the feeling that you have been taken advantage of. New car dealers are notorious for such behavior, which is why many people never return to a dealer once their new car or truck is out of warranty.

One item you should never ask a professional mechanic to do is to install parts you do not buy from him. You would not walk into a restaurant with a bag of groceries and ask the chef to fix you a meal, so do not ask your mechanic to install parts you bought elsewhere.

Another mistake many people make is trying to tell the mechanic how to do his job. You do not go to a doctor with a self-diagnosis, so do not tell the mechanic what he should or should not do. He knows more about your vehicle than you do, so let him make the diagnosis and recommend the necessary repairs. Just describe the symptoms and answer his questions.

THE BEST REPAIR VALUE FOR YOUR MONEY

The best overall repair value for your money is often found at an independently owned repair garage or service station. The local garage or service station tends to be more in tune with the needs of their customers because they are a small operation. They do not have the advertising power of a franchise behind them or the guaranteed market of a new car dealer. Consequently, they try harder to please their customers. They usually only have a few mechanics, so you can talk directly to the mechanic to describe your problem. If you have a misunderstanding, you can usually deal directly with the owner.

As a rule, dealerships charge the highest per-hour labor rates—$40 to $50 per hour is not uncommon. Independent repair garages often charge considerably less—$25 to $35 per hour. Service stations and tire dealers charge the least—$20 to $30 per hour. For some types of repairs, the best deals can be found by going to the automotive service center at a large retail store (such as Sears, Wards, K-Mart, etc.). These outlets specialize in fast-moving or popular replacement items such as shock absorbers, batteries, and mufflers. But beware of the "hook." They will often lure you in with an advertised special, then try to sell you additional parts or sell you a higher-quality component.

There is no such thing as a $19.95 muffler installed. It is a hook to sell you overpriced pipes and clamps. By the time they are through with your car, you'll have spent $80, $90, $100, or more for a nearly complete system. The reason why no one ever gets a $19.95 muffler installed is because exhaust pipes corrode very rapidly. By the time the muffler is shot, the pipes probably are likely too, and need to be replaced. So when the mechanic tells you he cannot install a muffler because the pipes are shot, he's telling you the truth, and you end up spending a lot more than $19.95 for your muffler.

The same applies to the famous $19.95 wheel alignment. Shops would quickly go broke if all they made on wheel alignments was $19.95. The profit comes from replacing the worn parts they know they will find on 9 out of 10 vehicles. No one is trying to cheat you because most misalignment problems are caused by worn suspension components. So when the mechanic tells you your ball joints are shot and the tie rod ends have to be replaced, he is only doing his job. Once again, you end up paying a lot more than you originally expected.

Deals can still be found when it comes to shock absorbers, MacPherson struts, and batteries. As long as you stick to the item advertised and do not let the salesman talk you into the higher-priced versions, you will get a bargain.

HANDLING PROBLEMS AND MISUNDERSTANDINGS

No, the customer is not always right. Many motorists have suffered untold verbal abuse from rude service personnel because they dared to challenge a repair or an amount charged. The outcome of such encounters usually depends on the personalities involved. Get two hot-heads confronting one another and the sparks are bound to fly.

How should you handle problems and misunderstandings? You obviously have certain legal rights, but you should not have to threaten legal action if your vehicle is not repaired to your satisfaction. If your car was not fixed properly, bring it back and ask the service advisor and/or mechanic to take a second look. Try to explain the problem as best you can. Do not try to tell them how to fix it or what they did wrong. If they made an admitted mistake, the garage should correct it and not charge any more for redoing it (unless extra parts are required that were not originally replaced).

The problem arises when the garage will not admit the mistake. Free repairs are obviously not profitable, so there is a very strong tendency to cover one's mistakes. Getting a second opinion

from another garage would not do you any good, unless you are involved in a legal action. So try to resolve the problem without implicating blame.

If you run into a situation, in which your car has not been properly repaired and the garage will not cooperate, you have several courses of action.

If it is a new car dealer, contact the customer service representative with the local zone office. They can sometimes put pressure on a dealer. If that fails, you can write to the automobile manufacturer or take your problem to a consumer arbitration board. Arbitration boards have been set up as intermediaries to solve such conflicts as a means of avoiding the unnecessary expense and hassle of a legal battle. The decision of the arbitration board is usually binding on the dealer, but not on you. If you do not like their decision, you can always call a lawyer and take your case to the court.

☐ You can take your business elsewhere. Do not give the same place a second chance to take advantage of you.

☐ File a complaint with your local Better Business Bureau. It might not do any good, but at least it can serve as a warning to others that the garage in question has a bad reputation for customer service.

☐ You can pay by check, then stop payment. Or pay by credit card, then dispute the charge when it shows up on your monthly statement. By disputing payment you can sometimes force a repair facility to right a wrong. But repair facility managers are wise to such maneuvers. If you pay for a large repair bill by check or credit card, they will often make you sign a document that waives your right to dispute payment. If the garage owner goes to court and wins, he can have a mechanic's lien placed on the title of your vehicle. Unless you think you have a legitimate complaint and can prove it, avoid this tactic.

One way to avoid problems is to make sure you understand the coverages and limitations of any warranties or repair guarantees. If you do not understand your rights or the requirements of the warranty, ask before a problem develops.

Appendix A:

Additional Sources of Help

In the repair sections of this book, I have frequently recommended that you refer to a shop manual for specific service procedures, tune-up specifications and/or fastener torque requirements. With so much diversity and complexity in today's vehicles, it is impossible to write a generic service procedure that covers all the potential variations and exceptions.

There are several sources for shop manuals. If you own an import vehicle you can usually buy a service manual for it from the dealer. Prices range from $25 to $95 for a factory import service manual. For American-made vehicles you generally have to write directly to the vehicle manufacturer or their manual supplier. Prices for the domestic manuals range from $15 to $75. Factory shop manuals are the most complete because they do not condense many different years, makes, and models into a single book as the general repair guides do.

General repair guides (Chilton, Mitchell, Motor, and others) are published by independent publishers who have no direct affiliation with the vehicle manufacturers. They take their service information from the factory manuals and condense five to ten years of material into a single book. A general repair guide will provide tune-up specifications (though the specifications listed are sometimes not very accurate), basic repair procedures (such as more detailed step-by-step procedures for relining the brakes on specific vehicles), and also include more advanced repairs (such as engine overhaul, etc.). The one advantage of owning such a book is that it does cover many different makes, models, and years. In this case, if you trade your car or truck, your service manual doesn't become obsolete. General repair guides are available at auto parts stores, book stores, and automotive retail outlets.

Should you buy a factory shop manual or a general repair guide? If all you are interested in is basic maintenance, this book is all you need. The same applies to doing your own light repair work (with possibly the exception of relining your brakes). If you think you need more detailed information for a light repair job, a trip to the reference or automotive section at your local library should give you all the guidance you need. The only time you will need a factory shop manual or general repair guide is if you contemplate doing more advanced repairs or working on other people's vehicles.

GENERAL REPAIR GUIDES

Chilton Publications
Chilton Way
Radnor, PA 19089

Mitchell Manuals
P.O. Box 26260
San Diego, CA 92126

Motor Publications
555 W. 57th St.
New York, NY 10019

FACTORY SERVICE MANUALS

AMC/Jeep/Renault:
AMC/Jeep/Renault dealer or
Myriad Services
8835 General Drive
Plymouth, MI 48170

BMW:
BMW dealer or
BMW of North America
Service Dept.
Montvale, NJ 07645

Buick:
Service Publications
Buick Motor Div., General Motors Corp.
P.O. Box 1901
Flint, MI 48501

Cadillac:
Helm, Inc.
P.O. Box 07130
Detroit, MI 48207

Chevrolet:
Helm, Inc.
P.O. Box 07130
Detroit, MI 48207

Chrysler (includes Dodge and Plymouth):
Chrysler Service Publications
Dyment Distribution Service
20026 Progress Drive
Strongsville, OH 44136

Ford (includes Mercury and Lincoln):
Helm, Inc.
P.O. Box 07150
Detroit, MI 48207

Isuzu:
Isuzu Retail Service Publications
2300 Pellissier Place
Whittier, CA 90601

Mercedes-Benz:
Mercedes-Benz of North America
Service Publications
1 Mercedes Drive
Montvale, NJ 07645

Mitsubishi:
Mitsubishi dealer or
Mitsubishi Service Publications
10540 Talbert Ave.
Fountain Valley, CA 92728

Nissan (includes Datsun):
Nissan dealer or
Pendant Industries
P.O. Box 387
Harbor City, CA 90710

Oldsmobile:
Lansing Lithographers
P.O. Box 26128
Lansing, MI 48909

Pontiac:
Helm, Inc.
P.O. Box 3518
Highland Park, MI 48203

Saab:
Saab dealer or
Saab-Scania of America
Technical Service Dept.
Saab Drive
Orange, CT 06477

Toyota:
Allied Graphics
750 West Victoria St.
Compton, CA 90220

Volkswagen:
Volkswagen Service Manuals
Robert Bentley Inc.
1000 Massachusetts Ave.
Cambridge, MA 02138

Volvo:
Volvo America Corp.
Publications Dept.
Rockleigh, NJ 07647

A WORD ABOUT WARRANTIES

All new cars carry a minimum one-year or 12,000-mile warranty. Some offer as much as 5 years or 50,000 miles on the engine and drivetrain. The longer the "free" warranty included on the vehicle, the better the deal for you. But these warranties are not really free. Their cost is built into, or hidden in, the selling price of the vehicle.

All new passenger cars since 1981 also have a government-mandated *Emissions Warranty* that covers all the emission control components (including the computer and fuel injection) for 5 years or 50,000 miles. Many people are not aware of this coverage, but if you search through your owner's manual and warranty information, you will find it.

Extended warranty packages can also be purchased at extra cost to provide additional coverage. The cost of these extended warranty packages is not fixed, despite what the dealer might tell you. There is always room to negotiate the price to help clinch the sale. Extended warranties can be through the vehicle manufacturer or through an independent insurance company. As long as the company backing the warranty is reputable—and is still in business when you try to cash in on the warranty—there is no reason not to go with an independent plan. Extended warranties can be expensive, but one major repair and they have paid for themselves.

Should you buy an extended warranty? Do not buy initially; wait until your new car warranty is about to expire, then decide. If you have had no major problems, the vehicle seems to be in good mechanical condition, and/or you think you might trade vehicles in another two years, save your money. It is unlikely you would ever need the extra coverage. But if you have been back to the dealer for numerous repairs, if you are concerned about the vehicle's condition, or if you plan to keep the car for more than two more years, an extended warranty is a wise investment.

As for used cars, some used car dealers will offer *limited* warranties that cover the engine, drive train, brakes, suspension, and cooling system. Typical coverage periods are 30, 60, and 90 days, 6 months, or 1 year. Sometimes the warranty will be included with the vehicle, other times it is sold separately.

Handling Warranty Problems

When you have a mechanical problem, your first course of action should be to take the vehicle back to the dealer who sold it to you. Let the dealer handle the warranty repairs. Vehicle manufacturers will not honor warranty repairs made by nonauthorized dealers, except in rare circumstances where an emergency was involved.

If the dealer is reluctant to perform the warranty work, or if he tries to charge you for work that you think should be covered under the warranty, contact the customer service department of the manufacturer's zone office (your dealer should give you the number). A factory service representative will try to arbitrate the dispute. Put your complaint on paper and keep a copy of any documents you mail or receive from the zone office and/or dealer. You might need them later to prove your case.

Customer Relations Offices

If the zone office gives you the run-around, your course of action should be to contact the Customer Relations Office of the vehicle manufacturer (see below):

AMC/Jeep/Renault
P.O. Box 442
Detroit, MI 48232

Audi
888 W. Big River Rd.
Troy, MI 48099

BMW of North America
Montvale, NJ 07645

Buick
902 E. Hamilton Ave.
Flint, MI 48550

Cadillac
2860 Clark Ave.
Detroit, MI 48232

Chevrolet
30007 Van Dyke Ave.
Warren, MI 48090

Chrysler
P.O. Box 1718
Detroit, MI 48288

Ford
The American Rd.
Dearborn, MI 48121

Honda
100 W. Alondra Blvd.
Gardena, CA 90247

Isuzu
P.O. Box 2280
City of Industry, CA 91746

Mazda
9451 Toledo Way
Irvine, CA 92714

Mercedes-Benz
1 Mercedes Dr.
Montvale, NJ 07645

Mitsubishi
10540 Talbert St.
Fountain Valley, CA 92708

Nissan
18501 S. Figueroa St.
Gardena, CA 90247

Oldsmobile
920 Townsend St.
Lansing, MI 48921

Pontiac
One Pontiac Plaza
Pontiac, MI 48053

Saab-Scania of America
Saab Drive
Orange, CT 06477

Subaru
7040 Central Hwy.
Pennsauken, NJ 08109

Toyota
19001 S. Western Ave.
Torrance, CA 90509

Volkswagen
888 W. Big Beaver Rd.
Troy, MI 48099

Volvo
Rockleigh NJ 07647

Consumer Arbitration Panels

If you do not get satisfaction from the vehicle manufacturer you should try a consumer arbitration panel. These are independent third-party groups who serve as a go-between for you and the vehicle manufacturer. They will listen to both sides, then try to settle the matter fairly. In most cases the decision of the panel is binding on the vehicle manufacturer if the panel decides in your favor. If the decision goes against you, it is not binding. You still have recourse through the courts if you are not satisfied.

Ford and Chrysler both have their own independent arbitration panels, but most of the other vehicle manufacturers will work with either of the following:

Autoline
Council of Better Business Bureaus Inc.
1515 Wilson Blvd.
Arlington, VA 22209
800-228-6505

Autocap
National Automobile Dealers Association
8400 Westpark Dr.
McLean, VA 22102
703-821-7144

Many states have passed *Warranty Enforcement Laws*, (better known as *Lemon Laws*), to protect consumers who purchase problem vehicles. The Center for Auto Safety (Ralph Nader's group), 2001 S. Street NW, Suite 410, Washington, D.C. 20009 (phone: 202-328-7700) sells *The Lemon Book* which describes the various state laws for $8.65.

REPLACEMENT PARTS WARRANTIES

When you buy a replacement part for your vehicle, new or rebuilt, there is usually a warranty or guarantee that provides free replacement if the part fails due to an inherent fault. That means you can exchange it for another if the part does not work or if it fails during the warranty period. It does not mean that you are entitled to another if you damage the part while installing it or cause it to fail through abuse.

Lifetime warranties are becoming a popular merchandising tool among parts remanufacturers as a way of competing against new parts and for building consumer confidence in their products. The lifetime warranty covers free replacement of the part for as long as you (the original owner) own it should the part fail. The warranty does not, however, cover the cost or labor involved in replacing the part. If you installed it yourself, you will not be reimbursed for your time and trouble. Nor is the manufacturer going to reimburse you for money you paid someone else to install the part.

All things considered, the lifetime warranty is a good deal. A part that carries a lifetime warranty is sometimes priced slightly higher, but if you plan to keep your vehicle for some time after repairs have been made, the lifetime part is well worth buying.

Appendix B

Maintenance Record Forms

Oil & filter changes

Date	Mileage	Comments (filter number & brand)	Oil type & brand

Air filter change

Date	Mileage	Comments (filter number & brand)

Fuel filter changes

Date	Mileage	Comments (filter number & brand)

Chassis lubrication

Date	Mileage	Comments (condition of boots, joints, etc.)

Tune-up

Date	Mileage	Comments (replace plugs. PCV valve, etc.)

Cooling system flush & refill

Date	Mileage	Comments (brand of antifreeze, hose condition)

Automatic transmission fluid change & filter

Date	Mileage	Comments

Other repairs

Date	Mileage	Nature of repair	Comments

Maintenance & repair cost record

Date	Description of service performed	Cost
		$
		$
		$
		$
		$
		$
		$
		$
		$
		$
		$
		$
		$
		$
		$
		$
		$
		$
	TOTAL	$

Glossary

AAA—Abbreviation for the American Automobile Association. AAA, in conjunction with various local motor clubs, often certifies various repair facilities. The approved facilities must meet certain minimum standards of service to be listed in the local AAA directory.

ABS—Acronym for anti-lock or anti-skid brake system. Vehicles equipped with ABS use wheel speed sensors and a computer-controlled brake pressure regulator to prevent wheel lock-up during sudden stops. When the computer senses one wheel is slowing faster than the others (indicating it is about to lock-up and skid), the computer reduces brake pressure to that wheel by momentarily pulsing the pressure regulator. By balancing the brake pressure to keep all the wheels braking at the same speed, the system prevents any wheel from locking and skidding. The car stops straight and the driver is able to maintain steering control, ABS brakes improve braking dramatically on wet or slick surfaces but make little difference on dry pavement.

active suspensions—A new type of computerized hydraulic suspension system that uses hydraulic "actuators" instead of conventional springs and shock absorbers to support the vehicle's weight. A "chassis computer" monitors ride height, wheel deflection, body roll, and acceleration to control ride and body attitude. Bumps are sensed as they are encountered, causing the computer to vent pressure from the wheel actuator as the wheel floats over the bump. Once the bump has passed, the computer opens a vent that allows hydraulic pressure to extend the actuator back to its original length. Such a system can provide a Cadillac-smooth ride on a rough road with Porsche-like agility on curves. The suspension can be programmed for antidive characteristics during braking and to lean the body into a turn like a motorcycle for faster cornering.

air conditioning—Your vehicle's air conditioning system works exactly the same as a home air conditioner. A compressor pumps Freon gas

173

(the refrigerant) to the condenser (the radiator-like heat exchanger in front of the radiator). Here the Freon sheds its heat and condenses into a high-pressure liquid. It then circulates through a restrictive metering orifice and enters the evaporator (the cooling fins under the dash), where it expands and cools the incoming air. Then it goes back to the compressor to start the journey all over again. Air conditioning service requires special tools and knowledge, but the do-it-yourselfer can add Freon if the system is low. Most air conditioning failures are due to loss of Freon (through leaks), plugging (caused by moisture entering the system and forming sludge), or compressor failure (due to loss of Freon or plugging). The system should be checked annually and Freon added as needed (Fig. G-1).

airflow sensor—A device that is used in many electronic fuel injection systems for measuring the volume of air entering the engine. Some use a spring-loaded vane while others use a hot wire filament to sense air flow.

air/fuel ratio—This is the relative proportion of air and fuel delivered by the carburetor or fuel injection to the engine. The ideal air/fuel ratio is 14.7 parts of air to every 1 part fuel. Less air or more fuel and the mixture is said to be rich. More air or less fuel and the mixture is said to be lean. Rich mixtures provide more power, but also use more fuel and increase exhaust emissions. Lean mixtures use less fuel, but if too lean cause misfiring at idle. An engine requires a richer mixture when starting and while warming up. The air/fuel ratio at idle can be adjusted by turning the idle mixture screw on the carburetor. To alter the mixture above idle, the main metering jets inside the carburetor must be changed. With electronic fuel injection, no changes can be made because the mixture is determined by the pulse time of the injector(s). The

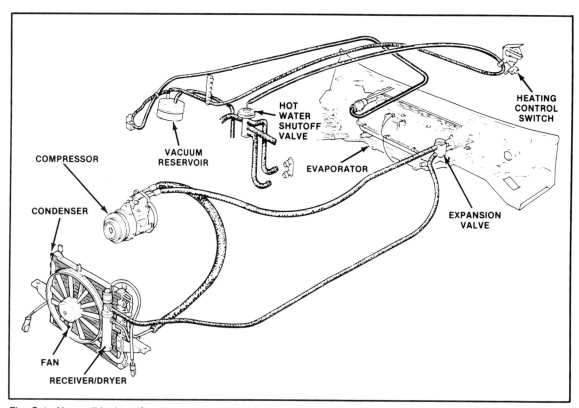

Fig. G-1. Air conditioning. (Courtesy of Ford Motor Company.)

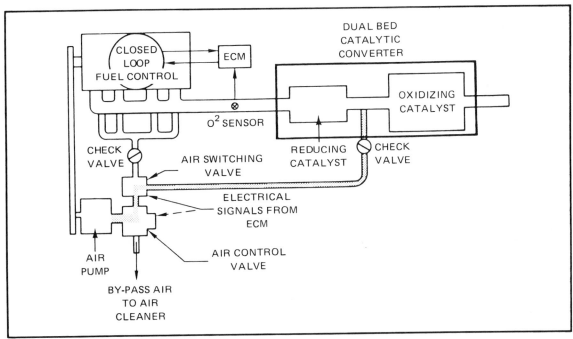

Fig. G-2. Air pump. (Courtesy of Chrysler Corporation.)

longer the injectors are on, the richer the mixture.

air pump—An emission control device on your engine that pumps air into the exhaust system so the catalytic converter can reburn pollutants out of the exhaust (Fig. G-2).

air shocks—A type of overload shock absorber that can be inflated with air to increase the suspension's load carrying ability.

alcohol—Alcohol is used as a gasoline additive to boost the octane rating of the fuel. Two types of alcohol are used: ethanol and methanol. Ethanol is the most commonly used alcohol. It is made by distilling fermented corn, sugar beets, or sugar cane. Methanol is made primarily from coal and is highly poisonous. Ethanol-blend fuels typically have a 10-percent ethanol content. Methanol blends are limited to 5 percent because methanol can be corrosive in higher concentrations. Will alcohol-blend gasoline harm your car? Not if the fuel is mixed properly and the amount of alcohol is limited to the percentages described.

alignment—Although most people think of the front wheels when alignment is mentioned, it actually refers to all four wheels. All four wheels should be perpendicular to the road and parallel to one another for the best handling, traction, and tire life. If the wheels are out of alignment, rapid or uneven tire wear and/or steering pull to one side can result. Four-wheel alignment, as opposed to the conventional two-wheel alignment, is very important today—especially on vehicles with independent rear suspensions. The three basic alignment angles are toe, camber, and caster, but on many new cars, caster and camber are not adjustable.

alternator—The component in a vehicle's charging system that makes electricity. The alternator's job is to keep the battery fully charged and to provide additional current to meet the demands of the ignition system, lights, and other accessories. Vehicles equipped with air conditioning and numerous electrical accessories require an alternator with a higher output capacity than a vehicle without such amenities. Alternator capacities are rated in amps with typical outputs ranging from 50 to 80 amps. When the

175

alternator or its control device, the voltage regulator, goes bad, the alternator light on the dash will glow red. If your vehicle has a charge indicator, it will show a continual discharge or low voltage. Without the supply of electricity to keep it charged, the battery soon goes dead along with your engine. Sometimes a slipping drive belt is all that is wrong, but usually the alternator and/or regulator need to be replaced.

antifreeze—Antifreeze protects the cooling system against both freezing and overheating. When used at normal strength (50% antifreeze/50% water) it can lower the freezing point of the coolant to – 34 degrees F. and raise its boiling temperature to 276 degrees F. Never use straight antifreeze in your cooling system, always mix it with at least 50% water. Antifreeze is 95% ethylene glycol. The only difference between brands of antifreeze are the type and/or quantity of anticorrosion additives used. Ethylene glycol never wears out, but the corrosion inhibitors do. That is why the antifreeze should be changed every two years.

ASE—Abbreviation for the National Institute for Automotive Service Excellence. ASE (formerly NIASE) certifies professional mechanics in various areas of repair expertise. A mechanic that has passed one or more tests is allowed to wear the ASE Blue Seal of Excellence on his uniform and any repair facility that employs certified mechanics can display the ASE sign.

automatic transmission fluid (ATF)—A special kind of oil for use in automatic transmissions. There are two main types: Dexron II and Type F. Most Ford transmissions use the Type F while everybody else uses Dexron II, but there are exceptions, so check your owner's manual recommendations. ATF breaks down if it overheats. Trailer towing is especially hard on it unless the transmission is equipped with an auxiliary oil cooler.

backfire—This is the popping or banging sound sometimes heard in the exhaust when decelerating. It can indicate a problem such as too-rich carburetion, a bad exhaust valve, or an ignition problem (retarded timing or a cracked distributor cap). If the backfiring occurs through the carburetor, it might mean overadvanced timing, a bad intake valve, or a cracked distributor cap.

back pressure—This is the pressure that backs up in the exhaust system as a result of the restriction caused by the muffler, catalytic converter, and tailpipe. The faster you drive and/or the greater the load on the engine, the higher the back pressure in the exhaust system. Back pressure inhibits the exit of exhaust gases so the engine has to work harder to push the exhaust out. This cuts down on engine power and fuel economy. Some of the causes of high back pressure include a clogged converter, a damaged or collapsed exhaust pipe, or a restrictive muffler.

ball joint—A flexible coupling in the vehicle's suspension that connects the control arm to the steering knuckle. A ball joint is so named because of its ball-and-socket construction. Some are designed to never require grease while others should be lubed every six months. As the joint wears, it becomes loose. The result is suspension noise and wheel misalignment (Fig. G-3).

battery—The battery is a storehouse of electrical energy for starting the engine. Unless you're driving an antique, your vehicle uses a 12-volt battery. Most batteries today are maintenance-free, meaning you do not have to add water to them periodically. Some even have built-in charge indicators. A green dot in the window means the battery is at least 75% charged, no

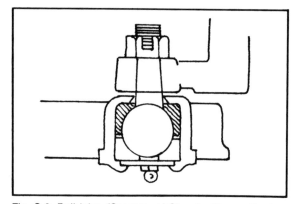

Fig. G-3. Ball joint. (Courtesy of Chrysler Corporation.)

dot means it needs recharging, and a clear or yellow window means you need a new battery because the water level inside is low. Do not try to jump start or charge such a battery. You might be able to salvage the battery if you can pry the sealed caps open and add water, but usually the battery must be replaced. Batteries are rated according to their cold cranking amp (CCA) capacity. As a rule of thumb, your engine needs a minimum of one CCA for every cubic inch of displacement and preferably two. The higher the CCA rating of the battery, the better. There is, however, no need to go overboard and buy a 650-amp battery for a four-cylinder engine.

blowby—A condition where combustion gases literally blow around the piston rings. When air and fuel are ignited inside the combustion chamber, the resulting explosion creates tremendous heat and pressure. The piston rings are supposed to seal against the cylinder walls to prevent the hot gases from escaping, but every engine suffers a small amount of blowby. If the rings and cylinders are worn, blowby can be a real problem. The gases are mostly water vapor and unburned fuel, so when they enter the crankcase, they contaminate the oil. Most of the gases are sucked out through the crankcase ventilation system before they can do much damage. In an engine with a lot of wear, however, excessive blowby can lead to rapid sludge buildup.

boots—Also called bellows. These are the protective rubber (synthetic or natural) or hard plastic (usually Hytrel) covers that surround CV joints. The boot's job is to keep grease in and dirt and water out. Split, torn, or otherwise damaged boots should be replaced immediately. Old boots should never be reused when servicing a joint; always install new boots.

brake bleeding—This is the process of removing air bubbles from the brake system by pumping fluid through the lines. Air bubbles are bad because they compress when pressure is applied resulting in a low or spongy-feeling pedal. The correct procedure for bleeding the brakes on most RWD vehicles is to start at the farthest wheel. Do the right rear, then left rear brake, followed by the right front and left front brakes. On a FWD vehicle with a diagonally-split brake system, do the right rear, then left front brake, followed by the left rear and right front brake.

brake calipers—The part of the disc brake that squeezes a pair of brake pads against the rotor. A caliper is nothing more than a casting with a piston inside. When hydraulic pressure pushes the piston out, it forces the brake pads against both sides of the rotor. Some calipers are floating in that they slide back and forth and self-center over the rotor. Others are fixed because they do not move in and out (Fig. G-4).

brake drums—The cast-iron housing and friction surface around a drum brake. The brake shoes expand outward and rub against the inside surface of the drums when the brakes are applied. Worn drums often take on a grooved appearance. The inner surface should be turned smooth on a brake lathe when the shoes are replaced. If the drum has worn too thin, is cracked, warped, or has taken on a bell-mouthed shape, it must be replaced. The spring around the outside of the drum on some vehicles absorbs vibrations and noise (Fig. G-5).

brake fluid—The brake system uses a special kind of alcohol-based hydraulic fluid. The fluid is *hydroscopic,* meaning it absorbs moisture over a period of time. Moisture lowers the boiling

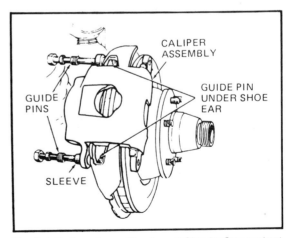

Fig. G-4. Brake calipers. (Courtesy of Chrysler Corporation.)

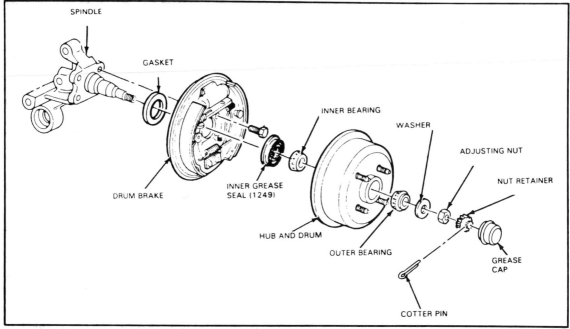

Fig. G-5. Brake drums. (Courtesy of Ford Motor Company.)

point of the fluid and causes internal corrosion in the brake system. This is the reason brake fluid should be replaced when brake repairs are made or every few years, whichever comes first. The best kind of brake fluid is silicone-based. It will not absorb moisture and does not require periodic replacement.

brake job—A typical brake job includes replacing the brake linings (new disc brake pads and shoes), resurfacing the rotors and drums, adding fresh brake fluid and bleeding the system, and inspecting/replacing any other worn components. If rotors or drums are worn beyond safe limits, they cannot be resurfaced and must be replaced. Leaky disc brake calipers, drum brake wheel cylinders, or the master cylinder should be rebuilt or replaced.

brake linings—The friction material on disc brake pads or drum shoes. A variety of materials are used including asbestos, semimetallic fibers, Fiberglas, and Kevlar. Asbestos linings are used on most older vehicles and on the rear drum brakes. Semimetallic linings are used on the front brakes of many front-wheel-drive vehicles.

Never substitute one for the other. The linings rub against the rotors or drums to create friction, producing a tremendous amount of heat. If the heat builds up faster than it can be shed, the brakes can fade. The linings are a high-wear item. Front brakes, especially those on FWD vehicles, receive the most wear. Average life for front brakes ranges from 30,000 to 60,000 miles, for rear brakes, 60,000 to 100,000 miles is the norm. Linings should be replaced when worn down to the lining rivet heads or when lining thickness is less than 1/8th inch.

brake pads—These are the linings used in the front disc brakes. They are called pads because of their flat pad-like shape. Each brake uses a pair of pads (one inner, one outer). Replacement pads are sold in two-pair sets and are easy to change. Calipers should be inspected for leaks and the rotors resurfaced to restore a smooth surface.

brake rotors—The flat disk-like plates that provide the friction surface in a disc brake. When hydraulic pressure is applied to the caliper, the brake pads are squeezed against both sides of

178

the rotor producing friction and heat. Some rotors have cooling fins between both faces and are called *vented* rotors. The rotors should always be resurfaced when new pads are installed. If worn beyond safe limits, cracked, or severely warped, they must be replaced.

brakes—The brake system uses hydraulic pressure to stop your vehicle when you step on the brake pedal. Pushing the pedal down pumps fluid from the master cylinder to the brakes at each wheel. This squeezes the brake linings against the rotors and drums, creating friction which brings the vehicle to a halt. The only maintenance the system requires is to check the fluid level periodically and to replace the fluid every few years or when brake repairs are performed (Fig. G-6).

brake shoes—The brake linings used in drum brakes (the rear brakes on most cars). Each drum contains two shoes: a primary or leading shoe and a secondary or trailing shoe. Replacement shoes are sold in sets of four, one pair for each brake. When shoes are replaced, the condition of the mounting hardware and return springs must be carefully inspected. Replace any worn, damaged, or stretched components. Drums should also be turned on a lathe to restore a smooth surface (Fig. G-7).

brake squeal—The annoying high-pitched screech that is sometimes heard when braking. A common ailment on many vehicles equipped with disc brakes, it is caused by vibration between the brake pad and rotor. It causes no harm, but metallic scraping sounds should be investigated, because it usually means the brake linings are worn down to their metal backing plates. If not replaced, the metal-to-metal contact can ruin the rotors or drums. Brake squeal can be eliminated by applying antisqueal compound to the backs of the pads and resurfacing the rotors. This rubber-like compound helps cushion the pads and soak up the annoying vibration.

BTU—Abbreviation for British thermal unit. One

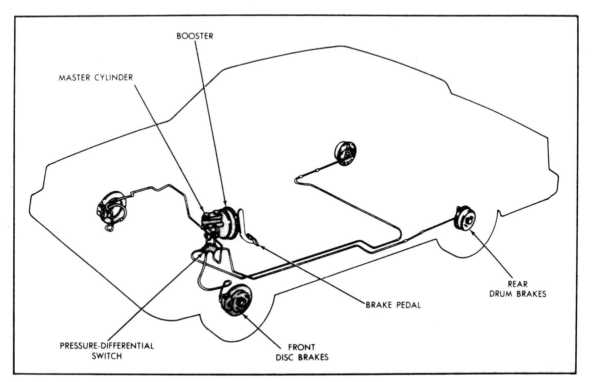

Fig. G-6. Brakes. (Courtesy of Chrysler Corporation.)

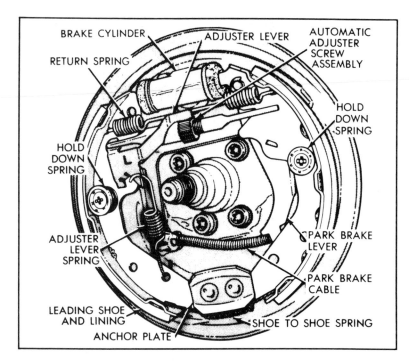

Fig. G-7. Brake shoes. (Courtesy of Chrysler Corporation.)

BTU is the amount of heat it takes to heat 1 pound of water 1 degree Fahrenheit. The energy value of various fuels is often expressed in so many BTUs per gallon. Gasoline, for example, has somewhere around 120,000 BTUs per gallon.

camber—A wheel alignment angle that refers to the inward or outward tilt of the wheels as viewed from the front. Outward tilt is called *positive* camber while inward tilt is called *negative*. Ideally, the wheels should have zero rolling camber (perpendicular to the road) when the vehicle is loaded. Camber changes as the vehicle is loaded and the suspension sags. To compensate, the static alignment specifications might call for a slight amount of positive or negative camber depending on how the suspension is built. On vehicles with independent rear suspensions, excessive negative camber often results when the vehicle is overloaded. Excessive camber can cause uneven tread wear on the tires. Camber can be affected by worn suspension components such as control arm bushings and ball joints, or by bent parts such as a MacPherson strut. Camber is changed by adding or subtracting shims from the control arm pivot mounts, or on strut cars by moving the top or bottom of the strut in or out (Fig. G-8).

camshaft—A shaft inside your engine that has lobes to operate the engine's valves. In "pushrod" engines, lifters ride on the cam lobes.

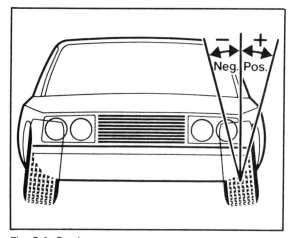

Fig. G-8. Camber.

The up and down motion is transferred through push rods and rocker arms to actuate the valves. In an "overhead" cam engine, the cam might push directly on the tops of the valves or work the valves through short rocker arms. Loss of lubrication (low oil) or dirty oil can cause scuffing and lobe wear on a cam. The result is loss of engine power because the affected valves do not open completely. The only cure is to replace the cam—a job that requires advanced skills. The cam can also be changed to improve performance and/or fuel economy. Aftermarket camshafts offer a wide range of different lobe profiles from which to choose. A higher-lift, longer-duration cam generally provides more power and moves the engine's peak power point up the rpm scale.

carbon monoxide (CO)—A deadly gas that results from the incomplete burning of gasoline inside your engine, carbon monoxide is considered to be a serious air pollutant. You cannot see it or smell it, but it can kill in very small concentrations. Because of this you should never run an engine inside a closed garage. Various means are used to reduce the amount of CO produced by your engine, and primary among these is the catalytic converter. The converter reburns CO in the exhaust and converts it into harmless carbon dioxide.

carburetor—This is the component that supplies fuel to your engine (unless you have fuel injection). It mixes air and fuel in varying proportions according to the position of the throttle opening and engine vacuum. Carburetor adjustments include idle speed, idle fuel mixture, and choke setting. Most carburetor problems are due to improper choke adjustment or dirty air or fuel. Dirt can plug the tiny metering orifices, resulting in a variety of driveability problems. Wear around the throttle shafts or warpage or vacuum leaks around the base plate can also cause problems. Overhaul kits are available to the do-it-yourself mechanic, but many carburetors can be very difficult to rebuild correctly. A better alternative is a factory rebuilt carburetor that can be easily installed.

cardan joint—Also known as a Hooke joint, universal joint or U-joint, it is a simple, flexible coupling using a double yoke and four-point center cross. Cardan joints are used as couplings in the driveshafts of rear-wheel-drive cars. Because they can produce uneven shaft speeds when operated at joint angles of more than a few degrees, they are usually not used with front-wheel drive (because the front wheels also steer and create large operating angles).

caster—A wheel alignment angle that refers to the forward or rearward tilt of the steering axis on the front wheels. A forward tilt of the steering axis is called "negative" caster, while a rearward tilt is called "positive." The caster angle has no affect on tread wear but it does affect steering return and stability. Most vehicles have a certain amount of positive caster. The higher the caster angle, the steadier the car feels at high speed. But the higher the caster angle, the greater the steering effort. The caster angle on many strut suspensions is fixed at the factory and is not adjustable (Fig. G-9).

catalytic converter—The converter is an emissions control device in the exhaust system that reduces the amount of pollutants produced by a vehicle. It does this by reburning certain pollutants and reforming others. Catalytic converters were first used on 1975 model cars to reduce hydrocarbon and carbon monoxide emis-

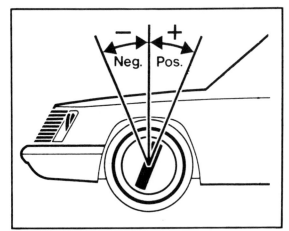

Fig. G-9. Caster.

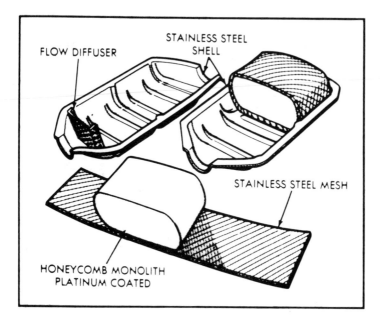

Fig. G-10. Catalytic converter.

FLOW DIFFUSER

STAINLESS STEEL SHELL

STAINLESS STEEL MESH

HONEYCOMB MONOLITH PLATINUM COATED

sions. In 1981 a new type of three-way converter was installed to also reduce oxides of nitrogen. The converter does a superb job of reducing pollutants, but it can be ruined by using regular leaded gasoline. Lead contaminates the platinum, rhodium, and palladium catalyst inside the converter and renders it useless (Fig. G-10).

centrifugal advance—A mechanism inside the distributor that advances ignition timing in response to increasing engine speed. The air/fuel mixture needs to be ignited earlier as engine speed increases, so the centrifugal advance mechanism uses a pair of spring-loaded flyweights to rotate the timing components inside the distributor. Late-model engines with computer spark timing do not have centrifugal advance units in the distributor (Fig. G-11).

charcoal canister—An evaporative emissions control component that traps fuel vapors from your vehicle's fuel tank and carburetor. The can-

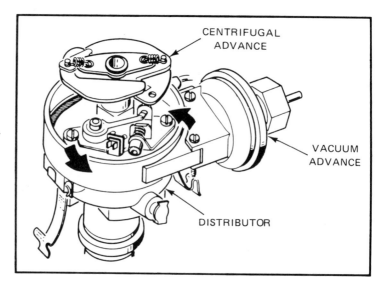

Fig. G-11. Centrifugal advance.

CENTRIFUGAL ADVANCE

VACUUM ADVANCE

DISTRIBUTOR

ister is usually located in the engine compartment and is connected to the carburetor and fuel tank with a maze of hoses. Charcoal crystals inside store the vapors until the engine starts, then a control valve opens, allowing the unburned fuel vapors to be sucked into the engine and burned. The canister is relatively trouble-free and requires no maintenance. Note: there are a few older cars that do require periodic canister filter replacements. Check your owner's manual (Fig. G-12).

charging system—The charging system includes the alternator, voltage regulator (which is often a part of the alternator itself), the battery, and the indicator gauge or warning light on the dash. The charging system's job is to generate enough current to keep the battery fully charged and to satisfy the demands of the ignition and electrical systems. The voltage regulator senses the demands on the electrical system and controls alternator output so that sufficient current is produced. A loose V-belt or a defective alternator or voltage regulator can cause the dash warning light to glow red (or the amp gauge to show steady discharge). If the problem is not corrected, the battery will run down and eventually go dead (Fig. G-13).

choke—A little flap-like valve in the top of a carburetor that opens and closes to control the amount of air entering the carburetor when the engine is cold. The choke's purpose is to artificially enrich the fuel mixture by choking off the air supply during starting and engine warmup. If the choke is not adjusted correctly, it can make the engine hard to start and or cause it to stall.

circuit breaker—A protective device that is often used in a wiring circuit to protect against overloads. A circuit breaker has a bimetallic arm and a pair of contact points. When the current exceeds its preset limits, the arm gets hot, bends, and opens the contact points. This shuts off the current through the circuit and protects against damage or fire. Most circuit breakers automatically reset themselves after they cool down, but some have a button that must be manually reset to restore power. You will find circuit breakers in the headlight and air conditioning circuits.

clutch—A device that couples the engine to the transmission. The clutch consists of a friction-

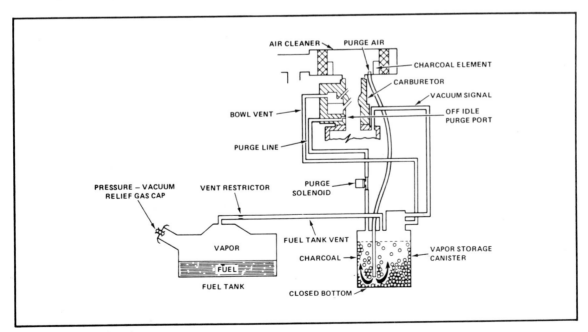

Fig. G-12. Charcoal canister.

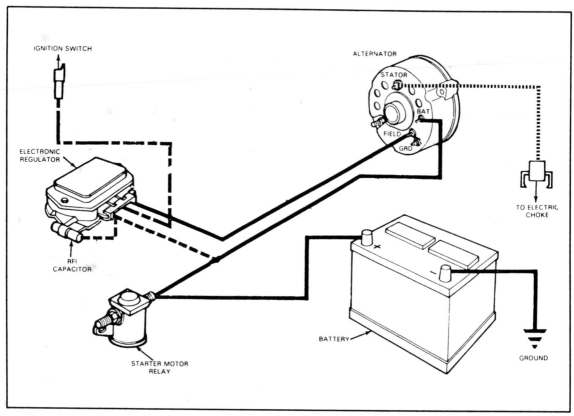

Fig. G-13. Charging system. (Courtesy of Ford Motor Company.)

lined disk, called the *clutch disk*, and a spring-loaded *pressure plate* that presses the clutch disk tightly against the flywheel. When the clutch pedal is pushed in, the linkage releases the spring pressure, allowing the clutch disk to slip. The clutch disk is subjected to a tremendous amount of friction and heat, which eventually causes it to wear out. At this point it starts to slip. Oil or grease on the flywheel, weak or broken springs in the pressure plate, or an overadjusted linkage can also cause it to slip. If it fails to release, the most likely cause is a broken clutch cable. Replacing the clutch is heavy work because it involves removing the transmission. Have this job done by a professional with the proper equipment.

compression ratio—As the pistons inside your engine travel up and down, they squeeze or compress the air/fuel mixture in the cylinders. This heats and mixes the fuel, which helps it to burn with greater force. The amount of squeeze is expressed as a numerical ratio and for a gasoline engine is usually between 8:1 and 9:1. This means the volume of the combustion chamber after the piston reaches top dead center is roughly 1/8 to 1/9 the volume of the cylinder when the piston was at the bottom of its travel. Generally speaking, the higher compression ratio, the more efficient the engine; but higher compression ratios are more prone to detonation. This requires higher octane fuel or special spark-retarding controls to control detonation.

computerized engine controls—Starting in 1981, domestic automobile manufacturers began using a new type of sophisticated engine control system that relies on a computer and various engine sensors to regulate fuel delivery, ignition timing, emissions control, and even automatic transmission lockup in new passenger cars and some light trucks. By combining these various functions into one master control system, manufacturers have been able to meet both the tough Federal antipollution standards and the Corporate Average Fuel Economy (CAFE) requirements set forth by Congress. General Motors calls their system Computer Command Control (CCC) and there are numerous different variations of it in use throughout General Motors' five divisions. Ford has gone through several generations of electronic engine control (EEC), the current one being EEC-IV. Chrysler started out with their Lean Burn system, which has evolved into the Spark Control Computer (SCC). The domestic systems all have a certain amount of built-in self-diagnostic capability and are able to detect gross problems in various computer control circuits. Problems are identified by various "trouble code" numbers that refer to specific diagnostic charts in the manufacturer's repair manual. Computerized engine control systems are beyond the abilities of most do-it-yourselfers, so if you are having problems with the system, take it to a competent professional (Fig. G-14).

constant velocity (CV) joint—A constant velocity joint is a joint that provides consistent driveshaft speeds regardless of the operating angle of the joint. CV joints are used primarily in the driveshafts of front-wheel-drive vehicles, and they come in two basic varieties: the Rzeppa ball-type joints (which you will find on the outer end of the driveshaft) and tripod joints (which are used on the inner end (Fig. G-15)).

coolant—The liquid inside the radiator and cooling system. It is called "coolant" because it helps to cool the engine. It circulates through the engine and absorbs the heat. The coolant then flows to the radiator where it sheds its heat. When the heater is turned on, coolant also flows through the heater core, which acts like a minia-

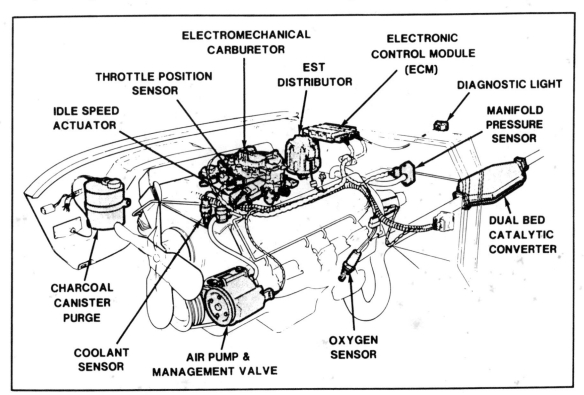

Fig. G-14. Computerized engine controls.

185

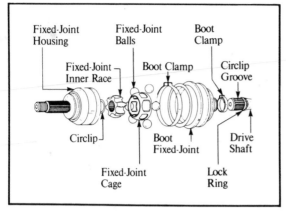

Fig. G-15. CV joint.

the radiator should be checked periodically to replace any that has been lost. The recommended coolant for most vehicles is a mixture of 50% water and 50% antifreeze. Straight water should never be used because it is extremely corrosive and offers no freezing or boilover protection.

cooling system—The cooling system consists of the radiator, water pump, thermostat, heater core, heater and radiator hoses, and the water jackets inside the cylinder head and engine block. An engine produces a tremendous amount of waste heat when it runs, so some method of cooling is needed to prevent the engine from self-destructing. Some engines—such as lawn mower and small motorcycles—are air-cooled. But liquid-cooling is used for most automotive applications because it is more efficient, it allows better temperature control, and it provides heat in the winter (Fig. G-16).

ture radiator, to heat air entering the passenger compartment. A low coolant level can result in overheating, no heat from the heater, and/or serious engine damage. The coolant level inside

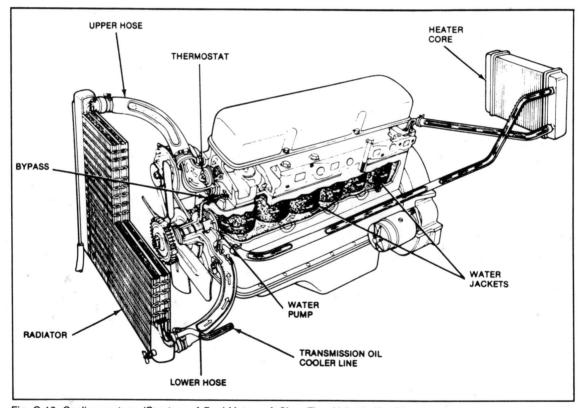

Fig. G-16. Cooling system. (Courtesy of *Ford Motorcraft Shop Tips*, Vol. 19, No. 2.)

crankshaft—The main shaft inside the engine that turns the up-and-down motion of the pistons into rotational torque. There are two types of crankshafts: cast-iron and forged steel. The cast-iron variety are used in most passenger car engines while the stronger forged crankshafts are used primarily in high-performance engines. When an engine is overhauled, the rod and main bearing journals are reground to restore a smooth surface. Crankshaft failures are, fortunately, not common, but when they occur they are usually caused by excessive internal engine vibration or defects in the crankshaft itself.

detonation—This is the pinging or knocking sound that is sometimes heard when accelerating. This noise is the result of erratic combustion inside your engine. Instead of burning normally, the fuel explodes in multiple flame front and the colliding fireballs inside the cylinders shake and rattle the pistons. Mild detonation is annoying but will not cause damage. Severe or prolonged detonation can ruin your engine. If switching to a higher octane fuel does not cure the problem, timing adjustments or other repairs might be necessary (Fig. G-17).

diesel engine—A type of engine that uses compression to ignite its fuel rather than a spark. A diesel engine has a much higher compression ratio than a gasoline engine (22:1 versus 8:1 for example) and because of this it is able to squeeze more usable power out of each drop of fuel. A typical diesel gets 30 to 50 percent better fuel mileage than a comparable gasoline engine of equal displacement. A diesel engine has no carburetor or throttle. Fuel is injected directly into the engine's cylinders through high-pressure mechanical injectors. Injector timing is very important because it affects idle quality, rattling, and exhaust smoke. Engine speed is governed by the injection pump, which controls the amount of fuel delivered. Most passenger car diesel engines have a glow plug starting system that preheats the combustion chamber. The fuel system can be contaminated by water, so many also have fuel/water separator filters.

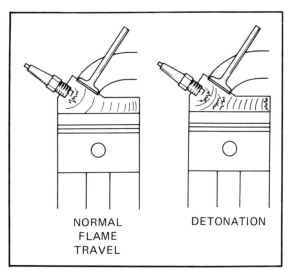

NORMAL FLAME TRAVEL   DETONATION

Fig. G-17. Detonation.

dieseling—Ever turn the ignition off on your car but the engine continues to run? That is called dieseling and it is caused by hot spots inside your engine that continue to ignite the incoming fuel. To prevent dieseling, most cars have a throttle stop solenoid on the carburetor that tightly shuts the throttle once the ignition is turned off. On other engines a fuel-shutoff solenoid is used.

differential—This is the gear box between the drive axles that transfers torque from the driveshaft to the axles and allows the drive axles to rotate at different speeds. This is necessary because the inner wheel follows a smaller arc than the outer wheel when the vehicle turns. The differential always provides power to the wheel that needs it least, because the gears always allow torque to follow the path of least resistance. Locking differentials that use spring-loaded clutch packs or fluid-encased disks are available as an option on some vehicles to prevent wheel spin. This is a "must" option for any high-performance or off-road vehicle.

disc brakes—A type of brake design that uses a flat disk-shaped rotor as the friction surface. A caliper squeezes a pair of brake pads against the rotor to stop the vehicle. Disc brakes are used on the front wheels of most passenger cars and sometimes on the rear.

distributor—The "brain" of your ignition system that "distributes" ignition voltage to each of the spark plugs. The distributor contains an electronic trigger or pickup device (older cars use contact points) that trigger the ignition coil. High voltage enters the distributor cap from the coil, travels down through the rotor to the appropriate spark plug terminal, and exits out the wire. On precomputer cars, the distributor also controls spark timing via centrifugal and vacuum advance units, but this function is performed by the computer in late-model cars. The only maintenance the distributor requires is periodic replacement of the rotor and cap (older cars need annual point replacements).

driveshaft—The propeller shaft that transmits engine torque to the differential or from the differential to the drive wheels. In front-wheel-drive vehicles the two driveshafts are often referred to as "halfshafts."

dynamometer—A machine that is used to measure the horsepower output of an engine. A chassis dynamometer has large rollers on which the drive wheels are placed. The vehicle is accelerated to a certain speed and put under load so the amount of power that is being delivered to the wheels can be measured. A dynamometer can also be used to simulate actual driving conditions when troubleshooting various driveability problems.

EGR valve—The EGR valve is the main emissions control component in the exhaust gas recirculation system. The valve is located on the intake manifold and opens a small passageway between the exhaust and intake manifold to allow a metered amount of exhaust to flow back into the engine. This reduces combustion temperatures and helps control the formation of oxides of nitrogen. The EGR valve is opened by the application of vacuum to its control diaphragm. Some EGR valves also require a certain amount of exhaust back pressure before they will open. The valve should remain closed while the engine is cold and at idle. It should only open once the engine has warmed up and is run-

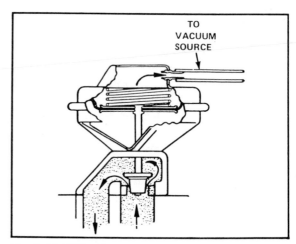

Fig. G-18. EGR value.

ning at part-throttle. If the valve sticks shut (or is disconnected), NOX emissions will soar and detonation will often result. If the valve sticks in the open position or fails to completely close, it acts like a vacuum leak, resulting in a rough idle, hesitation, and possible stalling (Fig. G-18).

electrical system—The battery, wires, and electrically-operated accessories in your vehicle. All modern passenger cars, light trucks, and most large motorcycles have 12-volt electrical systems. Farm tractors, most small motorcycles, antique cars, and pre-1967 Volkswagens have 6-volt electrical systems. Most heavy-duty trucks use 24-volt systems. The electrical system uses the battery and charging system as its power source with wires and switches routing the voltage to where it is needed. The metal body serves as the ground or return path for the voltage back to the battery. The electrical system is protected against damage by various devices. Most electrical problems fall into one of three basic categories: poor ground connections (loose or corroded), opens (breaks in circuit wires, connectors or switches), or shorts (grounded circuit wires or switches). A test light, ohmmeter, and/or voltmeter can be used to find the fault.

electronic fuel injection (EFI)—This type of system uses computer-controlled fuel injectors to spray fuel into the engine rather than mechan-

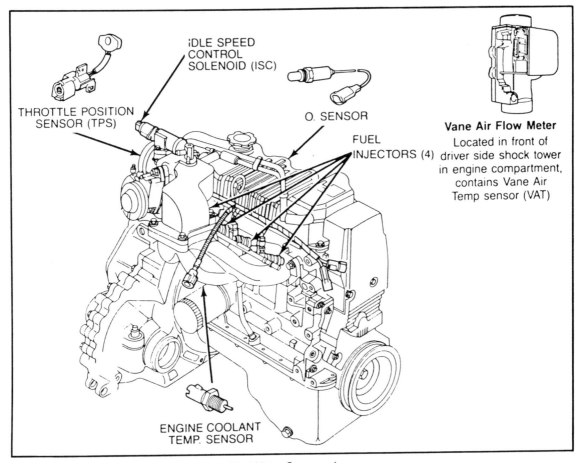

THROTTLE POSITION
SENSOR (TPS)

iDLE SPEED
CONTROL
SOLENOID (ISC)

O. SENSOR

FUEL
INJECTORS (4)

Vane Air Flow Meter
Located in front of
driver side shock tower
in engine compartment,
contains Vane Air
Temp sensor (VAT)

ENGINE COOLANT
TEMP. SENSOR

Fig. G-19. Electronic fuel injection. (Courtesy Ford Motor Company.)

ically controlled injectors or a carburetor. EFI comes in one of two varieties: throttle body injection or multiport injection. Electronic fuel injection is considered to be superior to carburetion because it allows more accurate fuel metering. The result is better mileage, easier starting, and better overall performance (Fig. G-19).

emission control system—The vehicle components that are responsible for reducing air pollution. This includes crankcase emissions, evaporative emissions, and tailpipe exhaust emissions. *Crankcase emissions* consist of unburned fuel and combustion by-products. These gases are recirculated back into the engine for reburning by the positive crankcase ventilation (PCV)

system. *Evaporative emissions* are the fuel vapors that seep out of the fuel tank and carburetor. They are prevented from escaping into the atmosphere by sealing the fuel system and storing the vapors in a vapor canister for later reburning. *Tailpipe exhaust emissions* consist of carbon monoxide (CO), unburned hydrocarbons (HC), and oxides of nitrogen (NOX) The formation of these pollutants is minimized by various engine design features, careful control over fuel calibration and ignition timing, and the EGR system. The pollutants that make it into the exhaust are reburned before they exit the tailpipe by the catalytic converter. The emission control system is an integral part of your engine, and should not be tampered with or disconnected. This is especially true on vehicles with computerized engine controls and/or those that must be subjected to annual emissions testing.

EPA—Abbreviation for the Environmental Protection Agency, the government agency responsible for enforcing antipollution rules. The EPA requires all vehicle manufacturers to certify their new cars as being in compliance with the applicable clean air standards for the year of manufacture. The manufacturer, in turn, must provide a 5 year/50,000 mile "emissions" warranty on every car they sell that guarantees free replacement of any emissions control device that might fail during that time. This coverage usually extends to such items as the computer control system, carburetion, fuel injection, and ignition system (except the spark plugs and normal wear items).

exhaust gas recirculation (EGR)—This is an emissions control technique for reducing oxides of nitrogen emissions in the tailpipe. A small amount of exhaust gas is recirculated back into the intake manifold to dilute the incoming air/fuel mixture. Contrary to what you would think, it has a cooling effect on combustion temperatures that helps reduce the formation of oxides of nitrogen. The EGR valve is the main control device in this system.

exhaust system—The exhaust system consists of the exhaust manifold, exhaust pipe, catalytic converter, muffler, and tailpipe. The system performs three important functions: it carries exhaust gases away from the engine, it quiets the engine, and it helps control pollution. The exhaust system's one weakness is its vulnerability to corrosion. Original equipment exhaust systems usually have stainless steel headpipes (the pipe between the exhaust manifold and catalytic converter) and converter shells, and aluminized pipe to resist corrosion. But after three or four years, the muffler and tailpipe often need to be replaced. Some new cars are now equipped with 100% stainless steel exhaust systems which, the car manufacturers hope, will last the life of the car (Fig. G-20).

flywheel—A large, heavy wheel on the end of the crankshaft that helps the engine maintain momentum when the clutch is engaged. The flywheel also helps dampen engine vibrations. The flywheel should be resurfaced when the clutch is replaced to restore a smooth surface. Oil or grease on the surface of the flywheel can make the clutch slip and chatter. On some vehicles, the ignition timing marks are on the flywheel and are observed by peering through a hole in the bellhousing. The teeth along the edge of the flywheel are for the starter to engage when the engine is cranked. Nicked, broken, or missing teeth can cause starting problems, so a damaged flywheel should be replaced. On vehicles equipped with an automatic transmission, the flywheel is lightweight stamped steel and resembles a spoked wheel. This is because the torque converter is quite heavy and provides the momentum.

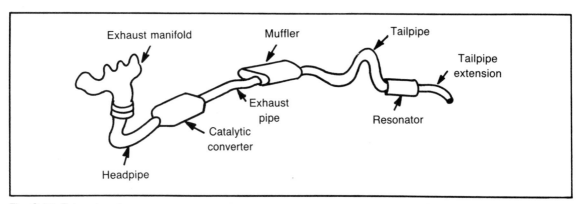

Fig. G-20. Exhaust system.

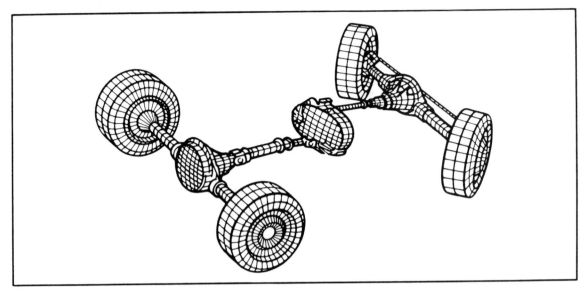

Fig. G-21. Four wheel drive.

four-wheel alignment—An alignment job that includes all four wheels, not just the front two. All vehicles can benefit from a four-wheel alignment, not just those with front-wheel drive or independent rear suspensions. The rear wheels have just as much influence over directional stability as those at the front and that is why many vehicles need to have all four wheels aligned. Many problems, such as a steering pull to one side, uneven tire wear on the rear tires, or poor tracking, can be caused by misaligned rear wheels. A four-wheel alignment job generally costs more than a conventional two-wheel alignment, but the results are often worth the extra cost.

four-wheel drive (4WD)—A method of driving a vehicle by applying engine torque to all four wheels. Various schemes are used for 4WD including part-time, full-time and variable four-wheel drive. The primary advantage of four-wheel drive is increased traction, which is especially useful for off-road excursions or severe weather driving, but is of little value for normal driving. Because of the added friction in the drivetrain, a four-wheel-drive vehicle typically gets significantly lower fuel mileage than a front- or rear-wheel-drive vehicle. To help cut the drag,

most 4WD drivetrains have a transfer case that allows the driver to select either two- or four-wheel-drive depending on driving conditions. In trucks, you will often find locking hubs on the front wheels that can be locked in the "on" or free-wheeling position as needed. The latest trend in exotic sports cars is to have full-time variable four-wheel drive, in which a special transfer case routes the power to where it is needed most (Fig. G-21).

four-wheel steering—A system that uses all four wheels to steer the car. Turning the rear wheels in the opposite direction to the front at slow speeds can allow faster maneuvering and a tighter turning radius. Turning the rear wheels in the same direction as those at the front at high speed allows sudden lane changes with much greater stability. Turning the rear wheels in the same direction as the front when parking makes parallel parking much easier.

freeze plug—An expansion plug located in the side of an engine block that is designed to protect the block against freeze damage. Water expands when it turns to ice and if the coolant doesn't have enough antifreeze protection, it can freeze and crack the engine block. The freeze plugs (there are several) are supposed to pop out under such conditions to relieve the pressure on the block. Freeze plugs can often be a source of troublesome leaks as a result of internal cooling system corrosion.

front-wheel drive (FWD)—A means of driving a vehicle by applying engine power to the front wheels instead of the rear wheels. There are advantages and disadvantages to front-wheel drive. The advantages are mainly to the vehicle manufacturers because it makes it easier for them to package a vehicle engine/drivetrain/body combination more efficiently. In other words, the same basic engine/drivetrain package can be installed under a variety of different model cars. The same basic engine/transaxle package Chrysler developed for the Omni and Horizon can be found under all their current front-wheel drives ranging from the mini-vans to the sports sedans. Thus, a manufacturer can save considerably in tooling and development of a new front-wheel-drive model. Some drivers will argue that front-wheel drive handles better than rear-wheel drive while others will argue exactly the opposite. Porsche and Mercedes seem to be unimpressed by FWD and most race cars are rear-wheel drive. On the negative side, some front-wheel-drive cars have a tendency to "torque steer" and transaxle problems can be costly to repair because they often involve pulling the engine (Fig. G-22).

fuel injection—A method of fuel delivery whereby fuel is sprayed into the intake manifold or intake ports through a nozzle instead of a carburetor. Fuel injection has long been popular with import car makers but only recently have the domestic manufacturers started using it. Bosch holds most of the patents on fuel injection, so the majority of cars use Bosch or Bosch-derived systems.

fuse—A fuse is a protective link in a wiring circuit that is designed to burn out in case of an overload. The fuse has a tiny wire inside it that is designed to melt if the current exceeds a certain value. When the wire melts, it breaks the circuit and protects against damage or fire. Most fuses are located in the fuse box under the dash, although "in-line" fuses might be hidden elsewhere. *Fuse links* are short sections of special wiring that are also used to protect wiring circuits. The locations of both in-line fuses and fuse links can be looked up in a wiring diagram for your vehicle. When replacing a blown fuse, try to determine why the fuse blew. Always replace a fuse with one of the same rated capacity. Never substitute one of a higher capacity because the circuit might not be able to handle it (Fig. G-23).

gas shocks—A type of shock absorber that's pressurized with nitrogen gas to reduce internal foaming and cavitation. Considered to be a premium-grade shock, gas shocks are often used as original equipment on sports sedans and even mini-vans. A gas shock usually provides notice-

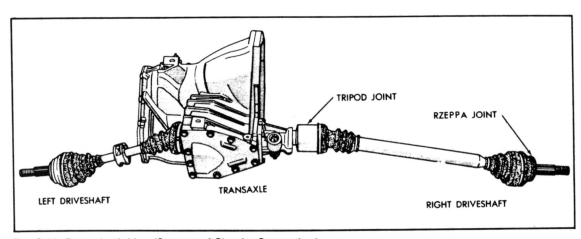

Fig. G-22. Front wheel drive. (Courtesy of Chrysler Corporation.)

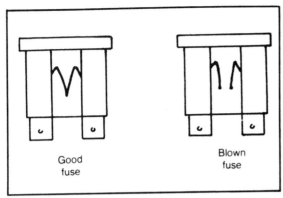

Fig. G-23. Fuse. (Courtesy of Chrysler Corporation.)

ably better ride control and flatter cornering. They are well worth considering if you are in need of replacement shocks.

gasket—A means of sealing the mating surfaces between various components. Gaskets are used between the various parts of your engine to keep oil, coolant, air, and fuel in their respective places. Rubber, cork, or a combination of cork/rubber gaskets are often used to seal the oil pan, valve covers, water pump, and timing chain cover. Metal gaskets are used between the cylinder head and engine block, and metal or asbestos gaskets are used to seal intake and exhaust manifolds. Over time, cork gaskets become brittle and break, allowing oil to leak out of the engine. Tightening the cover bolts will sometimes stop a leak, but usually the gasket must be replaced. Some late-model engines use various chemical sealers (such as RTV silicone) in place of conventional gaskets.

gas line freeze—When condensation builds up inside your fuel tank during the winter, water sometimes gets into the fuel line where it freezes in the low spots. The ice effectively blocks the flow of fuel and makes the car impossible to start. The only cure is to get the vehicle inside a warm garage where it can thaw. There are several ways to prevent gas line freeze. One is to keep your fuel tank full so there is little room for condensation to form. Another is to add an alcohol-based additive to your fuel tank every time you buy gas to absorb moisture (Fig. G-24).

gasohol—A gasoline-alcohol blend consisting of 90 percent gasoline and 10 percent ethanol alcohol. Gasohol was introduced in the midst of the 1970's fuel crisis as a means of extending limited fuel supplies. "Gasohol" as a name for alcohol-blend fuel is no longer used, but higher octane fuels based on alcohol blends continue to enjoy widespread popularity.

gasoline—A mixture of various liquid hydrocarbons derived from crude oil. It is a nonrenewable resource upon which we are overdependent and for which we will pay dearly if and when our supplies run short. Depending on how it is refined and what is added to it, the fuel's quality can vary greatly. Tetraethyl lead used to be used as a fuel additive to boost low-grade gasoline to a higher octane rating, but its use is now strictly limited. Leaded gasoline should never be used in a late-model car because lead can ruin the oxygen sensor and catalytic converter. Gasoline is highly flammable and should always be treated with respect. Never smoke when working on the fuel system (or when filling your fuel tank) and never use it as a cleaning solvent.

halfshaft—The name given to either of the two driveshafts that run from the transaxle to the wheels in a front-wheel-drive vehicle. Halfshafts can be of solid or tubular construction, and of equal or unequal length side to side.

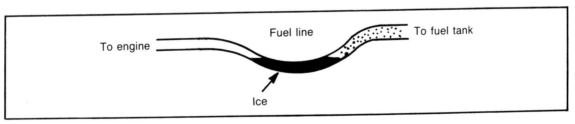

Fig. G-24. Gas line freeze.

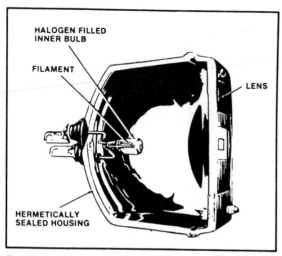

Fig. G-25. Halogen headlights. (Courtesy of Ford Motor Company.)

halogen headlights—A type of headlight that produces more light than an ordinary headlight. A halogen bulb burns brighter because it has a thinner filament. To keep the filament from melting, however, the gas mixture inside the bulb is altered slightly by adding a small amount of halogen gas (bromine, chlorine, flourine, iodine, or astatine) and sometimes krypton. Why they cost so much more than ordinary headlights has yet to be explained (Fig. G-25).

horsepower—A unit of measure for quantifying power output. Invented by James Watt, the term was originally used to describe how much effort a horse exerted when lugging coal out of a coal mine. One horsepower was the amount of effort one horse put forth in raising 33,000 pounds 1 foot in 1 minute. Engine horsepower ratings are determined on special equipment and are usually expressed as so much *brake* horsepower, which is the amount of horsepower the engine actually delivers after internal friction and parasitic loses are taken into account.

hub nut—The large hex nut on the outer end of a front-wheel-drive halfshaft that holds the shaft within the wheel hub. Most vehicle manufacturers recommend replacing this nut if it is removed for CV joint service.

hydrocarbon (HC)—A hydrocarbon (HC) is any kind of substance that contains hydrogen and carbon, such as gasoline and oil. When gasoline burns inside an engine, there is always a tiny amount that is left over. If an engine is misfiring because of a fouled spark plug or a leaky valve, or if it has worn rings or valve guides and uses oil, quite a bit of unburned HC can pass through the engine into the exhaust. Unburned HC is a major source of air pollution and is the primary source of smog in most urban areas. Various means are used to reduce the amount of HC an engine produces, the primary one of which is the catalytic converter. The converter reduces HC emissions by reburning and converting it into harmless water vapor.

idle mixture—The air/fuel ratio that is delivered through the carburetor when the engine is idling. It can be adjusted by turning the idle mixture adjustment screw(s) on the carburetor. The screw opens up a small passage that lets more or less fuel into the engine. On most late-model vehicles, the idle mixture screws have caps that allow only limited adjustment, or they are completely sealed to prevent tampering. The relative richness or leanness of the idle mixture has a big effect on tail pipe emissions at idle.

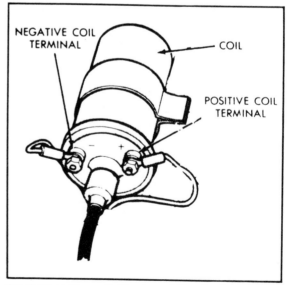

Fig. G-26. Ignition coil. (Courtesy of Chrysler Corporation.)

idle speed—Refers to how fast the engine runs when idling. It can usually be adjusted by turning a screw on the carburetor throttle linkage, or by turning an air bypass screw on a fuel injection throttle body. On many newer cars, however, it is computer controlled and nonadjustable.

ignition coil—The component in the ignition system that turns low voltage into high voltage to fire the spark plugs. When 12 volts pass through the coil's primary windings, it creates a strong magnetic field. Then, when the current is shut off (by the ignition module or the opening of the contact points in older ignition systems), the magnetic field causes a surge of high voltage (as much as 40,000 volts) in the coil's secondary windings. The high voltage passes to the distributor, then on to the spark plugs where it jumps the plug gap and fires the plugs. Coil problems include shorts or openings in the internal wiring, and cracks around the high-voltage terminal.

ignition module—The control box that replaces the contact points in an electronic ignition system. A magnetic pickup in the distributor is used to trigger the module, which in turn uses its transistorized circuitry to switch the ignition coil on and off to fire the spark plugs. The ignition module itself can be located inside the distributor (GM and some imports), on the distributor housing (some Ford applications), or in the engine compartment. Some modules also control timing advance and retard. If a module goes bad, it usually is completely inoperable. The engine will not run because there is no trigger voltage to the ignition coil. You cannot fix a bad module, it must be replaced.

ignition system—The various components that control the igniting of fuel in the engine's

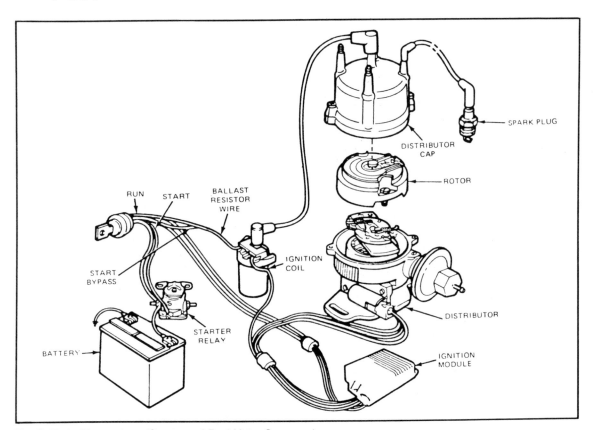

Fig. G-27. Ignition system. (Courtesy of Ford Motor Company.)

cylinders (Fig. G-27). The ignition system has two parts: the primary side (the distributor and electronic control module) and the secondary side (the ignition coil, distributor cap, rotor, spark plug wires, and spark plugs).

injector—The component in a diesel or gasoline fuel injection system that squirts fuel into the engine. In gasoline engines, the injector is usually electrically triggered. Varnish and dirt can build up in the nozzle opening, restricting the flow of fuel. Injectors can be cleaned by using various fuel additives. In diesel engines, the injectors are mechanical and deliver fuel under very high pressure directly into the cylinders. Clogging and leaking are two common problems with diesel injectors. Dirty injectors can be cleaned with fuel additives, but leaky injectors must be replaced.

inner or inboard CV joint—The CV joint closest to the transaxle in a front-wheel-drive car (Fig. G-28).

intercooler—A heat exchanger that is added to a turbocharged engine to cool the air after it leaves the turbo. This increases the air's density and means more air can be pumped into the engine. The result is roughly a 10 to 15 percent improvement in horsepower.

jounce—When you drive over a bump and the suspension is momentarily compressed, that is called jounce. When it springs back, that is called rebound.

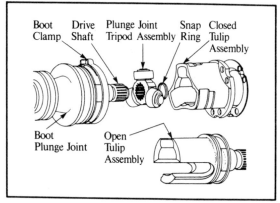

Fig. G-28. Inboard CV joint.

jump starting—A technique of starting one vehicle using another vehicle's battery. A pair of jumper cables are required to connect the terminals of both batteries together (positive to positive, negative to negative). The safest technique is to first connect the positive terminals on both batteries to one another and then to connect the negative terminal on the good battery to a ground (such as the engine block or frame) on the vehicle with a dead battery. The final jumper connection usually sparks, so keeping the spark away from the discharged battery avoids any danger of blowing up the battery. Once the jumper cables have been connected, the engine should be run at fast idle to help charge the dead battery for a few of minutes. Then the first attempt to start the car should be made. If it does not start within 15 seconds, stop and wait a minute before trying again. This gives the starter a chance to cool off. Continuous cranking can ruin the starter and drain the good battery.

LCD—A liquid crystal display is a type of electronic display that forms opaque or dull-colored letters or numbers on various backgrounds. LCD displays are popular for digital dashboards, but they are not as readable in direct sunlight as LED displays (see below).

LED—A light emitting diode is an electronic light bulb that produces a red-colored light. You will find LED displays used on everything from hand calculators to instrument panels. LEDs are also used in some vehicle speed sensors and in some electronic ignitions.

lifters—Also called "followers" or "tappets," they are the components that ride on the cam lobes and help "lift" the valves open. There are two basic types: solid and hydraulic. Hydraulic lifters are hollow and fill up with oil to take up slack in the upper valve train. Low oil pressure, loss of pressure from the lifters, or plugged oil holes in the lifters can result in a "clattering" sound that is referred to as "noisy lifters." Hydraulic lifters do not require periodic adjustment, but solid lifters do require adjusting to maintain the correct amount of valve lash.

MacPherson strut—A special kind of oversized shock absorber that is used as part of the vehicle's suspension. When used on the front suspension, it replaces the upper control arm and ball joint. Some struts have coil springs around them while others do not. Some struts have replaceable internal components that can be repaired by dropping in a new cartridge. A do-it-yourselfer can replace (or rebuild) a MacPherson strut, but it might require renting a spring compressor and/or having the wheels realigned (Fig. G-29).

master cylinder—When you step on the brake pedal, it pushes a piston inside the master cylinder that produces hydraulic pressure inside the brake system. The brake fluid reservoir is located on top of the master cylinder, and you will find both mounted on the firewall in the engine

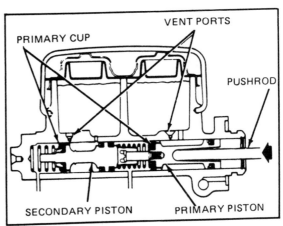

Fig. G-30. Master cylinder.

compartment on the driver's side of the vehicle. When the piston seals in the master cylinder eventually wear out, the cylinder might start to leak fluid and/or lose pressure. A brake pedal that gradually sinks to the floor is a sure sign of a bad master cylinder. The unit can be rebuilt or replaced Note: aluminum master cylinders should never be honed because doing so removes the protective anodizing from the inside of the cylinder (Fig. G-30).

MFI—Abbreviation for multi-port fuel injection, a type of fuel injection system that has one injector for each engine cylinder. Each injector sprays its fuel directly into the intake port in the cylinder head. Multi-port fuel injection is considered to be the 'hot' setup because it provides better cylinder-to-cylinder fuel distribution for more power.

motor oil—The lifeblood of the engine, it not only lubricates the engine, but also cools the crankshaft bearings and pistons. As an engine runs, combustion blowby into the crankcase contaminates the oil with moisture, soot, and unburned fuel. Moisture is the worst culprit because it forms acids and sludge. Additives in the motor oil (nearly a third of a can of oil is additives) fight the contaminants and give the oil special lubricating properties. The oil itself never wears out, but the additives do. That is why the oil must be changed periodically to replenish the additives. Adding in an occasional can of oil is

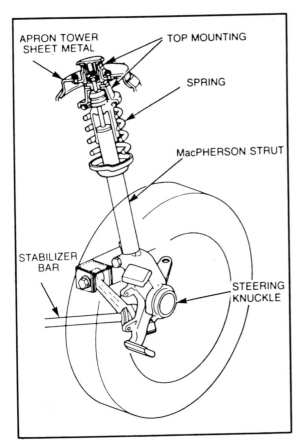

Fig. G-29. MacPherson strut.

197

not enough. The oil filter traps dirt (but not moisture) so it should also be replaced at every oil change. Use the recommended viscosity and type of oil listed in your owner's manual. The difference between competing brands of motor oil is mostly advertising. Any oil of the proper viscosity that conforms to the highest "SF" rating should be safe for your engine. Use of straight weight or nondetergent oils in late-model engines is not recommended.

MPG—Abbreviation for miles per gallon. A vehicle's fuel economy is determined by a number of factors including the size of the engine, the type of carburetion used, the weight of the vehicle, the type of transmission used (manual or automatic), the final drive ratio, the size and type of tires used, tire inflation pressures, aerodynamic streamlining of the body, the driving habits of the driver, the kind of road surface and terrain upon which the vehicle is driven, the speed at which it is driven, and environmental factors such as temperature, wind, and humidity. Taking all of these factors into consideration, it is no wonder the EPA says "the mileage you get may vary from the official EPA estimates."

muffler—The device in your exhaust system that quiets the roar of the exhaust. A muffler is nothing more than a steel can full of baffles. Some (the so-called "glass-pack" mufflers) use Fiberglas batting to soak up noise. Mufflers rust out because exhaust is roughly 50 percent water vapor. The further the muffler is located from the engine, the more prone it is to rapid rust-through because the water vapor has more time to cool and condense. The best mufflers use metal that is galvanized on both sides. Aluminized mufflers or those that use galvanized metal on the outside only are not as rust resistant. The worst mufflers are those with no protection at all. Changing a muffler usually requires a hacksaw or chisel because the connections are either welded or corroded tight. For what you would save on a do-it-yourself muffler job, you might be better off taking it to a muffler shop.

NHTSA—Abbreviation for the National Highway Traffic and Safety Administration. This is the government agency that is responsible for making and policing safety rules for all vehicles. NHTSA is the agency that can order a vehicle manufacturer to issue a recall.

NOX—Abbreviation for oxides of nitrogen. The "N" stands for nitrogen, the "O" for oxygen, and the "X" is scientific notation for the various combinations of the two. NOX is formed inside your engine when combustion temperatures exceed 2500 degrees Fahrenheit. NOX is considered to be a serious air pollutant because it is so irritating. NOX emissions are minimized by the EGR valve and by the catalytic converter in 1981 and newer model cars.

octane—This is a measure of a fuel's resistance to detonation. The higher the number, the better the fuel. Typical unleaded regular octane ratings range from 86 to 88. Premium-grade unleaded fuels start around 89 and go as high as 93 or 94. By comparison, leaded premium fuels of a decade ago often started at 95 and went to over 100. The octane rating of gasoline can be boosted by additional refining and/or adding octane boosting chemicals such as benzene, alcohol, or tetraethyl lead. Lead is a great octane booster, but it ruins catalytic converters and oxygen sensors. Because of this, leaded fuel should not be used in 1975 and later model cars.

oil consumption—All engines use a small amount of oil over a period of time. It gets past the piston rings and valve guide seals and is burned in the combustion chamber. A small amount escapes through the PCV system and a few drops usually manage to seep through a gasket or seal. The question is, at what point should one consider oil consumption to be a problem? Any engine that consumes less than a quart of oil every 3,000 miles is in excellent mechanical condition. If it uses less than a quart in 1500 miles, it is still in pretty good condition. But once oil consumption exceeds a quart of oil every 1000 miles, it signals that the engine is approaching retirement. Blue smoke in the exhaust or oil consumption on the order of a quart or more every

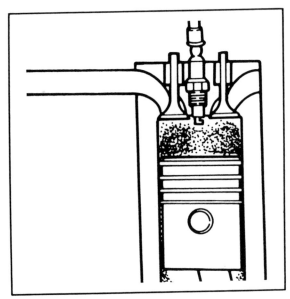

Fig. G-31. Oil consumption.

500 miles indicates serious oil burning problems (usually due to worn or broken piston rings, a cracked piston, or worn valve guides and/or seals). Sometimes a leaky seal or gasket can make an otherwise good engine use oil. The most frequent leak points are valve cover gaskets, crankshaft end seals, and oil pan gaskets. Tightening the valve cover or pan bolts can sometimes stop a leak, but usually the only remedy is to replace the gasket (Fig. G-31).

oil cooler—A heat exchanger for cooling oil. Most automatic transmissions are equipped with an oil cooler that is located inside the radiator. Because the radiator usually runs close to 200 degrees, the amount of cooling this kind of setup provides is questionable. An aftermarket oil cooler that can be installed outside the radiator can provide much better cooling and is recommended for towing or high-performance applications. Except for air-cooled engines (older Volkswagens, for example) and race cars, most engines do not use an oil cooler. The engine's cooling system is usually adequate to keep oil temperatures within safe limits.

oil pressure—The amount of pressure created in your engine's oil system by the oil pump. A cer-

tain amount of oil pressure is needed to circulate the oil throughout the engine and to maintain adequate lubrication. Low oil pressure or loss of pressure is serious because it can mean expensive engine damage. A low oil level in the oil pan, oil leaks, dirty oil, diluted oil (with gasoline), too low a viscosity oil, a plugged oil pickup screen or oil filter, a worn oil pump, or worn main bearings can all cause dangerously low oil pressure. Complete loss of oil pressure usually results from a broken oil pump drive-shaft (the pump is usually driven off the bottom of the distributor or the camshaft). Unless the engine is shut off immediately it will be ruined. Oil pressure is monitored by a sending unit mounted someplace on the engine block. Oil pushes against a spring-loaded diaphragm, which in turn is connected to a resistor or set of contacts that trigger the dash gauge or warning light. A low oil pressure indication should always be investigated immediately. If the oil level isn't low, you have a problem—especially if the engine is making noise. Sometimes a faulty oil pressure sending unit will give a false low reading, but usually it is something else.

overhead cam (OHC)—This refers to a type of engine design that positions the camshaft in the cylinder head over the valves. It is a popular design on many four-cylinder engines, but it is rarely used on V6 or V8 engines. Many import vehicles use engines with overhead cams. Many of these engines lack hydraulic valve adjusters, so periodic readjustment of valve lash settings is required. On engines that use a rubber belt to drive the overhead cam, the belt usually needs to be replaced somewhere around 60,000 miles (Fig. G-32).

oxygen sensor—A component in the engine's computer control system that monitors the amount of oxygen in the exhaust. The computer uses this information to change the relative richness or leanness of the air/fuel mixture. You will find the oxygen sensor in the exhaust manifold. It resembles a small spark plug on the outside, but inside it has a special zirconium element that produces a varying voltage once it gets hot. The

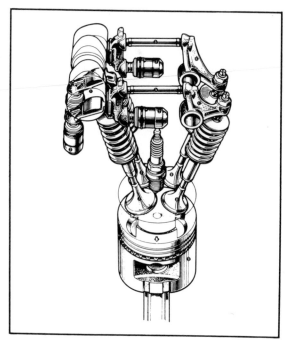

Fig. G-32. Overhead cam.

lower the oxygen content, the higher the sensor's output voltage. The oxygen sensor is vulnerable to contamination if leaded fuel is used and if it goes bad, the computer would not know how to set the fuel mixture. Consequently, your car would not run well because it is getting too much gas. The normal life of the sensor is approximately 50,000 miles (Fig. G-33).

outer or outboard CV joint—The CV joint closest the wheel in a front- or rear-wheel-drive vehicle.

overheating—When the temperature of the coolant exceeds the normal operating temperature range of the engine, it is said to be overheating. A number of things can cause this to happen. Idling for long periods of time in traffic during hot weather can cause overheating, because the water pump does not turn fast enough to circulate sufficient coolant through the system (put the transmission in neutral and rev up the engine to help cool it off). A defective thermostat can stick shut and prevent the coolant from circulating to the radiator (replace the thermostat). A leak that allows the coolant level to drop can

result in overheating (fix the leak, then refill the cooling system). A defective or inoperative cooling fan can cause the engine to overheat, as can a slipping or broken fan belt (find the fault and fix it). If your engine overheats, turning on the heater can sometimes help increase cooling capacity enough to cool it down. In most cases, though, you should shut if off and let it cool because running it hot can ruin the engine. Do not open the radiator until the engine has been off for at least an hour and then add coolant only after the engine has been restarted and is idling.

overload shocks—A type of shock absorber that is equipped with a helper spring to keep the suspension from sagging when a vehicle is heavily loaded.

oversteer—A handling trait in which a vehicle tends to overrespond to changes that are made in the direction of the steering wheel. The rear end on a vehicle that oversteers will tend to spin around when the vehicle is turned sharply.

parking brake—A mechanical brake for locking the rear wheels when parking. When you pull on the parking brake handle or step on the parking brake pedal, it pulls a pair of cables that ex-

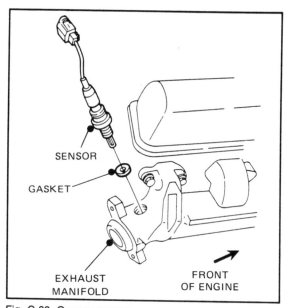

SENSOR

GASKET

EXHAUST
MANIFOLD

FRONT
OF ENGINE

Fig. G-33. Oxygen sensor.

tend to the rear brakes. The cables work a lever mechanism that binds the rear shoes against the drums or on rear disc brake-equipped vehicles, locks the pads (or a pair of minishoes) against the rotor. The most common problem associated with the parking brake is corrosion in the cable sleeves, which can prevent the rear brakes from releasing once the brake has been applied. The best way to prevent this from happening is to use the parking brake frequently (Fig G-34).

PCV valve—The positive crankcase ventilation valve is an emissions control device that routes unburned crankcase blowby gases back into the intake manifold where they can be reburned. The PCV system is one of the oldest emission control devices and also one of the most beneficial. Besides totally eliminating crankcase emissions as a source of air pollution, the constant recirculation of air through the crankcase helps remove moisture, which otherwise would cause sludge to form. Therefore, the PCV valve extends the life of your oil and your engine. The PCV valve requires little maintenance. The valve and filter should be replaced at approximately 30,000 miles (Fig. G-35).

PFI—Abbreviation for port fuel injection, another name for a multi-port fuel injection system. The system uses one injector for each engine cylinder. Fuel is sprayed directly into the intake port for better cylinder-to-cylinder fuel distribution and more power.

power brakes—Most vehicles use a vacuum booster to increase the pedal force applied to the master cylinder. Some use a hydraulic power unit that does the same thing with hydraulic pressure rather than vacuum. Power brakes require no special maintenance, but if the booster goes bad, pedal effort will be noticeably higher. A loose or leaky vacuum hose to the booster unit is often all that is wrong. But if the booster itself is bad, it must be replaced.

power steering—A means of hydraulically assisted steering. A belt-driven power steering pump creates system pressure. The pressurized fluid is then routed into a cylinder that helps push the wheels one way or the other when the steering wheel is turned. The two most common power steering complaints are noise and leaks. A slipping drive belt on the power steering pump can produce a loud squeal, especially when turn-

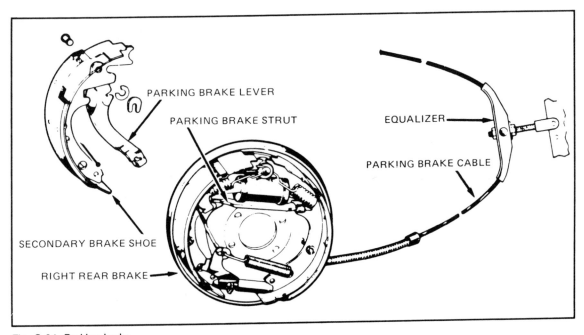

PARKING BRAKE LEVER

PARKING BRAKE STRUT

EQUALIZER

PARKING BRAKE CABLE

SECONDARY BRAKE SHOE

RIGHT REAR BRAKE

Fig. G-34. Parking brake.

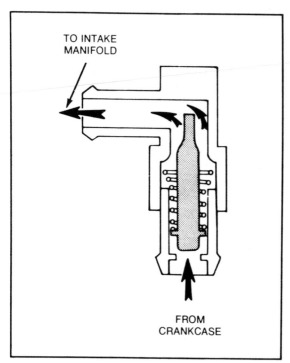

ing sharply. A bad valve or bearings in the pump itself can make a growling noise. Leaks most often occur at hose couplings or on the power cylinder seals. In power rack and pinion steering units, internal leaks can be a major problem (which require replacing the entire unit with a new or rebuilt assembly). The only required maintenance for this system is to check the level of the power steering fluid periodically. If low, check for possible leaks, then add fresh fluid to the pump reservoir. Running the system low can ruin the pump.

preventive maintenance—A method of preventing problems by maintaining wear items according to a regular schedule. Lubricating, adjusting, and replacing all wear items before they can cause problems contributes to trouble-free driving and longer vehicle life. Regular fluid checks and fluid and filter changes are the most important items on any preventive maintenance checklist.

PSI—Abbreviation for pounds per square inch. Usually used when referring to tire inflation

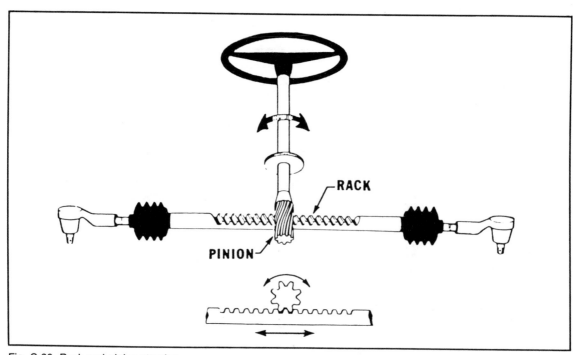

RACK

PINION

Fig. G-36. Rack and pinion steering.

pressures, cooling system pressure, or turbocharger boost pressure.

rack and pinion steering—A type of lightweight steering gear that uses a wormlike gear (the pinion) to drive a horizontal bar (the rack). The primary advantage of rack and pinion steering is that it is lightweight and uses fewer parts than a reciprocating ball steering gear (Fig. G-36).

radial tire—A type of tire that is constructed with the reinforcing belts sideways under the tread rather than lengthwise. This makes the tire more flexible, which reduces rolling resistance to improve fuel economy. A radial tire can be identified by looking for the letter "R" in the size designation on the tire's sidewall (Fig. G-37).

radiator—The part of your cooling system that rids the engine of heat. Coolant from the engine flows past the thermostat and into the radiator where it is cooled by air passing through the fins. Internal corrosion and hairline cracks caused by vibration are the two primary causes of radiator leaks. "Stop leak" can be added to the radiator to temporarily plug small leaks, but larger leaks usually require professional repair or replacement. *Recoring* a radiator means putting a new finned heat exchanger section between the end tanks. This is usually more economical than buying a whole new radiator.

rebound—This term refers to the suspension springing back after it has been momentarily compressed.

rebuilt parts—Rebuilt parts have been salvaged and reconditioned to good-as-new condition. Rebuilt parts include alternators, starters, water pumps, clutches, brake calipers, brake shoes, master brake cylinders, and fuel pumps. Savings compared to equivalent new parts range from 20 to 50 percent, but let the buyer beware. The quality ranges from exceptional to questionable. Some rebuilders do a complete overhaul and replace everything that is worn, while others only fix what is wrong. Rebuilts are fine, but buy a reputable name brand product backed by a written guarantee.

relay—An electrical device that uses an electromagnetic switch and contact points to turn on and off various high-amperage electrical accessories. Your vehicle likely has a horn relay, a headlight relay, a relay for the rear window defogger, and relays for various other items such as the blower motor. When an accessory goes dead, it is often the relay that needs to be replaced.

RPM—Abbreviation for revolutions per minute. Engine speed is often expressed as so many rpm.

rear-wheel drive (RWD)—A method of driving a vehicle whereby engine power is applied to the rear wheels. Power from the engine flows through the transmission, down the driveshaft, through the differential, to the rear axles and wheels.

rustproofing—The process of applying rust-inhibiting chemicals, waxes, or sealers to the underside and inside of the vehicle's body as well as any other rust-prone areas. Do not confuse it with undercoating, which treats only the underside of the vehicle. Commercial rustproofing treatments such as Rusty Jones, Ziebart, etc., usually include a guarantee that offers 5-year rust protection. Be aware of the fact that such guarantees usually require annual checkups to touch up any areas where the rustproofing might have peeled loose, worn away, or been damaged. Numerous rustproofing chemicals are available for do-it-yourself application.

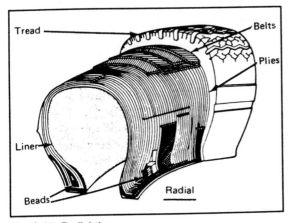

Fig. G-37. Radial tine.

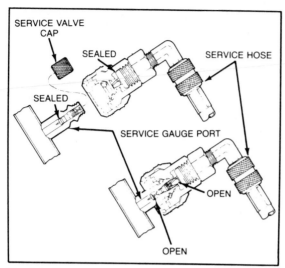

Fig. G-38. Schrader valve. (Courtesy of *Ford Motorcraft Shop Tips,* Vol. 19, No. 2.)

Schrader valve—A type of valve fitting that opens when depressed. Schrader valves are used in tire valve stems, on air conditioning hoses, and on the fuel rails of many fuel injection systems (Fig. G-38).

semimetallic brakes—A type of brake lining that uses steel wool instead of asbestos as a reinforcing fiber. Semimetallic brakes give better high-temperature performance and wear characteristics than conventional asbestos linings. They are commonly used on the front disc brakes of front-wheel-drive passenger cars. Asbestos pads should never be substituted for semimetallic pads when relining the brakes. Rapid brake wear will result.

serpentine belt—A type of flat rubber drive belt that is used to turn multiple accessories on the front of an engine. It is called a serpentine belt because of the way it snakes around the various pulleys. Many vehicles now have a single serpentine drive belt because it eliminates the need for several separate V-belts. A spring-loaded pulley maintains tension on the serpentine belt. This eliminates the need to retension the belt when it is replaced. Serpentine belts generally last 25 to 50 percent longer than conventional V-belts (Fig. G-39).

shock absorber—A part of your suspension system that is designed to dampen up-and-down wheel motions that result from bumps and chassis movement. Each wheel has its own shock absorber, which is nothing more than a fluid-filled cylinder with a piston and valving inside. The shock absorber's job is to provide a controlled amount of resistance every time the wheels bounce up and down or the chassis leans as it goes around a corner. The constant motion and the heat created by all the internal friction can wear out an original equipment shock in 15,000 to 25,000 miles. There are many different types of replacement shocks from which to choose and selecting the one that is right depends on the application. Oil on the outside of a shock is a sign that the seal is leaking and the shock might need to be replaced. A "bounce test" can also be used to tell if the shocks are worn (the vehicle should bounce no more than once or twice after rocking the bumper up and down vigorously).

smart suspensions—Any suspension that uses computer-controlled shock absorbers and/or air springs to vary ride characteristics and/or ride height. The advantage of such a suspension is that it can change the way the suspension reacts to changing road conditions. On a rough road, it can provide a smoother ride. On smooth roads, it can firm up to provide better handling. A computer-controlled solenoid on top of each

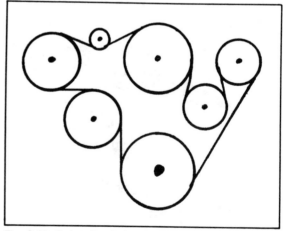

Fig. G-39. Serpentine belt.

shock absorber or MacPherson strut changes the internal valving of the shock to provide a stiffer or softer suspension as needed. On suspensions that use air springs, ride height sensors allow the computer to maintain the same ride height in spite of changing loads. Air can be added or bled from the air springs by computer-controlled solenoid valves. On some vehicles, the computer lowers the vehicle for better aerodynamics at high speed; on some four-wheel drive vehicles, the suspension can be raised for increased off-road ground clearance.

spare tire—There are several different types of spare tires: a folding spare (which must be inflated with an air canister prior to mounting), a compact spare (which is much smaller and narrower than the other wheels on your vehicle), and a lightweight spare (which is the same diameter as the other tires on your vehicle but thinner). All of these tires are labeled "temporary" spares because of their weight-saving construction. As such, they are intended for emergency use only—not for sustained or high-speed driving. Most carry a warning not to exceed 50 mph nor to travel farther than 50 miles. The only kind of spare tire that can be used without such restrictions is a conventional, full-size spare that is the same as the other tires on your vehicle.

spark knock—This is the pinging or rattling noise sometimes heard during acceleration that indicates detonation is occurring inside the engine. Spark knock can be caused by a variety of things including using low-octane fuel, overadvanced ignition timing, too much compression (often due to a buildup of carbon in the combustion chamber), by an inoperative EGR valve, and/or by too much heat. If switching to a higher octane fuel does not cure the problem, the cause should be investigated, because prolonged or heavy knocking can damage your engine.

spark plug—A component in the ignition system that ignites the fuel inside the combustion chamber. The spark plug is nothing more than a pair of electrodes with a gap in between. When high voltage from the ignition system reaches the gap, an electrical arc jumps across it and ignites

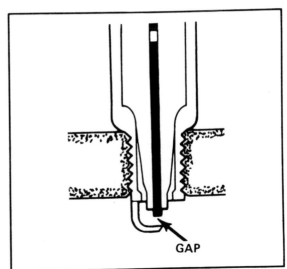

Fig. G-40. Spark plug.

the fuel. The distance across this gap is critical because if it is too wide, there might not be enough voltage to push the spark across. The center electrode gradually wears away as the spark plug accumulates miles and deposits buildup around the insulated tip that can short circuit the firing voltage. That's why spark plugs require periodic replacement. With unleaded fuel, average plug life should be approximately 30,000 miles (Fig. G-40).

solenoid—A type of electrical device that uses an electromagnet to move something. The starter on your engine uses a solenoid for engaging the flywheel. Power door locks use solenoids to pull and release the locks. A fuel injector has a built-in solenoid that opens and closes the nozzle. An idle stop solenoid might be used on the carburetor to close the throttle to prevent dieseling when the engine is shut off, or to increase idle speed when the air conditioner is running.

spoiler—An aerodynamic accessory that goes across the trunk or back of a vehicle to deflect the direction of airflow and reduce drag. A front spoiler is technically an "air dam" because it prevents air from getting under the car and increasing drag.

suspension—The part of a vehicle that carries the weight. This includes the springs, control arms, ball joints, struts and/or shock absorbers (Fig. G-41).

supercharger—Also called a "blower," a supercharger is a device that forces more air and fuel into the engine to increase horsepower. Unlike a turbocharger, a supercharger is belt or gear driven and provides instant boost pressure to the engine at any speed.

sway bar—A component that is often used in a suspension system to control body roll. A sway bar can be used on the front and/or rear suspension to help keep the body flat as the vehicle rounds a corner. This greatly improves a vehicle's cornering agility. Replacing the sway bar with one of a larger diameter can increase it even more.

TDC—Abbreviation for top dead center. This is the point at which the piston reaches its uppermost position in the cylinder. Ignition timing is usually expressed as so many degrees before top dead center (BTDC) or after top dead center (ATDC). A timing mark on the crankshaft pulley or flywheel corresponds to the top dead center position of the number one engine cylinder (Fig. G-42).

test pipe—A short piece of exhaust pipe that is designed to replace a catalytic converter in an exhaust system, supposedly while you test the results of the switch. There is some question as to the legality of test pipes because removing the catalytic converter is considered tampering with your vehicle's emission control system. A professional mechanic can be fined up to $10,000 if caught installing one on a customer's car, and although there is no law against a motorist installing one on his own car, it can be grounds for failing an emissions test. In spite of the law, test pipes have become a hot item because they enable people to save a few cents per gallon by burning regular leaded gas (except on 1981 and newer engines with computer controls, because lead will still damage the oxygen sensor). A test pipe is also a less expensive alternative to buying a new converter, but now that leaded gasoline is disappearing, the market for test pipes might be starting to cool.

thermostat—A temperature control device in your engine's cooling system that speeds engine warm-up and helps the engine run at a consistent operating temperature. Thermostats come in various temperature ratings but most engines today use a thermostat that opens between 190 and 195 degrees. The thermostat is usually located in a small housing that connects the upper radiator hose to the engine. Sometimes a

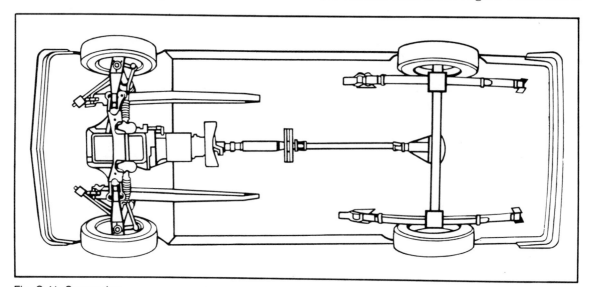

Fig. G-41. Suspension.

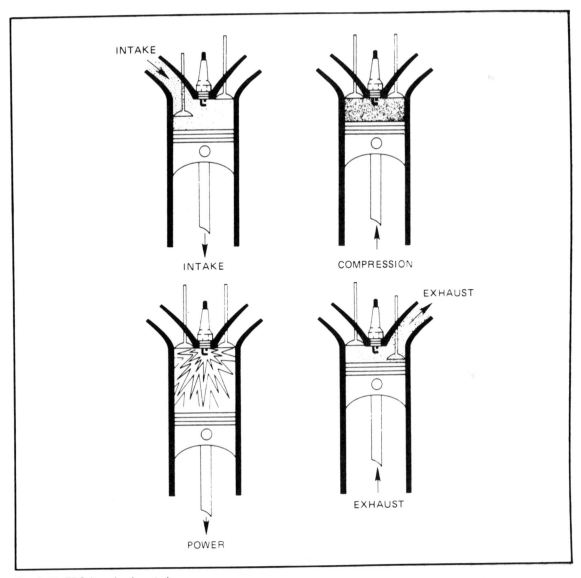

INTAKE

INTAKE

COMPRESSION

EXHAUST

POWER

EXHAUST

Fig. G-42. TDC (top dead center).

thermostat will stick shut, causing the engine to overheat. Overheating occurs because the thermostat blocks the flow of coolant back to the radiator. If a thermostat sticks open, the engine will warm up slowly and might never reach its normal operating temperature. This can result in little or no heat from the heater. Running an engine without a thermostat is not recommended because excessive cooling can lead to increased blowby and ring wear (Fig. G-43).

throttle body injection (TBI)—A type of electronic fuel injection system that uses a single injector or pair of injectors mounted in a centrally located throttle body. The throttle unit resembles a carburetor except that there is no fuel bowl, float, or metering jets. Fuel is sprayed directly into the throttle bore(s) by the injector(s) (Fig. G-44).

throttle position sensor (TPS)—A little gadget on the carburetor throttle linkage or fuel injec-

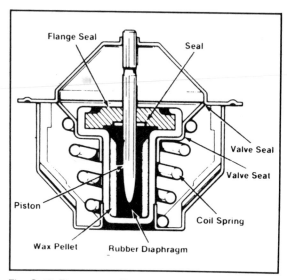

Fig. G-43. Thermostat. (Courtesy of *Ford Motorcraft Shop Tips,* Vol. 19, No. 2.)

tion throttle body that keeps the engine control computer informed about the throttle opening. The TPS is a variable resistor that changes resistance as the throttle opens wider. The computer needs this information to change the air/fuel mixture. Adjustment is very critical and is best left to a qualified professional.

tie rod end—A flexible coupling in the steering linkage that connects the tie rods to the steering knuckles. Some require periodic greasing (twice a year or every 6,000 miles) while others are sealed. A loose or worn tie rod will cause a feathered wear pattern on tires and is probably the leading cause of rapid tire wear. Worn tie rod ends can be detected by raising the suspension and rocking the front wheel back and forth. If there is any free play, it probably means the tie rod ends are bad. Replacement can be a do-it-yourself job, but front toe alignment must be reset once the new tie rods ends have been installed. (Fig. G-45).

timing light—A strobe light for checking ignition timing. The light is connected to the number one spark plug wire, so every time the plug fires the light flashes. The light is then aimed at the timing marks on the crankshaft pulley or flywheel to read timing.

tire ratings—On the sidewall of every tire is information about tire size, maximum load rating, maximum inflation pressure, tire construction, and performance standards. Tread wear is a comparative rating of how long the tire will last compared to other tires. The higher the number, the longer the predicted life of the tread. A tire with a 200 rating should go twice as many miles as one with a 100 rating. The numbers do not correspond to a fixed mileage figure, because there are so many variables that affect the life of the tread (maintaining the correct inflation pressure is one of the most important). The traction rating is a measure of the tire's ability to stop on wet pavement. An "A" is the best rating, "B" is average, and "C" is the lowest acceptable rating. The temperature rating is an indication of how cool the tire runs at highway speeds. Performance tires also carry a speed rating: "H"-rated tires are good for speeds up to 130 mph, and "V"-rated tires are certified for speeds above 130 mph.

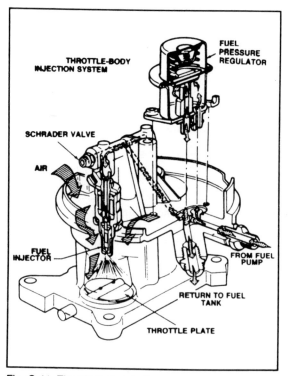

Fig. G-44. Throttle body injection.

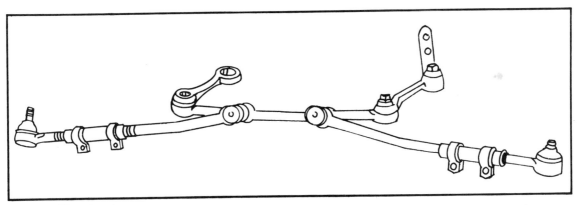

Fig. G-45. Tie rod end.

toe—A wheel alignment angle that refers to the parallelism of the tires as viewed from above. Toe-in means the leading edges of the tires are closer together than the rear edges. Toe-out means the leading edges of the tires are farther apart than the rear edges. A vehicle should have zero running toe (perfect parallel alignment) when driving. But because the rubber bushings and joints in the suspension give a little (called "compliance"), most rear-wheel-drive vehicles call for a slight amount of toe-in when the wheels are initially aligned. Front-wheel-drive vehicles are just the opposite; most call for a slight amount of toe-out because the drive wheels tend to bow in as they pull the vehicle down the road. Toe alignment is very important because it greatly affects tread wear. If toe alignment is off, it will produce a feathered wear pattern across the tire tread. Toe is adjusted by turning the tie rods or tie rod ends to shorten or lengthen the steering linkage. On front-wheel-drive vehicles, the rear toe setting can often be changed by adding shims behind the wheel hub or by changing the pivot position of the control arms (Fig. G-46).

torque—Turning or twisting force. Torque is usually expressed as so many foot/pounds (a 1-pound force exerted on a lever 1 foot in length). A torque wrench measures the amount of twisting force being applied to a nut or bolt. The torque output of an engine is expressed as the maximum force exerted by the engine at a given engine speed. Large cubic inch displacement en-

gines and engines with long throw crankshafts produce high torque outputs.

torque converter—A fluid coupling that connects the engine to an automatic transmission. The torque converter contains three sets of bladed wheels that face one another. One wheel, the impeller, is attached to the converter housing and turns at the same speed as the engine. Another wheel, the turbine, is attached to the transmission input shaft. As the impeller spins, it slings automatic transmission fluid at the turbine and makes it turn. The third wheel, the stator, is positioned between the turbine and impeller to redirect fluid flow. When starting out, the stator remains stationary and multiplies torque from two to two-and-a-half times (much

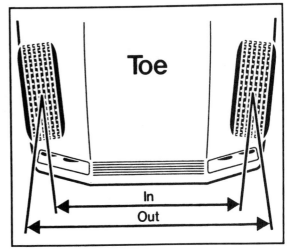

Fig. G-46. Toe.

like a reduction gear) by recirculating fluid back through the impeller. But when the speed of the turbine wheel starts to catch up with the impeller, the stator starts to spin and the converter "locks up," becoming a direct drive fluid coupling. Many late-model vehicles are equipped with a "lockup" torque converter that contains an electrically operated computer-controlled clutch mechanism. The mechanical clutch eliminates the slight amount of slippage that occurs in an ordinary torque converter fluid coupling to improve fuel economy. The lockup solenoid is engaged when the vehicle reaches a predetermined speed and/or engine load (Fig. G-47).

torque steer—The annoying tendency of some front-wheel-drive vehicles to pull to one side when engine torque is applied. In other words, you step on the gas and the car wants to steer right or left. By redesigning the power train to use equal length halfshafts between the transaxle and wheels, the tendency toward torque steer can be greatly reduced. The other remedy is to keep off the gas.

torque wrench—A special wrench with a built-in indicator that shows you how much force you are applying to a bolt. A torque wrench should always be used when doing any type of major engine work, when tightening fasteners on the brake system or suspension, when tightening wheel lug nuts, or when you do not want to risk breaking a bolt.

towing—Most vehicles can tow a moderate amount of weight (1000 pounds or less) without too much trouble. But for heavier loads, the suspension and cooling system might require beefing up (see your owner's manual for towing recommendations and load limits). Overload or air-assist shocks can keep the rear end from sagging and a stabilizer bar on the trailer hitch can reduce swaying. Automatic transmissions should be equipped with an oil cooler to protect the transmission against overheating. A larger radiator or a larger fan might be required to keep the engine from overheating.

transaxle—The transmission in a front-wheel-drive vehicle. It combines both transmission and differential into one assembly (Fig. G-48).

transmission—The gear box that multiplies engine torque by gear reduction and/or torque conversion. A typical manual transmission has four or five speeds, with the final or highest gear being either a direct 1:1 drive ratio or an "overdrive" ratio (less than 1:1). An automatic transmission first multiplies engine torque as it passes through the fluid coupling, known as the torque converter, and then through three or four separate gear ratios. A manual transmission usually gives slightly better fuel economy than an automatic, because there is a certain amount of slippage that occurs in the automatic's torque converter. A manual transmission is usually trouble-free, except for the clutch, which can be very troublesome if adjusted incorrectly or abused. With automatics, the leading problem is fluid breakdown from overheating. Fluid and filter changes every 24,000 miles can avoid premature transmission failure, but few people heed such advice. Consequently, automatics often expire after only 40,000, 50,000, or 60,000 miles when they could last the life of the vehicle.

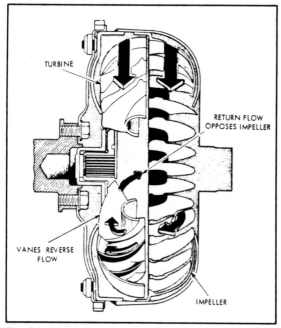

TURBINE

RETURN FLOW
OPPOSES IMPELLER

VANES REVERSE
FLOW

IMPELLER

Fig. G-47. Torque converter.

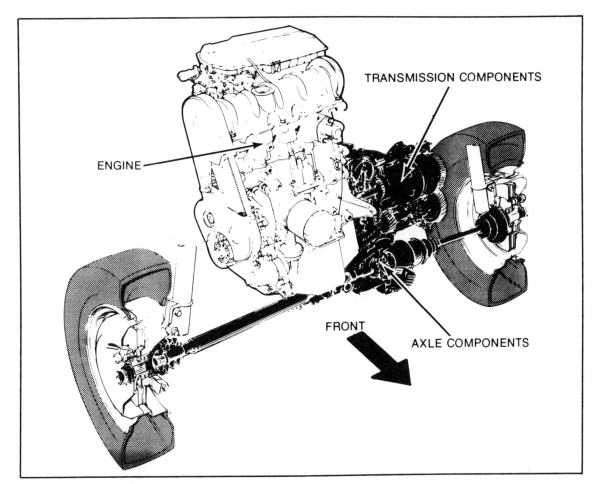

Fig. G-48. Transaxle. (Courtesy of Chrysler Corporation.)

trouble codes—A code number generated by a vehicle's onboard computer that corresponds to a specific fault. Most computerized engine control systems have a certain amount of self-diagnostic capability. When the engine is running and the computer detects a problem in one of its sensor or output circuits, or even within itself, it triggers a trouble code. In some systems, the code number is retained in memory. In others, the code is not stored but is regenerated when a mechanic runs the system through a special self-diagnostic test. Your only indication of trouble is when the "Check Engine" or "Power Loss" light on the instrument panel lights up. What does it mean? It depends on the problem.

Sometimes it is nothing serious, but it could signal a failure that might lead to further problems. To understand trouble codes, you have to have a reference manual that tells what the numbers mean and explains the step-by-step diagnostic procedure for isolating the fault. Codes are usually read out of the computer by grounding the computer's diagnostic connector. By counting the flashes of the dash light, you can determine the number. On some systems, special test equipment is needed to read the codes and to monitor the various control circuits. It is a complex subject for a do-it-yourselfer, and even some professional mechanics do not fully understand it.

tune-up—An obsolete term used to describe the

211

periodic maintenance that is performed when tuning an engine to its original specifications. With today's electronic ignition systems that require sealed carburetors and nonadjustable fuel injection, and no periodic adjustments, there is not much left to adjust. Today's tune-up, therefore, consists primarily of replacing the spark plugs and checking timing and idle speed. It might also include replacing the air and fuel filters and inspecting the emissions control system, but as far as "tuning" is concerned, there is little left to tune.

turbocharging—A means of increasing horsepower (up to 50 percent or more) by using an exhaust-driven air pump (the turbocharger) to force more air and fuel into the engine. Hot exhaust gases coming out of the engine spin an impeller on one end of the turbocharger. On the other end is a second impeller that pumps air into the engine. A *wastegate* (a small trap door that opens to bleed off exhaust pressure) limits the amount of pressure boost the turbo can produce. A little boost is a good thing, but too much boost can destroy the engine. The higher the boost pressure, the greater the horsepower produced. It is a way of making a little engine breathe like an engine of much higher displacement. Turbochargers spin at extremely high speeds, sometimes over 100,000 rpm. A steady supply of clean oil is essential to lubricate the turbo shaft bearings. Because of this, a turbocharged engine should never be revved up and shut off abruptly. The high temperatures in the turbo are hard on oil, so frequent oil changes are usually recommended. Special turbo oils are also available that offer better high-temperature resistance. If the turbo bearings go bad, the impellers would not turn freely and boost pressure will drop. A turbo can be inspected by removing the plumbing from either side and seeing if the impeller spins freely when turned by hand. Any looseness, roughness, or sign of rubbing means it is worn out and needs to be replaced (Fig. G-49).

undercoating—The application of a sound-deadening and/or rust-inhibiting chemical, wax,

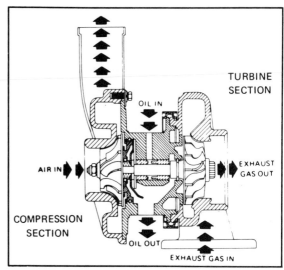

Fig. G-49. Turbocharging.

or sealer to the underside of a vehicle. Do not confuse it with rustproofing, which includes coating the inside body panels and other rust-prone areas of the vehicle.

understeer—A steering condition during which the vehicle does not respond quickly to steering changes. If a vehicle understeers, it wants to continue going straight when the steering wheel is turned. Under normal driving conditions understeer is not a problem. But when the vehicle is driven at high speed into a curve, the front of the car will tend to plow to the outside. Some vehicles are more prone to understeer than others. Front-wheel-drive vehicles fall into this category as do overpowered rear-engine Porsches.

V-belt—More commonly known as a fan belt, a V-belt is the rubber belt that drives the alternator, air conditioning compressor, power steering pump, and water pump. It is called a V-belt because of its V-shaped cross-section. The sides of the belt grip the pulleys. Some belts have notches in them to increase grip, to help cool the belt, and to relieve stress as the belt bends around small-diameter pulleys. Some vehicles use a single flat belt to drive multiple accessories. Cogged rubber timing belts are used on

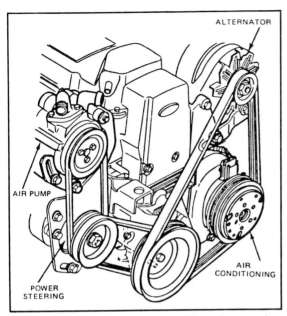

Fig. G-50. V-belt. (Courtesy of Ford Motor Company.)

many overhead cam engines to drive the camshaft. After three or four years of flexing and countless cycles around the engine's pulleys, most V-belts need to be replaced. Due to the method in which many belts are constructed today, you can't determine a belt's true condition by a visual examination. Time and mileage must also be taken into consideration. That is why most experts now recommend replacing the belts as a preventive measure every three to four years regardless of the appearance (Fig. G-50).

vacuum advance—This is the name of a device on the distributor that changes ignition timing in response to engine load. When an engine is cruising under light load, there is very strong vacuum in the intake manifold. This pulls on the vacuum advance diaphragm and advances timing for better fuel economy. When the engine is under heavy load, the throttle is opened wide and vacuum falls. This releases the diaphragm and eliminates the extra timing advance. If the extra advance is not canceled, the engine will probably experience spark knock.

valve job—Reconditioning the engine valves. It requires removing the cylinder head, disassembling the head and checking it for cracks or warpage (a common problem on aluminum cylinder heads), regrinding the valve faces and seats, replacing or restoring the valve guides, installing new valve guide seals, inspecting the springs and other valve hardware, then reassembling the heads and putting them back on the engine. It is a complicated job that requires a lot of special equipment and knowledge. The actual machine work on most valve jobs is performed in a jobber machine shop. The mechanic only removes the head and sends it out. The job can be expensive, especially if parts are needed, so plan on spending several hundred dollars or more if your engine needs a valve job.

vapor lock—When gasoline overheats and boils inside the carburetor bowl or fuel pump of a hot engine, it ceases to flow. This can cause stalling or hard starting. This is called vapor lock and it usually happens during hot weather. If a hot engine would not start, all you can do is let it set and cool. Check your cooling system to see if anything is causing your engine to run unusually hot (a bad thermostat or cooling fan, for example). Switching brands of gasoline sometimes helps because some brands are formulated to resist vapor lock better than others.

variable rate springs—A type of spring that changes stiffness as it deflects. A variable rate spring uses coils of varying thickness or spacing to provide a soft ride when the vehicle is lightly loaded, but a firmer ride when the load increases. Only a few vehicles have variable rate springs as original equipment. On most vehicles, the rear coil springs can be easily replaced with variable rate springs to reduce bottoming and to increase the vehicle's load carrying capacity. Variable rate springs are also available for the front suspension.

viscosity—This is a term used to describe the thickness of motor oil. The higher the number, the thicker the oil. Common straight grade viscosity ratings are 10, 20, 30, and 40, with 10 being the thinnest and 40 the thickest. A low-viscosity oil provides better lubrication at low temperatures and reduces internal drag on the engine, but they lack the staying power for high temperature or high speed protection. The heavier grade oils such as 30 and 40, on the other hand, are much better for high speed and high-temperature lubrication, but they might be so thick at low temperatures as to inhibit easy cranking. The best motor oils take advantage of each; these are the multiviscosity oils such as a 5W-20, 5W-30, 10W-30, and 10W-40. By using a blend of different viscosity oils, they have the flow characteristics of a low-viscosity oil when cold, but offer the protection of a heavy oil when hot.

VIN—Abbreviation for vehicle identification number. This is the vehicle's serial number that can be found stamped on a small metal plate affixed to the dash at the base of the windshield. The number might also be stamped on various body parts, the engine, and transmission. It is sometimes necessary to refer to the VIN number when ordering replacement parts.

voltage regulator—A part of your vehicle's charging system that controls how much electricity the alternator produces. The voltage regulator on today's cars is an electronic black box, which means you cannot adjust it or repair it if anything goes wrong. On many vehicles (primarily General Motors) the voltage regulator is located inside the alternator and cannot be replaced separately. A defective regulator can cause the alternator to produce too much voltage (which can damage the battery, lights, and electronic components) or it can prevent it from making enough voltage to keep the battery fully charged. The toughest challenge when diagnosing a charging problem is to determine whether it is the voltage regulator or alternator that is at fault. Using a procedure called "full fielding the alternator," which causes the alternator to put out maximum current, will tell a mechanic which is at fault.

warranty—The basic guarantee that comes with a new vehicle. All vehicle manufacturers offer a one year or 12,000 mile (whichever comes first) warranty that virtually covers anything that goes

wrong with the car. All vehicle manufacturers also provide a special government-mandated 5-year/50,000 mile "emissions" warranty that covers the emission control components (which also includes the engine's computer because it is considered to be an emissions control device). Some offer 2-year/24,000 mile or longer warranty protection on the engine and drivetrain, and a 3-year unlimited mileage warranty coverage against rust. New car and truck dealers also sell "extended" warranty packages that extend the time and mileage of coverage. Extended warranties are expensive but can easily pay for themselves if the vehicle requires major repairs. Should you buy an extended warranty when you purchase a new vehicle? No. Wait until your basic warranty is about to expire. If you have not had any serious problems already, chances are you would not. Put the money you save toward your next down payment. But if the car has been in and out of the shop for numerous warranty repairs, you would better buy an extended warranty. Before your basic warranty expires, you will receive a mail offer from the manufacturer offering you the option of extending your coverage.

wastegate—A trapdoor-like device on the exhaust side of a turbocharger that limits the amount of boost a turbo can produce. The wastegate consists of a spring-loaded diaphragm. A vacuum hose connects the diaphragm to the intake manifold. When boost pressure starts to exceed the rating of the wastegate, the diaphragm pulls open a bypass flap in the turbo housing. This allows some of the exhaust to go around the turbo impeller, which slows it down. A wastegate can be checked by applying pressure to the hose with a hand-held pump. If it does not move at the specified pressure (which you can look up in a manual), the diaphragm is probably ruptured and the wastegate needs to be replaced (Fig. G-51).

water jacket—This term refers to the hollow space inside the engine block and cylinder head where coolant flows.

water pump—A small impellerlike pump that circulates coolant through your engine's cooling

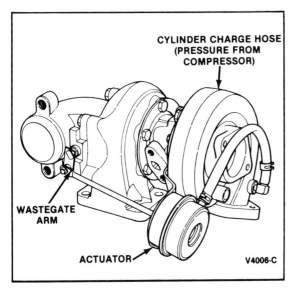

Fig. G-51. Wastegate.

system. The water pump is mounted on the engine and is driven by the fan belt, alternator belt, or overhead cam timing belt. The pump shaft has a large bearing and seal, which after 40,000 miles or so usually starts to leak. The pump can be replaced with a new or rebuilt unit, but the degree of replacement difficulty varies, depending on pump accessibility (Fig. G-52).

wheel bearings—Inside the wheel hubs are either roller or ball bearings that carry the vehicle's weight. On RWD vehicles with solid axles, the rear wheel bearings are mounted on the axles. Because of the loads they carry, most wheel bearings require periodic cleaning and repacking with grease. A recommended interval is every two years or 24,000 miles. Off-road vehicles or those that are driven through hub-deep water should be repacked more frequently. The front wheel bearings on some FWD cars are sealed and do not require any maintenance, but the rear wheel bearings on most FWD cars do require periodic greasing. A bad wheel bearing will typically make grinding, whining, or squealing noises and you can often feel the looseness or roughness if you raise the suspension and rotate the wheel by hand. Worn wheel bearings should be replaced, because when they fail, they

can sometimes cause the wheel or axle to separate from the vehicle.

wheel cylinder—This is the hydraulic component that pushes the brake shoes out in a drum brake. The wheel cylinder consists of a small casting with two outward-facing pistons. When hydraulic fluid from the master cylinder is forced into the cylinder, it pushes the two pistons out and applies the brakes. Leaks sometimes develop around the cuplike piston seals. The most inexpensive way to fix a leaky wheel cylinder is to install a "kit" that contains new piston seals.

wheel spin—This occurs when one drive wheel spins uselessly while the other does not turn. It can happen when one wheel is on a slippery surface (ice, snow, mud, slush) and the other on dry pavement. The reason it happens is because the differential always routes power to the wheel that needs it the least. The only way to eliminate it is to buy a vehicle with a locking differential.

winterizing—The process of preparing one's vehicle for the ravages of winter. The annual fall ritual includes checking, replacing and/or replenishing the antifreeze in the cooling system, mounting the snowtires, waxing the body to protect it against road salt, and sometimes tune-up to aid starting.

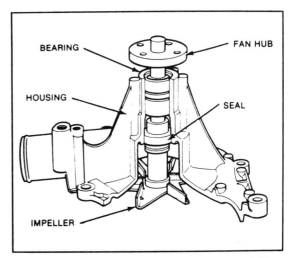

Fig. G-52. Water pump. (Courtesy of *Ford Motorcraft Shop Tips*, Vol. 19, No. 2.)

Index